Mathematics Solutions
An Introduction to Dyscalculia

Part A
How to Identify, Assess and Manage
Specific Learning Difficulties in Mathematics

by

Jan Poustie et al
B.Ed.,(Dunelm), Cert Ed., R.S.A. Diploma SpLD,
Sharma Cert., A.M.B.D.A.

(The text in this book has been set out with an irregular right hand margin to aid those with visual/reading difficulties. Much of Part 1 was originally printed as Chapter 4 of the first edition of the 'Solutions for Specific Learning Difficulties: Identification Guide.)

NEXT GENERATION UK 2000

ISBN 1 901544 45 1

A NEXT GENERATION PUBLICATION
First Published in Great Britain in 2000
Part 1 © Copyright Jan Poustie 1996
Parts 2–4 © Copyright Jan Poustie 1999

The moral rights of the author have been asserted.

Printed by Taunton Printing Company

Published by Next Generation
68 Hamilton Road, Taunton, TA1 2ES
E-mail jan.poustie@virgin.net Tel: 01823 289559 Fax: 01823 289566

Page

Acknowledgements | v
Word from the Author | 1
(Please read this section first)

Part 1   Identification | 5
Chapter 1   Indicators and Causes of Mathematical Learning Difficulties | 7

Chapter 2   Dyscalculia | 15

Part 2   The Specific Learning Difficulties Profile and Mathematics
Introduction   The Specific Learning Difficulties Profile | 35

Chapter 3   How the SpLD Profile Conditions Affect Mathematics | 47

Chapter 4   Dyspraxia | 59

Chapter 5   Auditory Dysfunctioning (including Central Auditory Processing Disorder) | 75

Chapter 6   Specific Language Impairment | 81

Chapter 7   Dyslexia | 101

Chapter 8   Attention Deficits | 105

Chapter 9   Behavioural Problems | 113

Chapter 10   Assessment | 133

Chapter 11   Living with Dyscalculia | 147

Chapter 12   Conclusion | 157

Part 3   Resources
Appendix 1:   Help & Support Agencies | 161
Appendix 2:   Photocopiable Resources | 163
Appendix 3:   Useful Resources | 171

Indices
General Index | 177
Resources Index | 187

Jan holds the RSA Diploma Specific Learning Difficulties/ Dyslexia, Professor Mahesh Sharma's Diagnosis and Remediation of Learning Problems in Mathematics Certificate and is an Associate Member of the British Dyslexia Association. Her company 'Next Generation' is a corporate member of the British Dyslexia Association.

Jan Poustie is the creator of the 'Next Generation' books and teaching packs. She runs a private practice (based in Taunton, Somerset) where she teaches, assesses, advises, lectures and designs teaching materials for Specific Learning Difficulties.

Jan has taught for twenty plus years a variety of subjects up to and including HNC level. Her teaching experience includes playgroup, primary, secondary and Further Education establishments. She has extensive experience in the field of special needs (including having been Head of a Special Needs Department).

Besides her professional interest in Specific Learning Difficulties she also has considerable personal experience of this field of which not the least part is her own Dyspraxia, Dyscalculia and Attention Deficits; hence her very strong interest in these fields.

Acknowledgements

Many grateful thanks go to the following people whose work has helped and encouraged me:

Professor Mahesh Sharma (Provost and Executive Vice President of Cambridge College, Mass., USA and Director of Teaching/Learning of Mathematics Centre, Wellesley, Mass., USA) to whom I am greatly indebted. Attending his course 'The Diagnosis and Remediation of Mathematical Learning Difficulties' (hosted by Patricia Brazil) set me on the road to overcoming my own mathematical learning difficulties and so enabled me to pursue a career which involves helping those who have mathematical learning difficulties.

Many thanks also go to:
Dr Steve Chinn
Principal, Mark College, Somerset.

Richard Ashcroft
Head of Mathematics, Mark College, Somerset.

Keith Holland
Behavioural Optometrist.

Martin Turner
Head of Psychology, Dyslexia Institute.

Dr Catherine Caulfield
Clinical Psychologist at the Brain and Behaviour Clinic, Maudsley Hospital.

Dr Ian Frampton
Clinical Neuropsychologist at the Brain and Behaviour Clinic, Maudsley Hospital.

Norma Corkish
AFASIC ex-Chief Executive.

Patricia Clayton
Irlen Diagnostician.

Denise Caferelli-Dees
Audiological Scientist and Speech Pathologist.

The views expressed by the author are her own and do not necessarily represent those who have assisted with the writing of this book.

'Mind Maps' is a registered trademark of Tony Buzan

Madeleine Portwood
Specialist Senior Educational Psychologist, Durham.

Dr Josephine Marriage
Paediatric Audiological Scientist.

Mary Nash-Wortham
Speech Therapist.

Rosemary Sassoon
Specialist in the educational and medical aspects of handwriting.

Dr Pauline Smith
Psychometric Consultant, NFER-NELSON Publishing Company.

I am also very grateful for the co-operation, assistance and encouragement that I have received from the following agencies and organisations and their staff:
- AFASIC
- The Dyspraxia Foundation
- The British School of Optometry, AD/HD Family Support Group UK
- Dyslexia Institute
- Division of Educational and Child Psychology of the British Psychological Society
- Fragile-X Society
- The Hyperactive Children's Support Group.

Finally,
My thanks and love go to my family who have let me have the peace to write this! Many thanks to Pam Brooks (and her family) for her encouragement and work on the original document that is the basis for Part 1 of this book and for giving me the faith to keep writing. Also grateful thanks to Pam for designing the template for the stunning new layout of this book. (No doubt she will find all the spacing and non-alignment errors that I have made when I finally laid out the text!)

Jan

This book is dedicated to

my lovely daughter

Alexandra

without whom

it would never have been

written.

Word from the author

This book has been incredibly difficult to write partly because one knows that most of the readers will be totally new to this subject and partly because of the need to decide what had to be included and what could safely be omitted. During this process the focus of the book (and its title) have changed many times but hopefully what you see before you now will be what you need in order to ensure effective provision for the student affected by difficulties in learning mathematics.

It was realised that several aspects of Dyscalculia needed to be included in this book for it to be an effective tool for the reader. However, early on, it was realised that there was too much information for one book. Thus information on Specific Language Impairment was kept in this book but a separate title *An Introduction to Mathematics and Language* (ISBN 1 901544 96 6) which includes the problems of mathematical language itself and how to deal with them was published in 1999. There was still too much information for one book and so we decided to publish two complementary titles.

Part A: How to Identify, Assess and Manage Specific Learning Difficulties in Mathematics.

This has been designed to be the reference manual which explains how the different conditions found within (and associated with) the SpLD Profile affect the acquisition and use of mathematics. By referring to this manual at the start of tuition teachers etc. will be able to implement the strategies necessary for dealing with the conditions which are causing the difficulty in learning mathematics.

Part 1: Identification
The recognition of a specific learning difficulty in mathematics is still fairly new to many people. Information on how to identify the presence of Dyscalculia was essential as one cannot provide for what one cannot recognise.

It was also realised that, when reading this book, some people would have to come to terms with the realisation that more conditions were present than they had realised and/or that they themselves have one or more of the conditions. This may be quite devastating for the reader. However it may be helpful to

Many readers will buy both parts of *Mathematics Solutions*.
It may be very tempting for the reader to 'dive in' to the teaching strategies outlined in *Mathematics Solutions - An Introduction to Dyscalculia Part B* when faced with a student who needs help quickly. However, the reader will gain a better understanding of Dyscalculia (and will be able to offer more effective help) if s/he reads Part A first.

In order to enable everyone to feel that they are getting a fair deal when they buy both *Mathematics Solutions - An Introduction to Dyscalculia Part A* and *Literacy Solutions* we offer a discount on the second book purchased. (At the time of going to print this discount was £6. Proof of purchase of the first book is required to obtain this discount, Tel: 01823 289559 for details.)

remember that there has actually been no change in you and/or your student since you picked up this book – just a change in perception.

Although we lack a national support group in the UK for Dyscalculia there is a network of help, support and advice which focuses on the other Specific Learning Difficulties Profile conditions. This book can enable you to access this network and the agencies which provide assessment and intervention. The information that you gain from this book is not the end of your hopes, dreams and aspirations but it may be the first step towards the realisation of them.

Part 2: The Specific Learning Difficulties Profile
A core of information on how the presence of the conditions found within, and alongside, the Profile affect the learning of mathematics was essential. This was the most difficult section to deal with as it was realised that the sister publication to this book – *Literacy Solutions* shared much of this core (but looks at it in the context of literacy skills). Initially, much of this section was left out because it was realised that some people would buy both *Literacy Solutions* and *Mathematics Solutions* and I did not want them to feel let down when they found out that both books shared some common information. In the end I realised that it was vital for those looking at mathematics to have this information.

Part 3: Appendices
Finally, as with all of my titles, I wanted the reader to look beyond the horizons of this book and so this section enables the reader to access information on a wide range of help and support agencies (which can help professionals, parents and students) plus useful resources.

Part B: How to teach students who have specific learning difficulties in mathematics
This has been designed as a practical teaching manual. Those who work with a particular student will find that their teaching is more effective if they refer to the pre-requisite skills chapters first. They are likely to need to refer to this manual on a regular basis throughout the period of tuition.

Part 1: The prerequisite skills for mathematics
This section explains what the prerequisite skills are and how to develop them.

Part 2: Teaching strategies
There was a need to include a large section on teaching strategies so that the reader could help the student more effectively. This section contains a wealth of information on what to do including:

▶▶   Helping the student
▶▶   Prioritising provision
▶▶   Teaching tips
▶▶   Place value
▶▶   Passing examinations
▶▶   How to achieve success
▶▶   Levels of knowing mathematics (Professor Mahesh Sharma)

Part 3: Resources
Includes a wide range of resources that can help our students.

* * *

The problems faced by students when Dyslexia is present have been recognised for some time. The problems caused by the presence of Dyscalculia are no less damaging. We cannot hope to help these students unless we start to learn more about the condition and the aim of this book is to enable the reader to start to understand this complex field.

The effects of Dyscalculia (and Dyspraxia plus Attention Deficits) in my own childhood were quite devastating. These conditions continued on into adulthood – each of them makes life more stressful but it is the Dyscalculia that irritates and frustrates me the most. In that, I am not alone, for in my consultancy I see adults (and children) who feel inadequate and unable to achieve their life goals purely because of the presence of Dyscalculia. Dyscalculia has made the writing of this book both a labour of love and one of hate. The need to check and re-check the information contained within it (and to check that I had correctly calculated the examples within it) made it both stressful and frustrating! However, the need to play my part in enabling children and adults not to have the same struggle to gain qualifications and a worthwhile career has spurred me on.

I was lucky. I unwittingly developed strategies that helped compensate for some of my mathematical problems and so I was able (by overworking to a great extent) to gain my degree. I was

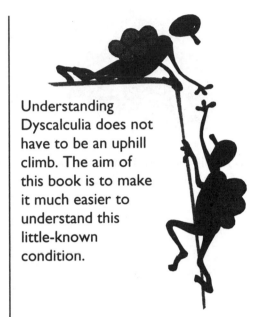

Understanding Dyscalculia does not have to be an uphill climb. The aim of this book is to make it much easier to understand this little-known condition.

Mathematics Solutions – An Introduction to Dyscalculia Part A by Jan Poustie et al   ISBN 1 901544 45 1

Dyscalculia can make many areas of one's life very difficult.

When something is strange to us we can feel threatened by our lack of knowledge and feel that we do not have the power to help. Taking the first step towards understanding Dyscalculia gives confidence in one's own abilities to help these students. It also provides a basis for discussion of both the problems and the provision that is most likely to be effective for each student.

very lucky when I met Professor Mahesh Sharma who enabled me for the first time to understand my condition and understand why so many aspects of mathematics had not made sense to me.

I was also lucky because my need to help one particular child overcome her mathematical difficulties (and the parents who asked me to help their children) resulted in me being able to overcome my own considerable anxiety regarding maths and to enable my students to achieve mathematical success. Others are not so fortunate. I hope that this book can make a contribution to changing the future of those for whom Dyscalculia makes life 'hell' and for those who want to help them.

Despite:

▸▸ a house and premises move which took over eighteen months to achieve (and where the 'chain' broke down five times),

▸▸ an old computer that crashed continuously (e.g. every ten to thirty minutes) over a period of eight months and so kept on deleting my information,

▸▸ the incredible stress of trying to buy a new computer over a period of four months where three different companies sent between them six new computers all of which had faulty parts. (That this book has been finished at all is thanks to the superb service of the Taunton based computer supplier 'Future Resources, Tel: 01823 351138.)

▸▸ two bouts of flu in one month,

▸▸ ongoing severe family illness and an even more exhausted author than I was when I finished *Literacy Solutions,*

I have actually managed to finish this book. I hope that it meets your needs.

Best wishes

Jan

Part 1

Identification

(Much of this section was originally printed as Chapter 4 of Solutions for Specific Learning Difficulties: Identification Guide written by Jan Poustie in consultation with Professor Mahesh Sharma.)

The identification of mathematical difficulties is not a simple task because there are many aspects to the learning of mathematics. In order to decide the cause of an individual's mathematical difficulties each of these aspects will need to be explored so that the individual's weaknesses and strengths can be assessed. Only once such an assessment is made can appropriate and adequate provision be given. Teaching must always be based upon using the student's strengths to enable her to overcome her weaknesses. If this strategy is not used and a thorough assessment of the student's difficulties is not made then provision is likely to be very much a 'hit and miss affair' which if one is lucky may achieve something but otherwise may well be a complete waste of time.

Mathematics Solutions – An Introduction to Dyscalculia Part A by Jan Poustie et al   ISBN 1 901544 45 1

Indicators and Causes of Mathematical Learning Difficulties

A. INDICATORS THAT AN INDIVIDUAL HAS MATHEMATICAL LEARNING DIFFICULTIES AND THE CAUSES OF SUCH DIFFICULTIES

GENERAL INDICATORS

Some of the most obvious indicators that someone is struggling with mathematical tasks are as follows.

1. Indicators which are noticeable at school and which will carry on into adulthood

A. Difficulties in fully understanding new concepts unless they are introduced using concrete apparatus (things that they can touch).

B. Becoming angry/frustrated with any mathematical task/game.

C. A dislike of any leisure games that involve numbers and/or spatial concepts; e.g. Rummikub®, dominoes, draughts and snakes and ladders. If spatial skills are weak the individual will find chess and othello® extremely difficult.

D. Rarely checking change when shopping.

E. Finding cooking stressful.

F. Frequently pressing the wrong keys on a calculator.

G. Failure to understand and use money.

H. Difficulties in understanding and using statistical information.

I. Miscounting of objects and/or misreading of text/numerals. This can cause difficulties when first introduced to number. Individuals may miss out numbers when counting and/or may fail to include all the objects. They can also write one thing but read it back as another. These difficulties can be found as part of Dyslexia and/or Dyscalculia.

J. Difficulties in learning to read the time.

Difficulties in learning to read the time may be present. Once learnt, this skill may never be totally reliable, especially when using an analogue clock/watch (where the numbers are set around the edge of a circle). Analogue clocks require the person to have good spatial skills, so those affected by Dyspraxia may have more of a difficulty with reading them. The author still frequently misreads the time on analogue clocks and miss-sets timers.

Mathematics Solutions – An Introduction to Dyscalculia Part A by Jan Poustie et al   ISBN I 901544 45 I

Frequently misdialling on the telephone can be a problem all of one's life and can be very frustrating!!

K. Difficulties with understanding fractions and/or algebra.

L. Individuals having difficulties in planning and organising their lives, their environments and/or a mathematical task.

M. Difficulties with understanding and using the language of mathematics.

N. A dislike and/or fear of mathematics. Individuals can also have combined attention span and information processing difficulties. If both these difficulties are present then the individual is likely to be slow at recalling basic arithmetic facts or even be unable to do so. Such individuals may rely on inefficient and very basic methods to work out calculations; e.g. serial counting. They may:

   a. *Work very slowly and still get the answerwrong*
       This can occur for a wide variety of reasons; e.g. loss of confidence, poor planning skills, slow recall of numbers and imperfectly learnt processes etc.

   b. *Work erratically*
       Failure to internalise concepts and methods can cause individuals to make what appear to be 'careless errors' in sums that they were having no difficulties with a few minutes earlier. This is common to several of the conditions within the Specific Learning Difficulties Profile; e.g. Dyslexia, Dyscalculia and Attention Deficits.

   c. *Avoid doing mathematics*
       Thus the student may misbehave, day-dream, offer to do jobs outside of the classroom, forget his/her books etc.

   d. *Tire easily when doing mathematics*
       This can be very noticeable at the end of the day/week/term. A huge amount of effort can be required to cope with the simplest of calculations. Often the only indicators that the student is tiring when doing mathematics are:

       ▸▸ more frequent illness,
       ▸▸ less work being produced and/or more untidy work as the effort to present work well is just too much.

       (Note: Some students will produce beautifully presented work but there will be hardly any of it.)

Mathematics Solutions – An Introduction to Dyscalculia Part A by Jan Poustie et al   ISBN 1 901544 45 1

2. Difficulties which will be present when young but are likely to be more noticeable in adulthood

A. Frequently missing appointments because they have been written down incorrectly and/or the amount of time spare before the appointment has been miscalculated.

B. Difficulties when travelling; e.g. going to the wrong platform, getting on the wrong bus, finding it difficult to read a map, remember road numbers etc.

C. Difficulties with working out how much wallpaper/ paint etc. is needed for a DIY task.

E. Preferring to cook meals that require only one pot or the oven rather than those that require various elements which have different cooking times but must all be ready at one time. Preferring to make up a recipe as one goes along rather than follow the recipe in a book.

B. DIFFERENT CAUSES OF MATHEMATICAL LEARNING DIFFICULTIES

Teaching and learning styles
The best mathematicians use both sequential and global strategies. Ideally concepts should be introduced via the learner's natural style and then reinforced, revised etc. via the opposite style. Two of the most important aspects of mathematics are its sequential nature (which is based upon a foundation of early skills and knowledge[1], and the fact that all of mathematical knowledge interrelates to its other parts and as such no topic can be seen in isolation. Each new topic has to be related to those areas already covered and to those which will be introduced in the future.

Therefore, in order to teach mathematics the teacher needs to be aware of where mathematically the individual has been, where s/he is now, where s/he will be going shortly and where s/he will be going in the far future. S/he also has to be aware of what information has been internalised by the individual; i.e.

▸▸ What has been accepted as making sense

▸▸ What has been understood as a concept

THE TWO EXTREMES OF LEARNING STYLE

Global
qualitative, grasshopper.
They jump from one thing to other.

Sequential
quantitative, inchworm.
They like to do things brick by brick.

Mathematics Solutions – An Introduction to Dyscalculia Part A by Jan Poustie et al   ISBN 1 901544 45 1

Each teacher will also have his/her own way of teaching mathematics which is often based upon his/her own way of learning it and sometimes the teaching method does not suit the student. This occurs when the methods used for delivering the mathematical curriculum are incompatible with the learner due to the learner's natural learning Style.

▸▸   What can be used by the learner in any situation.

If the teacher lacks this awareness it will be more difficult for the individual to place the new information into his/her 'schema' of mathematics. (This 'schema' is the system by which the individual has organised, arranged and connected each piece of mathematical information.)

Learning styles vary between the two extremes of needing information to be presented globally or sequentially. Global learners learn by looking at the topic as a complete whole and then looking at the parts in any order. Sequential learners learn the information in an ordered step-by-step manner.

Qualitative and Quantitative Learning Styles
(Derived from the work of Dr Steve Chinn, Professor Mahesh Sharma and Bath et al.)

The qualitative (global) learner
This learner is sometimes called a global learner or a 'grasshopper'. S/he needs to see the whole of a concept first and then learns by 'jumping in a non-sequential manner' from one part of the whole to another (this style may appear disordered to the onlooker). Such learners rely on their intuition to learn and understand. They can easily miss out a vital part of the 'whole' because of this disordered manner of working. However, the advantage of such a learning style is that they may be able to see the 'whole' of a concept in a way that other people cannot see it or make unusual connections between pieces of information. Such learners can find that school teaching techniques are in conflict with their learning style. Their preferred choice of learning style may be that of open learning where they have more control over the learning process.

By the time that extremely global learners reach secondary school they can either become disruptive, or seem very passive, as they do not understand the concepts being used but fear teacher/peer group criticism/rejection if they ask questions.

Mathematical tuition in the UK has tended to be based upon sequential teaching methods where a series of step-by-step processes is taught. Some students can follow/carry out the process; i.e. make few errors, but have no understanding of the concept. Other students will neither be accurate nor understand the concept.

Qualitative (global) students learn by asking a lot of questions.

They are intuitive learners. Their work can be inaccurate because of their way of working.

Some school textbooks are very out-of-date – in 1995 the author saw in use, in a secondary school, a set of textbooks that were over thirty years old! Teachers who are still using such outdated materials will only be using sequential methods unless they introduce a great deal of supplementary work. Such textbooks are also very off-putting to the student who has mathematical learning difficulties. They tend to contain vast amounts of small text and examples crammed on to one page with few illustrations – and all of it in black and white.

Quantitative (sequential) learners
This learner must take the concept a step at a time in an ordered (sequential) manner just like an 'inchworm'. S/he cannot see the whole until s/he has built up all the parts.   S/he prefers teacher-directed learning to open learning methods and so is likely to find that school is not in conflict with his/her learning style. S/he may be able to follow, apply and transfer the concept but may have only one way of explaining it to another student. Sequential learners may easily learn the process by which they do a sum but may find explaining concepts with apparatus such as Cuisenaire Rods very difficult.

Most people's learning style[2] is somewhere on an imaginary line between the two extremes. Few people are actually at the extreme end of the line but, as much of teaching is done in a sequential manner, it is often those who are closest to the 'grasshopper' learning style that are at the greatest disadvantage in our educational system. Some individuals are able to adopt the learning style of their teacher and this gradually replaces (to a varying extent) their natural learning style. However, others are totally unable to adopt another style and perhaps this is more common in those who are qualitative (grasshopper) learners.

Each person also has a natural way of learning through his/her senses; e.g. visually (by looking at things and by visualising information in his/her mind), auditorally (listening) and kinaesthetically (by moving parts of the body; e.g. the hand, the mouth, limbs).

The four main sensory channels of learning. Movement includes movements of the organs of speech, hand, eyes, body and limbs

Mathematics Solutions – An Introduction to Dyscalculia Part A by Jan Poustie et al   ISBN 1 901544 45 1

C. TEACHING THE RIGHT THING

When we look at a student who has mathematical learning difficulties (no matter what the cause of them) we tend to see the problems and then design a lesson to deal with them. We prioritise our provision based upon what we believe the student needs to be taught. However, the self-esteem of the student is likely to be low.

It is vital that we first boost self-esteem and enable the student to achieve success in areas which s/he regards as important. Thus it may be that we simply enable the student to score highly on the next tables test (even though we know that there is a good chance that it will go out of memory very quickly). It may be that s/he actually needs some support to stop being bullied or that we enable him/her to produce a neat chart etc., or even that we move the student to a better position in the classroom. The only way we can find out just what the student wants help in (and the priority s/he attaches to it) is by asking him/her. That is often not such an easy task and so the 'How I feel' sheets in Part 4 of this book have been designed to help the tutor and parents know the areas to concentrate on first.

D. OTHER CAUSES OF MATHEMATICAL LEARNING DIFFICULTIES

Some people regard Dyscalculia as being the cause of all mathematical difficulties. However, this is not the case and very few individuals will actually be affected by this condition. Each learner has his/her own set of difficulties/differences which will affect his/her ability to learn by the methods used by the teacher. The learner's differences/difficulties vary tremendously, from those which are easily resolved to those that require a great deal of provision. If we look at all of the circumstances that surround, or are part of, the learner we can see any (or all) of the following as being the cause of an individual's mathematical learning difficulties:

1. Limited mathematical experience
This can be due to various factors; e.g.

▸▸   frequent absences from lessons due to illness

▸▸   working slowly

Teachers may associate a difficulty in dealing with number with difficulties in dealing with all aspects of mathematics. When this occurs the student's mathematical experience may be limited by the teacher's expectations.

➤ being withdrawn from maths lessons in order to attend specialist tuition for difficulties caused by conditions such as those found within the SpLD Profile. (Absence from lessons may be unavoidable; e.g. illness, or may be due to attendance for specialist intervention such as physiotherapy which may not be easy to change because of timetabling restrictions.)

➤ not being allowed to progress to the 'problem solving' aspects of mathematics. This can occur when the teacher has an incorrect perception of the individual's mathematical ability which is based upon the fact that s/he is unable to do simple number work with any accuracy.

Teachers are aware that, just as a house will collapse if built upon weak foundations, so the ability to acquire higher 'mathematical knowledge' will collapse if the foundation is not both complete and secure. However, mathematics contains two elements – number (arithmetic) and mathematical concepts. The ability to cope with number can be weak but there can still be a fair (if not excellent) ability to understand highly developed mathematical concepts. Once appropriate strategies/ equipment are given to the learner to overcome his/her difficulties in number then s/he is able to progress to his/her correct mathematical level.

2. <u>The learner and the tool being incompatible</u>
This occurs when the student is at a learning stage which is incompatible with the 'tool' being used/provided to explain the concept and/or carry out the calculation. Thus s/he may be offered a picture when s/he needs something concrete which s/he can handle to help work out the answer.

3. <u>Maths anxiety</u>
The student who can remember the exact incident which started the anxiety is likely to need counselling to overcome it. The student affected by maths anxiety may need counselling to overcome his/her fear as otherwise the anxiety will prevent the student being able to learn effectively.

4. <u>The teaching does not suit the student</u>
This occurs when:

➤ The methods used for delivering the mathematical

The *Take off with Number* teaching pack (published by Next Generation) has been designed to reduce students' anxiety whilst encouraging the development of classification, number, planning and organisation, and sequencing skills.

All lessons and homework tasks should include some element of revision. Individuals with severe mathematical difficulties will initially need lessons/homework in which only a small amount of time is used for introducing new concepts with the rest of the time being devoted to revision.

Notes:

1. Mathematics for dyslexia, a teaching handbook by Chinn and Ashcroft. (Pub. Whurr.)

2. Different professionals use different terms; e.g. Sharma uses the terms qualitative/quantitative and Chinn uses the terms first used by Bath et al; i.e. grasshopper/inchworm.

curriculum are incompatible with the learner due to a variety of factors; e.g. use of a teaching style/method which does not suit the individual.

▸▸ Use of inappropriate teaching materials such as pictorial-based materials when the individual needs concrete-based ones and/or materials unsuitable to the individual's learning style.

▸▸ The teacher lacks enough knowledge of number/ mathematics to teach it well. (Mathematics is part of all teacher training courses in the UK. Teachers of mathematics in secondary schools and above can be expected to be mathematics specialists. However, most class teachers in primary schools are expected to teach mathematics regardless of whether they have a particular expertise in this field.)

▸▸ The teacher failing to notice that the individual does not understand the concept. This can occur when the teacher does not mark the work on a regular enough basis, does not involve individuals in enough discussion about how they work out a sum and when continuous revision is not used as an ongoing strategy.

Individuals may appear to know and understand the concept when it is taught but it is not internalised and so does not go into long-term memory. Such individuals may do well in class but have poor homework marks in comparison to class work and may have poor marks in examinations.

5. The presence of a condition which is found within, or alongside, the Specific Learning Difficulty Profile
This is explained in detail in Part 2 of this book.

Dyscalculia

(This chapter has been derived from Professor Mahesh Sharma and from Focus on Learning Problems in Mathematics – Dyscalculia, *extended and edited by Jan Poustie.)*

PART A: THE USE OF THE TERM 'DYSCALCULIA'

Although research has been conducted into it for many decades this is a little known condition in the UK. There are hardly any books on the subject, relatively few articles about it, no national UK agency dealing with it, relatively few conferences/lectures, and very few teaching materials designed for it in this country. (For details of some of these materials see Appendix 2.) The term 'Dyscalculia' has been used *historically* in two ways:

1. To describe a <u>Specific Learning Difficulty</u> (SpLD) in numeracy/ mathematics. As the condition is present from birth its correct name is *Developmental Dyscalculia*. It is one of a group of conditions which are part of the Specific Learning Difficulties Profile. Like Dyslexia, one does not 'grow out of it' but one can be taught strategies to help overcome some of the difficulties that it causes.

2. To refer to <u>all kinds of learning problems in mathematics</u> caused by various factors including *Developmental* and *Acquired Dyscalculia*.

In Part 2 of this book the term 'Dyscalculia' is used to refer to both Acquired Dyscalculia (caused by ME etc.) and to Developmental Dyscalculia (caused by the presence of one, or more, of the SpLD Profile conditions).

Acquired Dyscalculia

This term can be used to describe difficulties that are caused by non-developmental factors. This group of students have an acquired form of the Specific Learning Difficulties Profile. Into this group would come those students who are affected by ME and those who have Childhood Hemiplegia. ME is regarded by some as being one of the illnesses which comes within the term Chronic Fatigue Syndrome/Post Viral Fatigue Syndrome and by others as being a separate illness in its own right. ME stays within the bloodstream of the person and so s/he may appear to

The conditions found within the Specific Learning Difficulties Profile are Dyslexia, Attention Deficits (AD/HD), Dyspraxia (DCD), Specific Language Impairment, Central Auditory Processing Disorder, Autistic Spectrum Disorder and Dyscalculia.

Some of the conditions seen alongside the SpLD Profile are: Meares-Irlen Syndrome, Chronic Fatigue Syndrome (including ME), Childhood Hemiplegia and Non-Verbal Learning Deficit.

recover from the illness but stress and later episodes of illness may cause the problems to return. It appears to affect the student's ability to process numbers even though s/he may have had no difficulties (or even have been very good) at number work prior to the illness occurring. There is some evidence that those affected by Chronic Fatigue Syndrome where ME is not present may make a full recovery.

Those affected by Acquired Dyscalculia may have:

» a range of the difficulties associated with Developmental Dyscalculia,

» difficulties associated with the other conditions within the SpLD Profile (the acquired form of such conditions since the person was not born with them but acquired the difficulties due to another causal condition).

The student will also always have difficulties which are associated with the causal condition. Thus if ME is present we would expect to see fatigue as well. Only if the severity of the ME reduces (or the student makes a recovery/has a good day) will real improvement be seen in mathematical functioning.

Those affected by Childhood Hemiplegia are likely to have visio-spatial difficulties which will cause problems in many aspects of number plus other areas of mathematics; e.g. geometry, the reading of charts etc. Such students may have very severe problems with mathematics. This appears to occur because when the 'insult to the brain' (e.g. a brain haemorrhage – bleed into the brain) happens the brain prioritises language as being the function of the brain which must be protected. Another important factor is that the areas of the brain which relate to mathematical functioning are scattered across the brain unlike the language centres which are basically located in two areas. Thus there are many more areas of the brain relating to mathematics than there are to language. Therefore, as there are more areas relating to maths the odds are greater that any bleed will have a chance of affecting one of them rather than an area relating to literacy. Consequently, a student affected by Childhood Hemiplegia may have his/her literacy skills functioning

Dyscalculia can affect every area of one's life. The author always allows an extra half hour for every long car journey. She knows that once she has left the motorway she will spend at least half an hour misreading the map and getting totally lost!

at a reasonable level but the mathematical skills may be severely affected.

***

The greater the severity of the conditions found within (or associated with) the Specific Learning Difficulties Profile (and the more of them that are present) the greater the degree of difficulty in acquiring and using mathematical skills.

Is Dyscalculia likely to be the cause of an individual struggling with mathematical tasks?

No, very few people are believed to have Dyscalculia with some research figures suggesting that some form of Dyscalculia is present in about six per cent of the population. However, as there seems to have been a general acceptance in the past amongst the UK population that:

▶▶ its okay not to be good at mathematics because you can't be good at everything

▶▶ that females are usually poorer than men at mathematics. Thus it may well be that many people's difficulties with mathematics have been unrecognised in the past and continue to be unrecognised in the present.. As was seen in Chapter 1, various other factors can also have an impact upon one's ability to learning mathematics; e.g. teaching and learning styles and missed opportunities for learning (e.g. because of illness etc.).

PART B: RECOGNISING DYSCALCULIA

Recognising Dyscalculia in the classroom

Any, or all, of the following can be seen:

1. Difficulties in reading the time (though the hours and ½, ¼ hours may be known)

2. Miscounting objects.

3. Forgetting the next step in the operation.

4. Production of very little maths work by the end of a lesson.

5. Careless mistakes.

6. Failure to check work and/or the checking of work does not markedly improve accuracy. (Such students will need to be taught strategies for checking their work.)

Children, adults, different races, all academic abilities, female and male can all be affected by Dyscalculia. Some individuals will have problems in number but can cope with higher mathematics, others will have difficulties in every area.

7.   Difficulties in understanding the logic and/or the language of mathematics.

8.   Repeating a number, a symbol and/or a process that has been used in a previous sum or in a previous part of the operation.

9.   Bizarre errors; e.g. write a number/symbol that seems to come 'from nowhere'.

10. Slow responses. (Can be especially noticeable in mental arithmetic tasks and times tables tests). The commonly slow mental response of the student affected by Dyscalculia, or alternatively, the impulsive incorrect response of the Attention Deficits/gifted pupil, is likely to result in great frustration for all concerned is likely to be a major problem for both teacher and student in the UK's national numeracy lesson. .

11. Counting on fingers. This being present AT ANY AGE indicates a reliance on 'counting on' strategies and the need for concrete apparatus. (Finger-counting older teenagers are likely to have the most difficulty with conceptualising higher mathematics.)

12. Appears to understand the concept in classwork but not in homework.

13. Difficulties in learning number bonds to 10 and 20 and in learning times tables.

14. Cannot remember numbers.

15. Difficulties in planning/organising and carrying out mathematical tasks/processes.

16. Difficulties in reading a map.

17. Difficulties in learning some basic operations and in applying them to activities outside of the maths classroom; e.g.

    ▸▸   interpreting dials

    ▸▸   interpreting numerical read-outs

    ▸▸   calculating length/quantity.

18. Difficulties in explaining and applying concepts.

It is important to note that students affected by Dyscalculia may be found in any set/stream of the school. The highly intelligent

All of these difficulties can cause the person to become extremely frustrated and very tired when doing any task which has a mathematical content.

Mathematics Solutions – An Introduction to Dyscalculia Part A by Jan Poustie et al   ISBN 1 901544 45 1

pupil may be able to develop strategies to compensate for his/her Dyscalculia to a certain extent. The older the student the less likely s/he is to be in the top sets. However, if specialist help and a sympathetic mathematics teacher is provided the student may well be able to 'hold his/her own' in the top set in the early years of secondary school.

How do we recognise Developmental Dyscalculia?
Developmental Dyscalculia is 'a difficulty in number conceptualisation, understanding number relationships and outcomes of numerical or spatial operations.'[1] which is present at an early age. 'It is characterised by substantially lowered arithmetic achievement; i.e. several years below the appropriate level'[2] as compared with their peers of similar chronological age and intellectual ability. The person may be able to read fluently (or even exceedingly well).

Relatively little research into Developmental Dyscalculia has been conducted (as compared with research into literacy difficulties). Thus, much is not known about Developmental Dyscalculia and what is known is based on only a small amount of research.[3] Some research indicates that Developmental Dyscalculia (like Dyslexia) is caused by a difference in the way in which the brain works. It is believed by some professionals that few individuals have only a specific problem with number. Some believe that mathematical and language difficulties occur concurrently, especially when Dyslexia is present.[4] Some believe that difficulties in number/mathematics are part of a language dysfunction; e.g. Specific Language Impairment, or part of other conditions found within the Specific Learning Difficulties Profile such as Dyspraxia and Autistic Spectrum Disorder.

If an individual is affected by Developmental Dyscalculia any, or all, of the following types of arithmetic disorder (that were identified by Luria in 1966[5]) may be present.

1. Defects of logic
   Difficulties in holding and processing information in the mind. (*Forgetting where you are in the calculation, failing to carry a number accurately into the next part of the procedure.*) Luria linked some of these difficulties to spatial problems.[6]

The failure to integrate spatial and visualisation skills causes difficulties in understanding calendars and reading clocks and geometry. (As spatial difficulties are seen as part of Dyspraxia it seems likely that this condition is present when this sub-group of Dyscalculia is found.)

Mathematics Solutions – An Introduction to Dyscalculia Part A by Jan Poustie et al   ISBN 1 901544 45 1

A 'wall' can appear which seems to stop some of the elements (e.g. signs/numerals) existing during the mathematical operation.

2. Defects in planning

Difficulties in planning and a failure to check one's answer. (The individual attempts the task before making a preliminary analysis of what it requires and does not check that the answer is right.) Various skills are needed in order to plan so an individual may have difficulties in any, or all of the following.

Understanding the information within the problem
If individuals have difficulties in any of the areas of memory, language, reading and comprehension they are likely to find it difficult to understand information which is presented in a symbolic and/or textual (or oral) manner. Until the information is understood the mathematical problem cannot be solved.

Organisation of the information and planning the steps needed to reach a solution
Individuals may not be able to work out which pieces of information are related and/or the order in which certain operations need to be carried out. One cannot plan if one cannot see the whole of the task. A person affected by Dyscalculia can know exactly what all the signs and numerals mean in the sum and can know how to use them but a 'wall' can appear which seems to stop some of the elements (e.g. signs/numerals) existing during the mathematical operation. Although these elements are 'not seen' by the individual there is an awareness that 'something is wrong' but the individual has no idea what it is. It is as though the whole of the task is not seen accurately and only the fragments can therefore be worked upon.

This fragmentation of the task also applies to the reading of problems. Often the individual is unable to work out which parts of the information given are needed for the sum and which parts of it have been added in to make the sum harder but are not actually needed for the calculation. Since there is so much self doubt as to whether one is thinking clearly/ logically the individual can waste a lot of time going up mental 'dead ends' and may not recognise the correct 'path' when s/ he sees it.. The number stories mentioned in *Mathematics Solutions – An Introduction to Dyscalculia; Part B* can be helpful here.

Mathematics Solutions – An Introduction to Dyscalculia Part A by Jan Poustie et al   ISBN 1 901544 45 1

An inability to reliably check work.
Checking may achieve nothing for though the answer may be checked several times, the person may simply produce several different answers and have no idea as to which one is correct! Thus individuals may:

- Not bother to check at all because they feel that it will not help.

- Keep on checking until the same answer appears twice (this can take ten 'checks' or more, and can still be wrong).

- Go by the 'feel' of the answer (it 'feels' as though it ought to be right).

- Cross/rub it all out and leave the answer blank, leave an answer which they know is incorrect or if Attention Deficits is also present the student may well tear it up in anger and throw it in the bin. (*Doing the task once can be very stressful – sometimes the individual just cannot face doing it again.*)

- Have no strategies by which they can check the answer because they either can only follow the procedure that they originally used (and which they have failed to internalise correctly) and/or have difficulties in following procedures.

3. Perseveration of procedures that are no longer appropriate
Perseveration is when an individual continues to use an approach/thought process which may have been appropriate when first introduced to the task (or at the initial stage of it) but which is no longer appropriate. Such individuals may also be unable to reverse concepts; e.g. can count forwards/do addition but have difficulties in doing subtraction/counting backwards. The individual may also not recognise a number if it is given in a different way; e.g. may habitually say the phone number 289559 as 28-9,55-9 and may find it very difficult to accept that it is the same number when it is grouped differently; e.g. 28-95-59.

Other aspects of perseverating are:

- writing the same number just after one has written it; e.g. 4 x 2 = 2,

A failure to be able to check work reliably (or even to know where to start in the checking process) can be very frustrating for the student. Repeated checking of the answer (resulting in just a lot of different answers with no way of knowing which one is correct) can make the student feel very confused.

Using a calculator to check work may not help as it too involves a procedure. The individual may also have such poor estimation skills that s/he does not know whether the answer that comes up is likely to be correct anyway!

Perseveration can cause individuals to become 'locked' into a behaviour/process. As some individuals can find internalising procedures extremely difficult they can find it very hard to stop using the time-consuming methods/processes that they were originally taught when they were young. They can 'feel safer' when using previously learnt methods/processes, or when just carrying on with the one that they first thought of, even though they suspect it may not be the best one for the task in hand.

▶▶ writing a number just because it is the next one in the sequence; e.g. 6 + 4 = 5,

▶▶ applying the rules of one operation incorrectly to another; e.g. the individual treats 24 x 2 and 24 – 2 in the same way.

Perseveration difficulties can make both the student and the teacher very frustrated!!!

4. Inability to perform simple calculations; e.g. + and – 'The person understands the logic of the arithmetic operations but cannot recall the facts automatically.'[7]

What other terms have been used for certain characteristics of Dyscalculia?

Paraphasic substitutions
This is when one number is substituted for another. It can happen when writing or using a calculator. In the case of calculators the person can be saying the number that s/he wants but his/her hand can still press a different number. This is not a case of inverting/reversing numbers or pressing a button on the calculator that is next to the one that is wanted.

Reversals
Digits are reversed (e.g. the student reads/writes 5 instead of 2 and vice versa), misordered (e.g. 453 is written/read as 435), or inverted (e.g. 6 is read/written instead of 9 and vice versa). The presence of such difficulties can also be an indicator of several other difficulties/conditions; e.g. visual difficulties, Autistic Spectrum Disorder, Dyspraxia and Dyslexia. (*See chapters 3, 9, 4 and 7.*)

Misalignment Operations performed incorrectly because numbers/symbols are placed incorrectly e.g. the decimal point. (*This can also occur as part of Near-vision Dysfunctioning. (See Chapter 3.)*)

What other difficulties are individuals affected by Dyscalculia also likely to have?

A wide variety of difficulties are likely to be present; e.g. difficulties in:

1. Naming, reading, or writing mathematical symbols and terms as compared with one's peers of similar intellectual ability and age

2. <u>Manipulating real or abstract/representational objects; e.g.</u>
<u>difficulties in algebra etc. and in *'seeing'* one's errors at the</u>
<u>time</u>
This can cause individuals to feel annoyed, stressed,
frustrated and upset when they cannot do simple
calculations. They can know that the answer *'feels wrong'* but
are unable to find the error, though two days later it may be
utterly obvious!

3. <u>The way that they react to mathematics emotionally</u>
Maths anxiety, and low self-esteem resulting from it, is likely
to be present. A fear of mathematics can be a very real
problem for some students. *Anxiety can take several forms; e.g.*
a fear of anything related to numbers, fear when faced by a page
of sums (the student's face can visibly turn white), anxiety over
certain aspects of mathematics; e.g. fractions.

4. <u>Understanding absolute and relative positions of objects; e.g.</u>
<u>in each of the following, the digit '3' has a different value: 2.3,</u>
<u>23 and 2^3</u>

5. <u>Understanding new concepts unless concrete apparatus is</u>
<u>used to introduce it</u>
Concrete apparatus is apparatus that contains items that the
individual can touch, hold and manipulate (e.g. move the items
from one place to another) in order to work out the sum.
Individuals are likely to need such apparatus for a longer time
than their peers of similar chronological age and intellectual
ability.

6. <u>Remembering numbers</u>
Although individuals may be able to produce the correct
answer to a simple sum the difficulties that some have in
remembering any numbers can make it very difficult to:

➡ Answer complex and multi-step tasks correctly (e.g. long
multiplication and the sort of calculations that one has to
do when answering a complex word problem).

➡ Remember simple number bonds, e.g. the pairs of
numbers which equal either ten or twenty; e.g. 1 + 9 =
10 and 17 + 3 = 20.

➡ Remember numbers that are of personal importance;
e.g. one's own telephone number.

Slowness of responses can occur
This can be seen as taking longer
than normal (as compared with
peer group of similar
chronological age and intellectual
ability) to give a correct answer to
an addition/multiplication sum;
e.g. 1 + 9 = 10.

Note:
response time
could take
longer if any of
the following are present: Specific
Language Impairment, Dyslexia,
Central Auditory Processing
Disorder and/or Verbal
(Articulatory) Dyspraxia. (See
chapters 6, 7, 5 and 4.)

Mathematics Solutions – An Introduction to Dyscalculia Part A by Jan Poustie et al   ISBN 1 901544 45 1

Unlike many of those with literacy difficulties (e.g. Dyslexia) individuals affected by Dyscalculia may be able to learn their tables by rote learning methods.

However, difficulties in remembering isolated numbers may mean that they cannot use their knowledge of tables efficiently in calculations since it may involve having to 'say their table' from the beginning each time.

7. Grasping the logic of mathematics

The effort to understand, accept and internalise the logic behind a mathematical concept can be very great. If earlier methods of teaching have laid too small a foundation (or a faulty one) then individuals may be unable to easily adapt/ transfer the logic to a new level of learning and will fail to understand and/or internalise the new concept. An example of this can occur when there is a failure to introduce the 'area' method of multiplication[8] alongside the 'repeated addition' method (in which 'lots/groups' are used). A teacher using repeated addition might initially explain the multiplication sum $2 \times 3 = 6$ in the following way:

- ▸▸   2 apples on a tree (teacher draws it).
- ▸▸   How many apples are there?
- ▸▸   The student answers '2'.
- ▸▸   Teacher says 'We have one group (or 'lot') of apples.'
- ▸▸   Teacher writes the sum $(2 \times 1 = 2)$.

- ▸▸   Here is another tree with two apples on it.
- ▸▸   How many apples are there?
- ▸▸   Then the teacher writes the sum $(2 \times 2 = 4)$.

- ▸▸   Here is another tree with two apples on it.
- ▸▸   Each tree has 2 apples on it. We now have 3 trees.
- ▸▸   Count all the apples. $(2 \times 3 = 6)$.

Some individuals find that this method does not make sense as soon as they are asked to do sums such as $2 \times 0 = 0$ because they have started off with two apples so where have they gone! Even though to the teacher (and maybe to the rest of the class) the explanation that there are no trees to hang the apples on makes sense it will not help the individual affected by Developmental Dyscalculia. Such students know that from experience outside of the classroom that you can find apples without trees at every supermarket! However, an explanation using the area method will enable the individual to understand the concept.[9]

The area method of multiplication' is as follows
Multiplication is actually based on rectangles and squares. We have to find the area of the rectangle either by 'counting on' or

by multiplying. The area of the rectangle shown on the right is eight squares. In the sum 2 x 4 we are being told two sides of the rectangle. We are being asked to find the area of the rectangle. In division; e.g. 4 ÷ 2, we are being told the area of the shape and one side of the rectangle. We are being asked to find out the length of the other side of the rectangle.

8. <u>Solving 'magic squares' (see Figure 2.2), even those adding up to numbers less than 10</u>
This task is hard because there is no obvious starting point and even though the numbers may 'work' vertically they may not work horizontally/diagonally too. The stress of repeatedly working out the calculations when the individual is not at all sure as to whether each calculation is correct anyway can just be too great.

9. <u>Coping with mathematical tasks when under stress</u>
The student's mathematical ability may fall apart completely when under stress. It is known that the part of our brain which deals with symbolic information is called the neo-cortex. It is the last part of our brain to have developed as the human species has evolved. When under stress, this part of the brain starts to function less well and so we have the classic case of the student who performs erratically. Students are likely to perform erratically and/or badly when stress levels are too high (e.g. in examination conditions).

10. <u>Cognitive skill functioning and development</u>.
Individuals may be less efficient than their peer group of similar age and intellectual ability in **mathematical thinking** (cognitive) skills; e.g. reasoning, problem solving etc. A delay in mathematical cognitive skills is found 'in approximately 25% of people.'[10]

Mathematical thinking is based upon understanding mathematical concepts. There are various prerequisite skills (sub-skills) which are the foundation for the understanding and implementing of a mathematical operation and some of these may be absent or incomplete. If a sub-skill has not developed then any mathematical process to which it is linked will not be fully understood and internalised properly. This results in the individual appearing to learn a process (e.g. subtraction) but it becomes 'unlearnt' at a moment's notice. Sometimes the individual can become 'locked' into a process

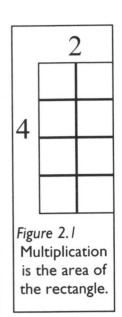

Figure 2.1
Multiplication is the area of the rectangle.

Figure 2.2
Fill in the blank squares to make a magic square in which each row and column adds up to 6
(*The answer is on page 34.*)

and is totally unable to come out of it as in the case of the ten year old who did the following

X̶0̶ X̶0̶ X̶0̶ 1̶ 2̶2   instead of $\overset{'}{2}$'2

14 -   1 4 -

___   ___

The student obviously knew part of the subtraction process (that she had to reduce the tens column by a ten and carry that ten over to the units column so that she could then take four from twelve). However, she became totally confused when she tried to record the 'carrying' part of the process and then could not progress to working out the sum. For all students it is vital that the tutor enables the pre-requisite skills to develop. (Comprehensive information on these skills and strategies to enable their development can be found in: *Mathematics Solutions – An Introduction to Dyscalculia; Part B: How to teach students who have specific learning difficulties in mathematics* by Jan Poustie et al, ISBN 1901544 72 9.)

C: A WIDER LOOK AT 'DEVELOPMENTAL DYSCALCULIA'

It is generally accepted that both Dyslexia and Dyscalculia are present because of a difference in the structure and function of the brain. Each of the other Specific Learning Difficulties Profile conditions (and the other conditions seen alongside the SpLD Profile) are also present because of such differences. It is also apparent that all of the conditions within the Profile overlap and because of this overlapping the author suggested in 1997 the use of the term 'Specific Learning Difficulties Profile' as a way of describing all of the conditions that come within it.

Research into Dyslexia (and into the brain) has caused the definition of Dyslexia to subtly alter and it will continue to do so in the twenty-first century. The latest development is that one branch of specialists are looking at a rather narrow definition which relates to the student's ability to read single words, with an emphasis on the skill of being able to break apart words and build them up using the sounds of the letters. All other difficulties present; e.g. comprehension of the written text etc. relate to other difficulties/conditions; e.g. the conditions with the SpLD Profile. Although this definition is used to develop an

The prerequisite skills are:

▸▸   Number
▸▸   Weight
▸▸   Area
▸▸   Volume
▸▸   Relationship between variables (e.g. problems such as 2 men dig a 5 metre tunnel in 10 minutes whilst 2 women dig a 3 metre tunnel in 4 minutes. Who digs fastest?)
▸▸   Classification
▸▸   Spatial
▸▸   Transivity (e.g. problems such as: John is older than Fred who is younger than Tom. Who is the youngest child?)

understanding of the different theoretical explanations and research findings relating to Dyslexia it is realised that it is not a self-limiting definition of Dyslexia.) Other groups are still looking at Dyslexia in its broadest sense so that the term includes difficulties in motor function, memory, sequencing, notation of all kinds and sometimes difficulties in mathematics. Both groups, however, realise that when we find that one condition is present then we must also look for other SpLD Profile conditions as there appears to be a strong likelihood that more than one condition is likely to be present in any one individual.

In the world of literacy, Developmental Dyslexia was recognised first as a cause of specific literacy difficulties and then the existence of a wider field of specific learning difficulties was accepted. Finally, the impact on literacy of each of the conditions within the SpLD Profile has been realised. It appears that with regard to the world of mathematics this transfer to looking at Developmental Dyscalculia in a wider context has not yet occurred but it may well be that in the future we will view Developmental Dyscalculia in a similar way to that of Developmental Dyslexia.

Dyslexia has been known about by large numbers of the population for some time but in the past some of the other SpLD Profile conditions may well have gone unrecognised as relatively few professionals would have known of their existence. (Dyspraxia was a relatively little known about condition in education until the late 1980s and professionals in the UK are only just beginning to learn about Central Auditory Processing Disorder.) Even the fact that Dyscalculia is a specific learning difficulty which affects the learning of mathematics was (and still is) not generally known by many members of the public.

It therefore seems very likely that some of the different SpLD Profile conditions have in the past gone unrecognised when investigations into a student's mathematical functioning have taken place. In the past, specialists have tended to look at a fairly narrow field; e.g. one particular condition that is part of the SpLD Profile and may have had little, or no, knowledge of the other conditions within the Profile. It was only towards the end of the twentieth century that this situation changed and some

The use of the term 'Acquired Dyscalculia'
This is pretty straightforward as the term can be used when the cause of the mathematical learning difficulties is a condition which can be seen alongside the SpLD Profile; e.g. ME and Childhood Hemiplegia.

The world of Dyslexia and the research into both this condition and the functioning of the human brain can enable us to have a greater understanding of Dyscalculia. It is becoming apparent to some specialists that both Dyslexia and Dyscalculia can be 'outcomes' rather than causal conditions of learning difficulties. In other words, the presence of other conditions can cause the specific learning difficulties that we know as Dyslexia and Dyscalculia.

Mathematics Solutions – An Introduction to Dyscalculia Part A by Jan Poustie et al   ISBN 1 901544 45 1

Historically the term Developmental Dyscalculia was used to refer to specific difficulties in understanding, processing and using numerical/mathematical information. It was believed that it was caused by a developmental condition other than the other conditions that are found within the Specific Learning Difficulty Profile. However, once one looks at individuals where various of the Specific Learning Difficulties Profile conditions are present it is apparent that each of the conditions can cause different difficulties in acquiring and using numerical/mathematical skills.

specialists started to look further afield. This could explain why Luria, in his four sub-groups of Developmental Dyscalculia, appears to include elements of Dyspraxia without mentioning it as the likely causal condition. (His 'Defects of Logic' sub-group includes 'spatial problems' which are often seen as part of Dyspraxia.) An examination of Sharma and Loveless' categories of Developmental Dyscalculia (which were published in 1986 in *Focus for Mathematics Vol. 8*) would also appear to support the view that the SpLD Profile conditions are at the root of some forms of Developmental Dyscalculia.

Basic forms of Developmental Dyscalculia
(These are based upon the system for the classification of computational disorders that was presented in 1970 by Kosc and based on his further work in 1970, 1979, 1981, 1982. These forms are set out in (and all quotes below are from) Part III Chapter 2 of Focus on Learning Problems in Mathematics: Dyscalculia Vol. 8 1986 *edited by Sharma and Loveless. which is published by Center for Teaching/Learning Mathematics. See page 171.)*

It should be noted that more than one form may be present in any one individual.

Verbal Dyscalculia
'A disorder in the ability to verbally designate mathematical terms and relations.'

'An inability to find the name for or to verbally name amounts and numbers of things, of terms, of digits, numerals, operational symbols.'

SpLD Profile conditions which may be present
These difficulties can occur when listening or when reading. This is akin to word finding, word labelling and receptive language difficulties that we see when Specific Language Impairment is present and so we need to look for that condition too.

Language difficulties are commonly associated with the presence of Dyspraxia, Autistic Spectrum Disorder and Dyslexia. Listening difficulties with or without receptive language difficulties (difficulties with understanding the language that we hear and/or read) are commonly associated with the presence of Attention Deficits.

Suggested strategies:
Teach mathematical word-finding and word-labelling as we do to Specific Language Impairment students; e.g. by plenty of practical concrete activities and by making an elaborate memory through the use of as many of the senses as possible. Encourage the use of charts and Mind Maps® to enable the student to see the relationships. See *Planning and Organisation Solutions* by Jan Poustie (page 174) for details of a variety of charts and details of Mind Map construction.

<u>Practognostic Dyscalculia</u>
'An impairment of the capacity for the mathematical manipulation of concrete or graphically illustrated objects.'

Difficulties with 'mathematical manipulations with real or drawn things (fingers, balls, cubes, staffs, etc.).' Problems will be present with addition, comparison of quantities; e.g. more and less, and comparison by size and tasks requiring spatial skills such as reading charts etc. Some of this group "may have no problems with writing and reading numbers and with operations (+ - x ÷) using numbers in script (e.g. word problems).

SpLD Profile conditions which may be present.
Since manipulations involve both movement and spatial skills we need to look for the presence of Dyspraxia. Autistic Spectrum Disorder. Attention Deficit students may also be affected by these difficulties.

Suggested strategies:
We know that improving spatial and co-ordination skills improves literacy functioning and this may be a worthwhile strategy for mathematics too. We do know that practical tasks which use the student's body help him/her to understand spatial relationships etc. Examples of this strategy are:

▸ position the student beside a much shorter or taller student and discuss who is taller/shorter,

▸ next use the smaller body parts; e.g. fingers of the student compared with fingers of the tutor.

▸ Then compare large and very small objects.

▸ Then progress to comparing a pair of Cuisenaire rods; e.g. the two-rod and the ten-rod. (Comparison using only pairs of rods enables the student to create a staircase of rods

The more forms that are present the more complex the programme of remediation will need to be if we are to help the student overcome his/her difficulties. An individual with Attention Deficits may show elements of several of these forms as s/he may not have listened to explanations (and so may not learn the terms and concepts).

Mathematics Solutions – An Introduction to Dyscalculia Part A by Jan Poustie et al ISBN 1 901544 45 1

Use the student's body to help him/her understand spatial relationships

which in its final form will start with the one-rod and finish with the ten-rod. See staircase in the margin on page 102.)

Lexical Dyscalculia

'A disorder of the ability to read mathematical symbols and their combinations.'

Difficulties in 'reading mathematical symbols (digits, numbers, operational signs and written mathematical operations).' As the student gets older reading 'fractions, squares, roots and decimal numbers' become a problem too. Similar looking digits will be confused; e.g. 3/8, 6/9 (or reversed; e.g. 2/5) plus two-digit numbers may be reversed; e.g. 21 confused for 12. The student may have problems with reading numbers written in a horizontal line and numbers which have more than one 0 in the middle of them; e.g. 2003.

SpLD Profile conditions which may be present:
This group of students may be affected by Dyslexia and/or occulomotor difficulties. The latter may be caused by Dyspraxia.

Suggested strategies
See panel on left of this page.

Graphic Dyscalculia

'A disorder of the ability to manipulate mathematical symbols in writing.'

The individual may not be able to write dictated single numbers, may write multi-digit numbers starting from right to left, may write '1284 as 1000, 200, 80, 4, or may ignore the zeros (i.e. 20073 written as 273 or 20730) or write in his own idiosyncratic manner.' The individual may be able to write down the number in the form of words; e.g. 7 written as 'seven'.

SpLD Profile conditions which may be present:
Dyslexia and Dyspraxia (including Verbal/Articulatory Dyspraxia and Occulomotor delay/Dyspraxia) and Central Auditory Processing Disorder (including Neuro-developmental delay).

Suggested strategies
Sharma's strategies for teaching place value are very helpful for multi-digit numbers (see Numeracy 1 video, page 171). If Constructional Dyspraxia is present then the following strategies can be helpful:

Lexical Dyscalculia
Suggested strategies

4

Using the 'Walking round a digit' strategy shown on page 32 whilst looking at the same digit shown by a pattern of dots can help:
➡ internalise the writing and reading of single-digit numbers
➡ reduce confusion between single-digit numbers.
(Also see Mathematics Solutions - An Introduction to Dyscalculia Part B.)

Mathematics Solutions – An Introduction to Dyscalculia Part A by Jan Poustie et al   ISBN 1 901544 45 1

1. Firstly, move the student's body through the digit (see Walking round a digit strategy on right).

2. Secondly, the student moves his/her hand round a very large version of the digit drawn on a very large sheet of paper (e.g. flipchart paper).

<u>Ideognostic Dyscalculia (also known as Dysymbolia)</u>
'A disorder of the ability to understand mathematical terms and relations and to calculate mentally.'

It is a difficulty with the basic concepts of mathematics as the student has difficulties in manipulating mathematical information because of difficulties in grasping mathematical principles or mathematical logic and thus lacks mathematical reasoning. The student is not able to 'calculate by heart on the level which is appropriate to his[her] age and educational placement. Young students will not be able to name the next numbers even in very easy number series; e.g. 1, 3, 5, 7. Older children and adults will have problems with slightly more complex number series; e.g. 2, 4, 8, 16.

SpLD Profile conditions which may be present:
Both those with Dyspraxia and with Dyslexia may have problems with sequencing. No number series comes automatically to the author except for the 2x table up to twenty-four (e.g. 2, 4, 6, 8, 10, 12, 14, 16, 18, 20, 22, 24). Difficulties with understanding the terms may relate to vocabulary acquisition difficulties linked to Specific Language Impairment and/or Central Auditory Processing Disorder.

Suggested strategies
A great deal of practical activities which use first the student's body and then which use concrete apparatus.
The pre-requisite skills for number need to be taught via games and practical activities see Mathematics Solutions - An Introduction to Dyscalculia Part B for further details.

<u>Operational Dyscalculia</u>
'A disorder of the ability to carry out mathematical operations.'

In order to complete a mathematical operation (do a sum) the student has to know rules that apply to that operation. This disorder is the 'inability to learn and appropriately apply these rules and carry out mathematical/arithmetical operations.'

Walking round a digit
Write a very large version of the digit on the floor or outside on the playground/patio. The student has to face front all of the time when walking round the digit.; e.g. to walk round the digit five s/he would:

▸▸ start at the top and move three paces to the left,

▸▸ move three paces backwards,

▸▸ move three paces to the right (in a slightly curving line)

▸▸ move two paces backwards

▸▸ move three paces to the left (in a slightly curving line).

Mathematics Solutions – An Introduction to Dyscalculia Part A by Jan Poustie et al   ISBN 1 901544 45 1

Operational Dyscalculia

Reducing the task by making lots of smaller (and easier sums) from a more complex one is the way that the author usually copes with complex sums. Thus when dealing with addition of a long column of numbers she will usually do as follows for each column:

▸▸ add up all pairs of numbers that make ten,

▸▸ put all other numbers into groups and does the appropriate multiplication sum; e.g. 7 x 4)

▸▸ add all the smaller numbers by counting on,

▸▸ add any spare large numbers (e.g. 9) by counting on. She pretends that there are dots on the numbers (set out in the pattern of the a long dice or playing cards) and 'touches' each dot with a finger/pencil.

▸▸ Finally she writes all the totals of the little sums to form another sum that she works out by going through the whole process again!

Operations may be interchanged; e.g. the student does an addition instead of a subtraction. There may be a reliance on finger counting when doing calculations. Complex sums may be changed to simpler ones thus
12 + 12 may be changed to smaller individual sums:

▸▸ $10 + 10 = 20$

▸▸ $2 + 2 = 4$

▸▸ $20 + 4 = 24$

SpLD Profile conditions
Attention Deficit students may appear to have this form of Dyscalculia because they:

▸▸ do not pay enough attention to learn the rules,

▸▸ may find the need to utilise a rule frustrating,

▸▸ may not read the signs carefully enough.

Suggested strategies
Explain the rule using Sharma's Levels of Knowing Mathematics (see Mathematics Solutions - An Introduction to Dyscalculia Part B).

***

When difficulties in understanding, processing and remembering numerical information are present, students find that mathematics does 'not make sense'. The individual feels that s/he is continually walking across a field under which rabbits have made a vast warren. At any minute one may find the ground disappears from underfoot and with it goes all understanding of where one is in a task, what the task actually is and how on earth one can progress to the next point! This makes even the simplest of numerical/mathematically based tasks stressful and basic computation skills (+, ÷ etc.) unreliable. This causes the person to frequently re-check work and feel unsure of him/herself whenever doing such tasks.

The need for research
It would be very useful if researchers into Dyscalculia included within their research the broader aspects of the student's functioning, including all SpLD Profile conditions that are present. This would enable us to extend our understanding of Developmental Dyscalculia and its relationship with the other SpLD Profile conditions. We would then know whether

Developmental Dyscalculia can be seen in isolation or whether it is always seen as part of the wider picture of the presence of more than one of the SpLD Profile conditions (and therefore could be regarded as the reflection of their presence). Of the SpLD Profile conditions so far only Dyslexia, and its associated mathematical difficulties, have been written about to any extent and books that cover this area can be found in Appendix 2.

Mathematical facts may be understood one minute and the next minute their meaning has slipped away silently into the night!

D: CAN THE DIFFICULTIES CAUSED BY THE PRESENCE OF DEVELOPMENTAL AND ACQUIRED DYSCALCULIA BE OVERCOME?

Yes, intervention involves using teaching methods that have been adapted to the student's needs, with early intervention being the most effective. Students affected by Developmental Dyscalculia are likely to have a range of difficulties according to which of the Specific Learning Difficulties Profile conditions are present. Success can only be obtained if provision is made for all the conditions which are present. Even those students who have severe difficulties can be helped to some degree or another.

Part 2 of this book enables the reader to have a greater understanding of the different SpLD Profile conditions and describes how each of them can affect the acquisition and use of mathematical skills. Part 2 enables the reader to look at the student as a 'whole' and each chapter contains useful strategies that can be used according to which condition is present. The problem of managing student behaviour in the classroom is becoming of increasing interest to many professionals and so Chapter 9 is dedicated to this aspect of education.

When reading this book parents and teachers may find that only a part of the picture has been identified/diagnosed and this may cause concern. However, it is worth remembering that this situation occurs simply because it is the most obvious conditions (e.g. the ones which are having the greater impact on behaviour or literacy) which are usually noticed first. Such difficulties are then likely to be referred for diagnosis, and the speciality of the professional who deals with that particular type of difficulty will determine what the diagnosis is. Unfortunately, it is still the case that not all UK specialists have a wide knowledge of the whole SpLD Profile. As a result, some of the conditions (which may be

Mathematics Solutions – An Introduction to Dyscalculia Part A by Jan Poustie et al   ISBN 1 901544 45 1

Figure 2.3:
A magic square in which each row and column adds up to 6.

2	3	1
1	2	3
3	1	2

Answer to the magic square found on page 26.

The second book in this series *Mathematics Solutions – An Introduction to Dyscalculia; Part B: How to teach students who have specific learning difficulties in mathematics* contains a host of teaching tips and information on useful resources. It looks in detail at the prerequisite skills for number (the foundation upon which other skills are built) and how to help students develop them.

(Note: Maths Notebook is published by Center for Teaching/Learning Mathematics. Their address is on page 171.)

having a much greater impact upon learning but which are being masked by other factors; e.g. high intelligence, other SpLD Profile conditions) are not recognised until much later.

It is when we have several moderate to severe forms of the Specific Learning Difficulties Profile conditions (and/or the conditions that can be seen alongside them) that we start to encounter major problems with acquiring mathematical skills. If CFS/ME is present then the student will need to have sufficient rest and this will require a very flexible provision; some students may attend school part-time; e.g. only attend school for as little as one to four lessons a week (plus a few hours per week of LEA provided home tuition), others may only be able to cope with a little LEA-provided home tuition plus support in the home via watching appropriate educational TV programmes, whilst other students will cope with a slightly reduced timetable.

Part 3 of this book contains useful help and support agencies plus a number of useful products and reference books.

Notes
1. and 2. *Math Notebook Vol. 8, Numbers 7, 8, 9 and 10* page 11 by Professor Mahesh Sharma (pub. Center for Teaching/Learning Mathematics).
3. and 4. See *Mathematics for Dyslexics: a Teaching Handbook* by Dr Steve Chinn and Richard Ashcroft (pub. Whurr Publishers Ltd.) Both are based at Mark College, Somerset.
5. 6. and 7. See *Math Notebook Vol.8, Numbers 7,8,9 and 10 – Dyslexia, Dyscalculia, and Some Remedial Perspectives for Mathematics Learning Problems* by Mahesh Sharma.
8. and 9. *The Math Notebook – Cuisenaire Rods and Mathematics Teaching Vol 10, numbers 3 and 4* by Mahesh C. Sharma. It explains the area method of multiplication and how it can be used for fractions. It also explains why 'of' means 'multiplied by'. Once this method is used it becomes obvious that any number multiplied by nought must equal nought!
10. Professor Sharma during his Certificate Course in the UK, 1995.

Part 2

The
Specific Learning
Difficulties
Profile

The Specific Learning Difficulties Profile

This chapter provides an outline of each of the Specific Learning Difficulties Profile conditions and their impact on numeracy/ mathematical skills. (Identification Solutions for Specific Learning Difficulties; Part A by Jan Poustie et al, ISBN 1 901544 14 1, provides comprehensive information on how to identify each of the conditions.)

OVERVIEW

When the Specific Learning Difficulties Profile is present individuals will have a subset of wide-ranging difficulties which can relate to any, or all, of the following: memory, visual and visual-perceptual skills, listening/auditory processing skills, planning/organisational skills, literacy, numeracy, music, practical tasks, concentration, behaviour, imagination and communication.

It is believed by many that the Profile conditions are related to each other primarily through the area of language. Thus inviduals affected by the conditions within the Profile are likely to have a combination of language-based difficulties which can be seen in any, or all, of the areas of written, spoken and heard language plus that of body language. The appropriate use of language, information processing, understanding and acquiring the areas of language (including mathematical language) can all be affected.

The conditions within the Profile affect the way in which the sensory input (information received) into the brain is perceived; e.g. the visual, listening input as well as the other senses of smell, touch etc. They can affect the processing of such input, the processing within the mind when thinking and the output produced by the mind. The output can take various forms; e.g. reading, writing, speaking and moving.

Associated with these difficulties are atopic conditions such as hayfever, eczema, asthma and nettle rash. Travel sickness can also occur and this is associated with the presence of certain aspects of Dyspraxia. The following conditions are found within the Profile.

No two individuals will be alike and many will have more than one condition.

Developmental conditions are present from birth.

Dyslexia
(*Also called Developmental Dyslexia.*)
In the past this has been used as an umbrella term for several of the conditions found within the Profile. Nowadays, it is more appropriate to use this term only in respect of a condition where the main difficulties are with the acquisition of spelling/ and or reading skills. (*Literacy Solutions* by Jan Poustie et al, ISBN 1 901544 20 6, looks at this condition and the impact of the SpLD Profile conditions on literacy.)

Dyspraxia
(*Also known as Developmental Dyspraxia, Developmental Co-ordination Disorder [DCD], Sensory Integration Disorder and Specific Developmental Disorder of Motor Function [SDDMF]. Note: the latter term is the one that will be used in future by NHS professionals.*)
There are various forms of Dyspraxia which all relate to difficulties in motor planning and organisation. This affects both gross motor skills (movements of the whole body and the limbs) and fine motor skills (movements of the organs of speech, hands/ fingers and the eyes). Sensory sensitivity often accompanies this condition and most have difficulties with acquiring dressing skills.

Difficulties are often present with regard to the planning and organisation of self, work and one's work environment. Both handwriting and the presentation of written work, charts etc. can be poor.

Spatial relationship difficulties associated with the presence of Dyspraxia can cause difficulties in understanding geometry. Fine-motor difficulties can affect the handling of the tools needed to construct shapes and measure angles, length etc. A 360° protractor (it is circular in shape rather than the usual half-circle) which has a handle on it for easier control can help. A pie chart stencil is also useful. Both are made by Helix (available from High Street shops). The majority of those affected by Dyspraxia are likely to have mathematical difficulties although there is some evidence that by late secondary school the majority are performing at a similar level to their peers.

Specific Language Impairment
(*Also known as Dysphasia.*)
A continuum of difficulties experienced by children and young

Dyspraxia
Many people do not realise that difficulties in acquiring gross motor skills such as kicking and climbing a rope etc. can affect the individual's acquisition of literacy skills. The omission of the crawling stage/crawling imperfectly indicates that there is likely to be a problem later on.

people who have not reached expected competence in communication skills in their first language, and whose teaching and learning is consequently affected. It causes difficulties with expressive language (that which you speak or write) and receptive language (that which you hear). Often this group is defined by exclusion: 'They are not autistic, the impairment is not the result of a physical, intellectual or hearing impairment'(Norma Corkish, AFASIC Ex-Chief Executive).

Dyscalculia
See Chapter 2.

Central Auditory Processing Disorder
A dysfunction of the processing of the auditory input (that which you hear) causing problems with understanding/processing what is heard.

Autistic Spectrum Disorder
(*Used to be called Autistic Continuum.*)
Difficulties in social interaction, social communication and in imagination-based activities/behaviour.

Attention Deficits
(*Also known as Attention Deficit Disorder, Attention Deficit Hyperactivity Disorder and Behaviour Inhibition Disorder.*)
Causes difficulties in concentrating and focusing attention. It affects behaviour and has several forms.The presence of this condition can result in the student lacking the patience to acquire many of the fine motor skills and/or failing to sit still long enough to do so. Delayed fine motor skills will affect various activities such as handwriting, mathematical drawings (e.g. charts, shapes etc.), recording mathematical information accurately (in columns etc.) handling small objects (e.g. making models, handling dice and counters etc.), painting, dressing skills (e.g. tying shoelaces, doing up buttons) etc.

This condition can affect the student's ability to concentrate on the teacher's explanation of a mathematical concept and his/her ability to write for any length of time. So the standard achieved in these activities may not reflect his/her intellectual ability.

These students often fail to give close attention to detail.
Thus they misread mathematical information.

ME can also cause such students to have co-ordination and attention difficulties and for them to feel hot or cold for no reason.

THE CONDITIONS WHICH CAN BE FOUND ALONGSIDE THE SPLD PROFILE

Meares-Irlen Syndrome
(*Also known as Scotopic Sensitivity Irlen Syndrome.*)
This is a perceptual dysfunction affecting reading and writing based activities as well as depth perception.

Chronic Fatigue Syndrome (CFS)
(*Also known as Post Viral Fatigue Syndrome [PVFS]and ME.*)
An illness characterised by fatigue, muscle pain and flu-like symptoms occurring after little or no mental/physical effort. It is usually a long-term illness which can last for several years. Children (from as young as five years) as well as adults are affected by it. It causes changes in the brain chemistry which result in the person developing an acquired form of the Specific Learning Difficulty Profile. Many areas of learning can be affected; e.g. literacy, numeracy, co-ordination and attention. Contacts for further advice: Action for ME (Tel: 01749 670799) and the ME Association (Tel: 01375 642466).

ME (Chronic Fatigue Syndrome/Post Viral Fatigue) can cause the student to have difficulties with number and other areas of mathematics. ME is an acquired condition (it is not there from birth) and so when this group of students have mathematical learning difficulties they have Acquired Dyscalculia. If the person is one of the twenty-five per cent of the people who makes a near full recovery from the ME then the Dyscalculia should no longer be apparent. However, if the individual is one of the seventy-five per cent who do not make a near normal recovery then s/he will continue to have difficulties of a Dyslexic/ Dyscalculic nature. Other difficulties may also be apparent because many aspects of the SpLD Profile are likely to be present (to one degree or another) when the person is affected by ME.

Childhood Hemiplegia
This is caused by brain damage as a result of haemorrhages in the brain just before birth, at birth or in the first few years of life. Most of these children who have moderate to severe damage are likely to be affected by specific learning difficulties.

Mathematics Solutions – An Introduction to Dyscalculia Part A by Jan Poustie et al   ISBN I 901544 45 I

Those with mild damage are less likely to be affected by SpLD. There can be difficulties in any, or all, of the following: reading spelling and arithmetic. Movement, behavioural, emotional and social skills difficulties may also be present.

Two-thirds of these children will be of normal intelligence; the other third are likely to be of less than normal intelligence. This condition affects various skills, non-verbal skills are most likely to be affected with language skills being preserved while visuo-spatial skills are lost to some extent. Thus similar difficulties to those found in NLD will also be present (see below). For further advice contact Drs Ian Frampton and Catherine Caulfield, Brain and Behaviour Clinic, Maudsley Hospital, London.

Bryon Rourke is a neuropsychologist based in Canada. Further information on NLD including Byron Rourke's answers to commonly asked questions on NLD can be found at the following internet site: www.nldontheweb.org/little_1.htm

Non-verbal Learning Deficit (NLD).

'This is associated with a deficiency of white matter in the brain. Such individuals have marked difficulties in the processing of visuospatial information' which will affect symbolic language, geometry, writing/layout, map reading, reading diagrams and the use of planning and organisational tools. (Martin Turner, Head of Psychology, Dyslexia Institute)

This term is currently being used in some quarters to include forms of Dyspraxia and Childhood Hemiplegia. For further information on this condition read *Syndrome of Non-verbal Learning Disabilities* by Byron Rourke (ISBN 0898623782 published by Guilford Publications).

GENETICALLY INHERITED SYNDROMES

A wide variety of genetically inherited syndromes exist of which several can include specific learning difficulties as part of their characteristics. One of the most common of these syndromes is Fragile-X. Students affected by this syndrome often show marked inattention, impulsive and overactive behaviours which require good student management skills on the part of the teacher. Difficulties in memorising information can also be part of this syndrome. Co-ordination difficulties (which affect writing) and speech and language difficulties (which may affect reading, creative writing and spelling) may also be present to varying degrees. There can be a considerable variation in reading skills

In the research into Fragile-X there is some evidence which suggests that such students learn better when visual strategies are used.

ranging from those who are unable to learn to read to those who learn to read quite well. Each student affected by a genetically inherited syndrome will have a different set of difficulties so the numeracy strategies will vary according to the areas of greatest difficulty. Attention will also need to be paid to any relevant research into effective strategies for learning with regard to the particular syndrome which is affecting the student.

OTHER ASPECTS OF THE SPLD PROFILE

What factors have caused the SpLD Profile to emerge?
There is now general recognition that a number of conditions are commonly seen together in various combinations. This recognition has occurred because:

1. People are looking beyond the horizons of their own discipline/interests to learn about (and recognise) other conditions.

2. The advance of research has caused definitions of conditions to both change and widen. The subsequent realisation that some of the characteristics (indicators of a condition) are shared by more than one condition has caused 'grey areas' to emerge between them.

How can the presence of more than one condition be recognised and how do we deal with such students?
Each of the conditions within the Specific Learning Difficulties (SpLD) Profile affect the learning and/or behaviour of the person in a different way. These characteristics (or indicators) enable the onlooker to recognise the presence of the condition. (These indicators are dealt with in great detail in *Identification Solutions for Specific Learning Difficulties; Part A* by Jan Poustie et al.)

If tutors wish to solve the mathematical learning difficulties of those students affected by Specific Learning Difficulties then the SpLD Profile conditions need to be addressed first.

What are the implications of recognising a combination of conditions?
A combination of conditions such as Dyslexia and Dyspraxia can have quite wide-ranging implications for the learner. If, for

Prioritisation of provision
If any form of ASD is present then that must be dealt with first. Those affected by ASD are likely to be the hardest students to teach. Not only are these students likely to be affected by a wide range of difficulties (including those of memory) but they also may not learn the information unless a way can be found to motivate them.

instance, Occulomotor Dyspraxia is present a concentration on teaching shapes is only going to achieve so much, but providing for the visual-perceptual and spatial difficulties which commonly accompany Developmental Dyspraxia (DCD) will achieve so much more. As each of the conditions within the Specific Learning Difficulty Profile can affect learning, behaviour etc. there is a need to both recognise and make provision for them all.

The following are some of the combinations which can occur:

▶▶ Attention Deficits alongside Dyslexia

▶▶ Developmental Dyspraxia alongside Dyslexia and/or Attention Deficits

▶▶ Specific Language Impairment alongside Dyslexia and/or Developmental Dyspraxia

▶▶ Central Auditory Processing Disorder alongside Dyspraxia

▶▶ Developmental Dyspraxia, Autistic Spectrum Disorder and Specific Language Impairment

▶▶ Attention Deficits alongside Central Auditory Processing Disorder/Receptive Language difficulties

▶▶ Developmental Dyspraxia alongside Autistic Spectrum Disorder

A wide-ranging provision is likely to be needed when two, or more, conditions are causing the student to have learning difficulties. The greater number of conditions the greater the difficulty in accessing appropriate and effective provision. It is not always realised that even a very low level of several conditions can result in considerable difficulties in learning.

The behavioural conditions
Behaviour must always be dealt with first as behaviour affects the student's ability to learn. The conditions which have behavioural aspects are Autistic Spectrum Disorder (ASD), Attention Deficits (ADD, ADHD) and Dyspraxia. It is now known that there is a 'grey area' in the middle of these conditions.

Dyslexia, Dyspraxia, Specific Language Impairment and Attention Deficits are seen alongside each other. So, when we look for one we must look for them all. Each condition can 'mask' the presence of the other conditions. High intelligence can also mask their presence and can itself be masked by these conditions. Thus highly intelligent students affected by one, or more, of these conditions may be regarded as being of 'average' ability by their teachers. This is especially likely if their oral work in school does not reflect their intelligence either because their language is affected by one of the conditions, or because they are shy etc.

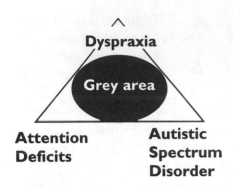

The *How I feel* sheets on pages 165 – 168 can help the tutor to monitor the student's self-esteem. Alternatively, the tutor may wish to use *B/G-Steem*, ISBN 1 873942 35 4, which is suitable for students aged 6 – 14 years. It is available from Lucky Duck Enterprises Tel: 0117 973 288 1.

The student may not be aware of his/her need to use the toilet.

A person may be diagnosed as being affected by one, or more, of these conditions, with elements of one (or more) of the others also being present. This is a very new area of research. In the UK at present, provision may not occur until identification/ diagnosis is made. However, some students who fall into this 'grey area' fail to meet all of the criteria for each of the conditions and so no provision at all is made for their difficulties.

Behavioural difficulties can create a vicious circle. The student has difficulties in learning due to conditions within the Specific Learning Difficulties Profile. Behaviour difficulties worsen when the student's difficulties in functioning are not provided for. The student loses self-esteem and either opts out (daydreams, truants etc.) or misbehaves.

We break the poor behaviour cycle by giving appropriate and effective provision plus raising the student's self-esteem. Sometimes behavioural difficulties are a reflection of the extreme anxiety/stress which can be found in students when any of the SpLD Profile conditions are present. As such students may lack the vocabulary to explain their anxieties it manifests itself in behavioural problems which results in the adult resorting to disciplinary measures. This, in turn, causes more anxiety which results in a downward spiral of behaviour.

How these behavioural conditions affect the recognition of body signals and so affect learning.
Those affected by Autistic Spectrum Disorder and Attention Deficits may not be aware of their own body signals. Such students may not associate a stomach pain with a need to eat or go to the toilet. They can fail to recognise the signs of their body being dehydrated (e.g. headache, dry mouth, irritability) and that they need a drink. This can result in the student becoming very irritable and exhibiting sometimes appalling behaviour because s/he is hungry/thirsty, or 'has had an accident' because s/he did not realise that s/he needed the toilet.

Students with any of the behavioural conditions (ASD, ADD, ADHD and Dyspraxia) may have very restricted diets, find it very difficult to try new foods and will not realise during growth spurts that they need to bring more food/drink to school.

Students with Articulatory (Verbal) Dyspraxia may be such slow eaters that only foods which are quick to eat (but which may be of less nourishment value) are included in their lunch box.

All of these students are likely to behave worse/have greater difficulties with concentration just before dinner-time and can go steadily down-hill all afternoon. This is made worse if they only have sugar-based foods at lunchtime. (Such foods only give a quick burst of energy and do not last for several hours as do mixed carbohydrates; e.g. sandwiches, pasta.) As soon as school finishes, these very irritable students rush home, raid the fridge and the biscuit barrel, flake out on the sofa and may take some hours to recover. If the teacher/parent sees this pattern occurring, opportunities/reminders to eat and drink must be provided if teaching is to be effective. These students may not be able to learn (or may only learn a little) until such provision occurs.

Students who are receiving after-school tuition may need sandwiches and a drink at the beginning of the session. Initially, many will need a sugar-based snack (e.g. chocolate) at intervals during the session as the brain uses 'sugar' when it is working and the intensive teaching demands more brain activity. (Note: mixed carbohydrate and protein snacks; e.g. a jam and peanut butter sandwich, rather than sugar-based snacks, will be necessary for those in whom sugar snacks cause hyperactivity/behavioural difficulties.)

Some schools use a 'withdrawal' system where the student is withdrawn from a lesson for specialist teaching. Students would benefit from being withdrawn from the first lesson of the morning if they eat breakfast, or straight after lunchtime or break if they are given opportunities to eat during the latter. Some students will eat part of their lunch at break time and then not have enough to eat at lunchtime. Always be alert for the student who does not bring enough food and/or drink to school and so consumes all, or most it, during break and is then extremely hungry/thirsty by the end of the day. (For further details see *Practical Solutions for Specific Learning Difficulties: Life Skills* by Jan Poustie ISBN 1 901544 50 8.)

The student's food intake will affect both performance and learning ability.

Most people do not realise how common ASD is. In 1997 it was believed that approximately one in a hundred people were affected by some form of it. However, we are now starting to see evidence indicating an increase in the incidence of this condition and considerable debate amongst professionals as to the:

▸▸   true figures within the community

▸▸   causes of the condition.

For further information see: The National Autistic Society websites (page 161) and http://osiris.sunderland.ac.uk/autism/

Autistic Spectrum Disorder (ASD)
(Including Asperger syndrome.)
If this condition is present it MUST always be dealt with first. This is a very specialised area of provision. ASD is often accompanied by profound learning difficulties, in which case it is usually recognised early and such students, along with those who have a moderate to severe form of this condition, are usually educated in special units/schools. However, the milder cases (and those who are more able) may go unrecognised and undiagnosed in mainstream schooling. This results in the students, and their parents, becoming distressed and their teachers becoming frustrated with a child that they cannot reach and teach. Much of this situation can be turned around once appropriate intervention occurs but this does require both parents and teachers to acquire greater knowledge of the condition.

(Information on this condition and effective strategies for dealing with it are available from the National Autistic Society – see Appendix 1.)

Delayed Motor Skills and Literacy
A delay in acquiring movement skills can have a 'knock on' effect on the development of literacy skills. Various factors can cause this delay; e.g. maternal problems during pregnancy, illness during critical periods of the child's devleopment and genetically inherited syndromes/conditions (Dyslexia is known to be eight per cent inherited and a genetic/inheritance factor is believed to be present to varying degrees in the other SpLD Profile conditions).

Neuro-Developmental Delay (NDD)
The term Neuro-Developmental Delay (NDD) can be used when there is a delay in acquiring the requisite motor skills at the appropriate age. NDD is believed to be significant in various SpLD Profile conditions; e.g.:

▸▸   Developmental Dyspraxia, Attention Deficits, Developmental Dyslexia

Movement-based difficulties are likely to affect self-esteem, especially in boys where skills on the sports field affect their status amongst their peers.

▸▸   Central Auditory Processing Disorder (CAPD) – see *Identification Solutions for Specific Learning Difficulties; Part A* by Jan Poustie et al for further information. There are a number of 'Sound Therapies' aimed at correcting CAPD which involve listening to specially made audio tapes (contact the Institute of Neuro-Physiological Psychology, Tel: 01244 311414 for further details). Other interventions include learning to sing in tune and to play a musical instrument, as these activities can speed up development of certain parts of the brain; e.g. the corpus callosum.)

Movement-based strategies can, in certain cases, be very effective for improving a variety of skills as the exercises establish new neural pathways in the brain which enable the mind to work more efficiently.

The term 'Neuro-Developmental Delay' was originated by Peter Blythe of The Institute for Neuro-Physiological Psychology (INPP) in 1983 and he defined it as being: 'The continued presence of a cluster (three or more) of the Primitive (baby) reflexes which should not be present after the first year of life and the lack of a cluster of Postural (movement control) reflexes which should be present after the first year of life'. It affects various aspects of learning; e.g. physical control of the body, auditory discrimination, the ability to follow text smoothly, binocular vision and behaviour.

Blythe (with David McGlown) developed a series of movement exercises (the 'Reflex Stimulation Programme') which the child could do, on a daily basis, at home. The exercises reproduce the movements that a very young baby would make. It is believed that they give the brain a second chance to control the 'baby' reflexes and release the Postural reflexes. Blythe has found that as the 'baby' reflexes are controlled by the brain so the child's presenting problems disappear and s/he can start to benefit from appropriate teaching methods.

There are now various versions of NDD movement exercises and another form of intervention is also in use where the Primitive Reflexes are 'brushed away'. 'Brushing' has a long history (it was used early in the twentieth century) and it does appear to have helped some children. However, various professionals have concerns about its use (especially in relation to the vagus nerve) and so it is a rather contentious area at present.

Movement-based strategies can be found in various books; e.g. *Developmental Dyspraxia*, (page A10), *Graded activities for children with motor difficulties* by James Russell (ISBN 0 521 33852 2) and *Take Time* by M. Nash-Wortham (ISBN 1 869981 50 2).

NDD interventions are not generally available on the NHS, though the INPP programme is currently being used in one NHS hospital. The length of the course means that it is an expensive intervention to obtain privately. Some practitioners of these techniques do not charge for a first appointment and advise the parents/adults at this first meeting as to whether they will be able to help or not.

How the SpLD Profile Conditions Affect Mathematics.

OVERVIEW

The SpLD Profile conditions can cause a wide range of problems and each of the conditions has a different impact upon numeracy and mathematical skills. The conditions can cause deficits in processing; e.g.

▸ **Memory:** arising from Dyslexia etc., causing difficulties in remembering times tables and the sequence of operations (addition, multiplication, division and subtraction) etc.

▸ **Language:** this can arise from Specific Language Impairment, causing difficulties in understanding mathematical language and usage. Other factors can also cause language difficulties.

Language is looked at in Chapter 6 and in *An Introduction to Mathematics and Language* – A Practical Guide to the Problems, Strategies and Solutions by Jan Poustie,   ISBN 1 901544 96 6.

Attention: arising from Attention Deficits (ADD, AD/HD) etc., causing difficulties in attending to each element of the calculation/teacher's explanation. (Note: Gifted children may also show attention difficulties if the subject/aspect of the topic does not interest them. Students who are under considerable stress also show attention difficulties. (This stress can often occur when the mind is in overload because the student's needs are not being met appropriately.)

▸ **An inability to integrate parts:** arising from Constructional Dyspraxia, causing difficulties in understanding calendars/clocks and geometry. Such students are likely to have difficulties in building age (and intellectually) appropriate models using construction toys such as Lego® etc.

▸ **Planning and organisation:** arising from Specific Language Impairment, Dyslexia, Dyspraxia, Attention

The Attention Deficit 'daydreamer' may be lost in a world of his own but his difficulties may be ignored as his behaviour (if noticed) is irritating rather than disruptive to the whole class.

Figures vary as to the incidence of arithmetical/mathematical difficulties in the Dyslexic population. They range from Professor Mahesh Sharma's belief that 'between twenty to twenty-five per cent of dyslexics also have difficulties with arithmetic/ mathematics'[1] to that of Chinn and Ashcroft who work with 'boys who have been diagnosed as dyslexic and find that upwards of seventy-five per cent of them are affected by such difficulties'[2] (see Chapter 7). Dr Ian McKinlay's research indicates that difficulties with number usually accompany Dyspraxia in childhood[3] (see Chapter 4).

Deficits. The gifted student, the global learner and the Attention Deficit student may intuitively work at tasks rather than plan and organise them.

▸▸ **Adapting, transferring and applying knowledge:** arising from the presence of Dyspraxia or Autistic Spectrum Disorder.

Each of the conditions within the SpLD Profile can affect the learning of arithmetic/mathematics. Various conditions are known to have a high incidence of associated mathematical difficulties; e.g. Dyslexia and Dyspraxia.

The following list contains the main indicators of difficulties in learning mathematics which may be found in individuals affected by the conditions that are found within, or are associated with, the SpLD Profile.

(If any of these difficulties are found the reader should investigate which of the possible conditions are also present. An identification of the likelihood of a particular condition being present can be made by referring to Identification Solutions for Specific Learning Difficulties; Part A *by Jan Poustie et al, ISBN 1 901544 14 1.)*

It should be noted that many indicators of mathematical learning difficulties cross over the boundaries between the different conditions that are found as part of the SpLD Profile. Thus an indicator can indicate that Developmental Dyscalculia (as defined in its narrowest context – see page 15) and/or another SpLD Profile condition is present.)

1. Difficulties in learning new mathematical skills
The first concept/process may be learnt but the individual may have great difficulty in acquiring new ones that build upon the first one and that require it to be adapted in some way. Some individuals may 'learn' the new concept/process in a one-to-one situation but are unable to transfer/apply it to other situations; e. g. within the classroom or daily life environments. *(This can be present as part of Dyscalculia; see Chapter 2. Also see Dyspraxia – Chapter 4 and Autistic Spectrum Disorder – Chapter 9.)* This difficulty may also occur when the teacher teaches via a learning style which is not compatible with the learning style of the student *(see Chapter 1 of this book)*. The presence of CFS/ME,

Childhood Hemiplegia and Non-verbal Learning Deficit may also cause such difficulties (*see pages 38 to 39*).

2. Planning and organisational difficulties

These can be present as part of Specific Language Impairment, Dyslexia, Developmental Dyscalculia, Dyspraxia, and Attention Deficits. (*See Chapters 7, 2, 4, 8 and 9.*) There can be difficulties in both planning and starting the task. Individuals may not be able to find a starting point, or may have several to choose from. As they do not know the correct starting point they cannot start the task at all. This behaviour can be misinterpreted by teachers/parents etc. as laziness.

3. Understanding the language of mathematics

This can be a major reason for the presence of mathematical learning difficulties/Developmental Dyscalculia. (*See Chapter 6 of this book and* An Introduction to Mathematics and Language – A Practical Guide to the Problems, Strategies and Solutions by Jan Poustie, *ISBN 1 901544 96 6.*)

4. Sequencing

Individuals can have difficulties in recognising and remembering sequences. They may not know the correct sequence of numbers/events (e.g. in counting, saying their times tables and the seasons of the year etc.). They can also have difficulties in carrying out multi-step mathematical processes; e.g. long multiplication. Such difficulties can be seen as part of Dyslexia (*see Chapter 7*) and Autistic Spectrum Disorder (*see Chapter 9*) and Chronic Fatigue Syndrome/ME (*see Chapter 2 and page 38.*)

If individuals have any combination of sequencing, remembering numbers and other memory difficulties present they will find it difficult (if not impossible) to learn their tables. Difficulties with carrying out a sequence as part of a practical task can also be found in those affected by Dyspraxia (*see Chapter 4*).

5. Concentration/attention difficulties

Individuals may:

▸▸   Not be able to attend to the task long enough to finish it and and/or may have difficulties in starting the task. (*See Attention Deficit Disorders Chapter 8 and Chronic Fatigue Syndrome/ME Chapter 2, and page 38.*) Those affected by

Strategies which can help students affected by planning and organisational difficulties can be found in *Planning and Organisation Solutions* by Jan Poustie (ISBN 1 901544 81 8, published by Next Generation).

Mathematics Solutions – An Introduction to Dyscalculia Part A by Jan Poustie et al   ISBN 1 901544 45 1

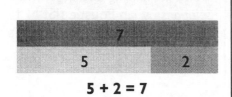

5 + 2 = 7

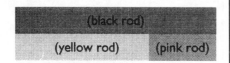

Yellow + pink = black

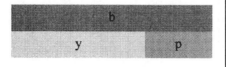

y + p = b

The sum 2 + 5 = 7 may be described as:
pink rod + yellow rod
= black rod
It may also be described as the initial letters of those words;
e.g. p + y = b

If Dyslexia is present use the end letter of black (k) when writing on the board to reduce visual confusion of p/b.

Autistic Spectrum Disorder (*see Chapter 9*) may have difficulties in starting the task because they have no interest in it.

Have difficulties in concentrating on instructions. *(See Attention Deficit Disorders Chapter 8, Central Auditory Processing Disorder Chapter 5, Specific Language Impairment Chapter 6 and Chronic Fatigue Syndrome/ME Chapter 2 and page 38 plus An Introduction to Mathematics and Language – A Practical Guide to the Problems, Strategies and Solutions by Jan Poustie, ISBN 1 901544 96 6.)*

▸▸ Refuse to co-operate with the teacher. This may indicate the presence of Attention Deficit Disorders (*see Chapters 8 and 9*) and/or traits of Autistic Spectrum Disorder (*Chapter 9*).

The student affected by Central Auditory Processing Disorder may mistakenly do the exact opposite of the teacher's verbal instruction and so may incorrectly be thought to be disobedient by adults. (*See Chapter 5.*)

▸▸ Have concentration difficulties due to visual/perceptual difficulties *(See Chapters 1, 4, 5 and section 9 below)* and/or stress and tiredness.

6. Failure to understand algebra
This difficulty may extend to even the simplest of equations. It can occur when early mathematics teaching did not extend concepts high enough and when the new concept is not related to present and past knowledge.

The individual may not understand where the 'letters' used in the equation have come from and it can make no sense at all that 'x' can mean one thing in one sum and something else in another. The strategy shown on the left is based on one used by Professor Sharma. (Just using this explanation once can be enough to make sense, and reduce the fear, of algebra.)
A failure in understanding the symbols used in algebra means that there is no chance of being able to solve such tasks. This lack of understanding can be avoided if concrete examples of the use of letters representing known numbers is used early enough e.g. via the use of Cuisenaire rods. This can be done at very early ages – in fact the rods can be used as soon as equations (sums) are first written down.

7. Difficulties in understanding fractions

There can be difficulties in understanding fractions once the units become smaller than quarters because they have not fully understood the concept of fractions. Previous knowledge of numbers can 'get in the way' of understanding the new concept. Thus individuals can:

▸▸ Have difficulties in knowing which is the bigger of a pair of fractions because 4 is bigger than 3 but in fractions $\frac{1}{4}$ is smaller than $\frac{1}{3}$.

▸▸ Find it illogical that when fractions are multiplied the result is smaller than the original fractions so equations such as $\frac{1}{2} \times \frac{1}{2} = \frac{1}{4}$ make no sense at all.

The student can become extremely anxious when presented with a task using fractions or even just the sight of a page of fractions.

(A combination of methods can enable the student to make sense of this; e.g. the area method of mathematics shown in Chapter 2 combined with the tutor taking a piece of paper to show 'a whole one' and folding it to create the halves and then the quarters.)

▸▸ Have difficulties in using/understanding the terms used for the parts of the fraction (or the terms used for the different types of fraction may not be known well enough).

8. Memory

There are many aspects to memory, and difficulties in a particular aspect will show itself in a particular way. Difficulties with memory are commonly associated with Dyslexia.

Individuals may have weaknesses in the memory skills which are needed to retain information in one's head whilst working out a calculation. Such difficulties can also cause the individual to forget all, or part, of the instruction for/explanation of a given task.

▸▸ *Auditory memory/processing difficulties*
These cause the individual to have difficulties in quickly recalling numbers; s/he may be able to cope with written sums but not with oral ones. (This can be seen as part of Specific Language Impairment, Dyslexia, Attention Deficit Disorder, Central Auditory Processing Disorder *(see Chapters 5, 6, 7, 8 9)*, Dyscalculia *(see Chapter 2)* and Chronic Fatigue Syndrome/ME *(see Chapter 2 and page 38.)*

▸ *Visual and symbolic memory*
These skills are needed to remember what the different signs mean and which way up/round etc. they should be. Individuals may be unable to remember the meanings of the symbols long enough to organise them and put them into the 'plan' of how to solve the question. Difficulties in understanding the use of symbols as representations of a concept etc. may also be present.

Memory difficulties may be present in Developmental Dyscalculia but they are also associated with Dyslexia, Attention Deficits and Autistic Spectrum Disorder. (*See Chapters 7, 8 and 9*.) Such difficulties can also found when CFS/ME is present (*see Chapter 2 and page 38*).Memory difficulties can result in slow working and what seem to be 'careless errors'.

9. Visual-spatial, spatial orientation and/or spatial relationships

Spatial difficulties can show as difficulties with geometry, shape discrimination, size and length. Such difficulties can affect the ability of the individual to find their place on the board/page and there may be difficulties in learning place value.[4] Spatial difficulties can be seen as part of Dyspraxia (*see Chapter 4*).

If both motor co-ordination difficulties and spatial-based difficulties are present, individuals may appear 'clumsy' and 'careless'. Such individuals may place objects on the edge of desks without realising that they are about to knock them off. They can also have difficulties in handling apparatus and constructing diagrams. Difficulties with visual-spatial skills can occur as part of Near-vision Dysfunctioning and/or perceptual difficulties.

(*The reader can gain further information on these conditions from Chapter 7 of* Identification Solutions for Specific Learning Difficulties *which provides comprehensive information on Near-vision Dysfunctioning and Chapter 12 in the same book which looks at Meares-Irlen Syndrome (also known as Scotopic Sensitivity Irlen Syndrome) which affects depth perception.*)

Near-vision Dysfunctioning can be seen as part of Occulomotor Dyspraxia and can exist because of Occulomotor delay. The following section explains how these difficulties can cause the

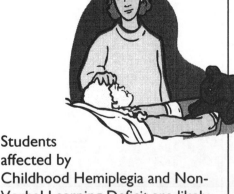

Students affected by Childhood Hemiplegia and Non-Verbal Learning Deficit are likely to have difficulties in these areas too whilst the student affected by CFS/ME may have intermittent visual difficulties with the greater difficulty being found when s/he is

student to underachieve and is extracted from Chapter 7 of *Literacy Solutions* 'Vision problems – their effects on learning, and how to help, both at home anc in the classroom' by Keith Holland and edited by Jan Poustie. Various factors will cause difficulties; e.g.

Only being able to take in information via a small visual area (and so the student will be distracted by information not required for the task that is outside of this visual area.)

▸▸ Stress will make it difficult to maintain focus on reading/ writing tasks, will lower the student's understanding of the material, the ability to think and will reduce concentration.

▸▸ The student is likely to have difficulties in visual imagery ('seeing in her mind' what she wants to write/draw. This can cause problems in remembering the correct layout of the sum etc. prior to writing it. It can also affect spatial development and so hinder the development of concepts in mathematics. It can cause problems with mathematical skills relating to space; e.g. shape, geometry, maps etc. Students with this difficulty may not absorb information presented visually so may listen to the teacher's instructions but ignore, or fail to fully absorb, the diagram on the board.

If the student cannot visualise space and volume then there are likely to be difficulties in understanding number concepts in concrete terms. The student may only 'succeed' in maths by slavishly following learned formulae and techniques, but without a real grasp of the effects that the formulae can have on the numbers themselves.

▸▸ Personality can affect the visual functioning of the student. Type A personalities respond to stress by trying harder, they become stressed and uptight. They overwork in order to achieve. They may have 'migraine-type' stress-related headaches and stress may cause changes in their visual functioning towards short- sightedness.

Type B personalities try to avoid the problem; e.g. not do the task, or do it poorly. Such students may show difficulties in bringing reading/writing material closer to their body.

The numbers in the left-hand column were written from dictation by a five year old boy. He had had one year of schooling and was of above average intellectual ability. The right-hand column shows the numbers which were dictated to him. His numeral construction was affected by his occulomotor and motor co-ordination difficulties.

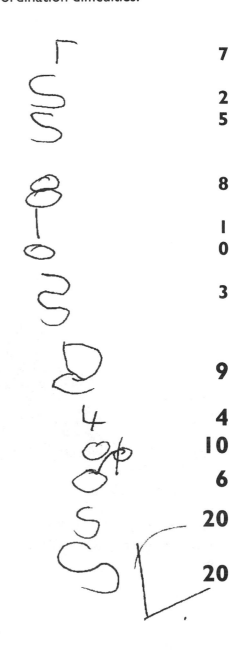

	7
	2
	5
	8
	1
	0
	3
	9
	4
	10
	6
	20
	20

Mathematics Solutions – An Introduction to Dyscalculia Part A by Jan Poustie et al   ISBN 1 901544 45 1

▸▸ Sometimes changing the colour of the paper can help.

▸▸ The use of coloured lenses/overlays (Institute of Optometry, Tel: 020 7407 4183) or Irlen lenses (The Irlen Institute, Tel: 01460 65555) is still regarded by some of the specialists in the field as being controversial. However, there is some evidence that these devices can help reduce the 'glare' and visual distortions that some students experience.

It should be noted that before lenses/overlays are used it is advised to have the functioning of the eye checked by an optometrist so that any underlying physical problem can be dealt with first.

Behavioural optometry exercises can help these students (contact British Association of Behavioural Optometrists, Tel: 01277 624916 or Keith Holland, Tel: 01242 233500 for details.

10. Writing difficulties

The individual may lay out sums/fractions etc. incorrectly and/or present work so badly that various errors occur in the calculation; e.g. incorrect following of a sequence of operations, misunderstanding of place value, misreading of the sum. In Chapter 6 of *Identification Solutions for Specific Learning Difficulties; Part A* the many causes of writing difficulties are described in full – all of which can apply in the writing of mathematical information of which the following are very important:

▸▸ Expressive language difficulties which are present as part of Specific Language Impairment and are often seen when Dyslexia is present (*see Chapters 6 and 7*). Such difficulties make it difficult for the student to know how to write the sum.

▸▸ Motor co-ordination and control difficulties caused by Dyspraxia, stress, anxiety etc. may make it difficult to write the symbols, numerals and diagrams (e.g. geometric shapes, graphs etc.) correctly (*see Chapter 4*).

Vision/perception difficulties will also cause problems in this area (see pages 52 - 54 of this book and *Chapters 7 and 12 Identification Solutions for Specific Learning Difficulties; Part A*).

When expressive language difficulties are present the individual may also have problems in stating which part of the task they are finding difficult. Such difficulties can also be seen when CFS/ME is present.

Mathematics Solutions – An Introduction to Dyscalculia Part A by Jan Poustie et al   ISBN 1 901544 45 1

The student affected by CFS/ME may have motor co-ordination difficulties and may also have difficulties in writing simply because s/he is just too tired to write or even to tired to hold him/herself in a position so that s/he can write.

▸▸ The person affected by Developmental Dyscalculia/ Dyslexia may not understand the significance of writing a particular part of a sum in a particular way; e.g. not fully understand why 2^2 cannot be written as 22

▸▸

11. Reading difficulties due to literacy difficulties (e.g. Dyslexia) and/or visual/perceptual dysfunction being present

The individual may either have great difficulties in reading any maths books, or only be able to read the words in the lower-level reading books and therefore may not progress to the more complex textbooks. S/he may find it very tiring to read which will slow his work down.

The Chronic Fatigue Syndrome/ME student may be too exhausted to read for more than a few minutes. Both slowness in work speed and being unable to read more complex text will result in the individual having less experience of mathematics (see *Chapter 7 plus* Identification Solutions for Specific Learning Difficulties).

12. Directional confusion

This can cause several types of difficulties which relate to the individual being unsure as to which direction to go next in either deciding which part of the sum to work on, or in constructing the numerals etc. Such difficulties are commonly associated with Dyslexia and visual and/or visual-perceptual difficulties. They can also be present as part of Dyspraxia and Autistic Spectrum Disorder *(See Chapters 4 and 9)*.

The individual has to know where s/he has to start the sum and where s/he has to put the answer and this varies according to how the sum is laid out and what type of sum it is. Thus, in the vertically written subtraction sum in Figure 3.1 the individual has to start at the right-hand bottom figure (with the answer going at the bottom) whilst in one form of division sum the starting point can at the left-hand side and the answer goes at the top.

The student may fail to understand which is the denominator and which is the numerator in fractions. (The denominator is the bottom number of the fraction which tells you how many parts the original thing was divided into. The numerator is the top number of the fraction which tells you how many parts you have.)

A vertically presented subtraction sum

34

11-

———

A division sum

2⟌8

Figure 3.1

Mathematics Solutions – An Introduction to Dyscalculia Part A by Jan Poustie et al   ISBN 1 901544 45 1

Directional confusion can make life very difficult for the student. Reading maps, drawing angles, letters, numerals etc. can be a nightmare and writing is likely to be laboured.

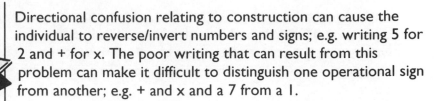

Putting a bar across the 7 as is done on the continent can make it much easier to distinguish between 1 and 7. This is especially important if a lot of numbers have to be written on a regular basis e.g. when doing book-keeping.

Directional confusion relating to construction can cause the individual to reverse/invert numbers and signs; e.g. writing 5 for 2 and + for x. The poor writing that can result from this problem can make it difficult to distinguish one operational sign from another; e.g. + and x and a 7 from a 1.

Directional confusion can cause a variety of difficulties; e.g. the individual may:

▸▸ have difficulties with visualisation (the ability to 'see in your mind' what it is you want to write). The *Language of Position Teaching Pack* published by Next Generation contains a visualisation section which may be helpful here.

▸▸ not be able to 'spell' the equation correctly as s/he cannot remember what it should look like.

13. Comprehension of the written and spoken word
Individuals may know how to do the calculation but produce an incorrect answer because they do not understand mathematical language.

The individual affected by Developmental Dyscalculia may be able to read the words in a mathematical word problem but can struggle to understand the meaning of the words and struggle to write it as a sum. Interestingly enough, literacy comprehension may be perfect. However, difficulties in literacy-based reading comprehension can also be present if the individual is affected by Dyslexia and Specific Language Impairment (*see Chapters 7 and 6*). Difficulties in understanding the spoken word can also be part of Specific Language Impairment (*see Chapter 6*), Dyspraxia (*see Chapter 4*) and Central Auditory Processing Disorder (*see Chapter 5*).

Those affected by CFS/ME can find that when the illness is severe they cannot tolerate noise or even speech. They can also find that they can have periods of time (which can occur quite suddenly) when they are unable to process the spoken and written word.

14. Motor co-ordination difficulties in practical tasks
Even though it may be essential for the individual to use concrete apparatus, those individuals affected by Dyspraxia may well find it difficult to use such apparatus without their peer

group teasing them. They are not likely to neatly throw the dice when working out probability tasks and can easily knock everything over when using equipment (*see Dyspraxia - Chapter 4.*)

15. The individual is reluctant, or struggles, to look at written/visual information

The individual can find looking at this sort of information painful and tiring if Near-vision Dysfunctioning/visual perceptual/ perception difficulties are present (*see pages   32–34.*) The person affected by CFS/ME may only be able to look at the book for just a few minutes at a time before becoming very tired. Occulomotor difficulties can also make the text 'swim' and be unpleasant to look at.

CASE STUDIES

The various conditions within the SpLD Profile can affect the student in a variety of ways as the following case studies show.

Case Study 1: fourteen-year-old girl

The student with Dyspraxia may have difficulties in transferring his/her knowledge to situations outside of the classroom. Thus the student when faced with having to use mathematics in cooking and sewing may need to be guided step-by-step through the maths s/he needs. An example of this was an extremely bright fourteen-year-old girl who had Articulatory Dyspraxia, gross motor difficulties, dressing difficulties, Specific Language Impairment and Developmental Dyscalculia. (*See Chapter 4 for details of Dyspraxia and Chapter 6 for details of Specific Language Impairment.*)

This student was in the set below the top set for mathematics and so her teachers would not expect to see the sort of problems that presented themselves. She decided to do some cooking and she needed to make twice the quantity stated in the recipe. Initially, she found this difficult to do and had to be talked through each part of the task. Similarly, a few weeks earlier she had needed to halve the ingredients in a recipe and had difficulties with that task too. In sewing she decided to make a animal's-head pyjama case. The outline was drawn but she needed to add an extra bit for the seam which was going to be two centimetres. She knew she should add two centimetres but had a struggle to

Besides the indicators mentioned in this chapter the reader should also note that the prerequisite skills described on page 26 of this book may be absent or delayed.

Dyscalculia can cause problems with basic household tasks.

Mathematics Solutions – An Introduction to Dyscalculia Part A by Jan Poustie et al   ISBN 1 901544 45 1

When she was younger this student would not have understood what she needed to do unless she had:

▸▸ the material in her hand,

▸▸ physically moved/marked out the material,

▸▸ pretended to sew the seam.

Case Study 2:
This woman had huge difficulties in constructing the Cuisenaire Rod staircase (shown on page 101) because she could not automatically grade the rods by size just by looking at them in a group. She had to be taught to compare two rods and then compare another two rods until eventually the staircase was formed. (This difficulty in grading by size can also be seen when Dyspraxia is present.)

get her head round the task. She knew that in actual fact she needed to add four centimetres in total because she needed two centimetres all the way round. Again it was a case of talking her through the task but this time a drawing was also needed.

Three of the Specific Learning Difficulties (Dyspraxia, Attention Deficits and Autistic Spectrum Disorder) are associated with differences in behaviour as compared with their peers of similar chronological age. This is looked at in Chapter 9 of this book.

Case Study 2: thirty-year-old woman
Some students have great difficulties in acquiring mathematical skills because of memory difficulties (this can occur when Attention Deficits or Autistic Spectrum Disorder is present). The latter group of students like repetition and those who find memorising lists easy may learn their times tables. However, one of the main difficulties is in trying to remember concepts. One thirty-year-old woman could only remember concepts during the lesson in which she was learning them. Although she was covering work close to GCSE standard she remembered virtually nothing of it once the lesson finished. She showed one of the classic signs of autism in that she had difficulties in releasing gaze (e.g. she stared for several minutes at a time at the face of the person who was talking to her).

Notes:

1. Professor Sharma at his Certificate Course in the UK 1995.

2. Information supplied by Chinn and Ashcroft. The large difference between their figures and Sharma's may be attributed to a variety of factors including that of the population with which they deal; e.g. children attend Sharma's centre because of their arithmetic/ mathematical difficulties and some may be undiagnosed Dyslexics whereas all of Chinn and Ashcroft's students are affected by Dyslexia.

3. Dr Ian McKinlay at the Dyspraxia Foundation's Professional Conference 1996.

Mathematics Solutions – An Introduction to Dyscalculia Part A by Jan Poustie et al   ISBN 1 901544 45 1

Dyspraxia

THE COMORBIDITY OF DYSPRAXIA

We know that when Dyspraxia is present we are also likely to find associated difficulties with numeracy, and commonly we will find difficulties in literacy and language too. (Dr Ian McKinlay's research indicates that difficulties with number usually accompany Dyspraxia in childhood.) We also know that we will often see difficulties in learning mathematics when Dyslexia is present.

The British Dyslexia Association's definition (see page 101) includes 'motor function' skills. Madeleine Portwood, Senior Educational Psychologist in County Durham and Chair of the Dyspraxia Foundation's Education Committee, states the following regarding the incidence of Dyslexia and Dyspraxia.

> 'Where there is evidence of motor difficulty and perceptual problems it is likely that there is evidence of Developmental Dyspraxia, some members of the medical profession refer to this as Developmental Co-ordination Disorder (DCD). Some medical professionals use neither term and refer to co-ordination difficulties instead. The comorbidity of dyslexia and dyspraxia is high (between 30 – 40%).'

Dyspraxia can be diagnosed as young as four years once identified by the pre-school professional/teacher/parent and referred to the appropriate specialists. At the same age, the likelihood of Dyslexia being present can also be identified. Therefore, when 'concern' is raised regarding the child's educational progress in respect of either motor function or Dyslexia, the assessment should include tools that can identify the likelihood of Dyslexia, Dyspraxia and Dyscalculia being present. (See Identification Solutions for Specific Learning Difficulties *by Jan Poustie et al, ISBN 1 901544 14 1 for further details of these conditions.*)

Most people who know a little about Developmental Dyspraxia assume that it only affects certain types of movements; e.g. gross motor skills (whole body, arms and legs) and fine motor skills (hands/fingers, organs of speech and eyes). However, it can also

Dyspraxia is also known as Developmental Dyspraxia, Developmental Co-ordination Disorder [DCD], Sensory Integration Disorder and Specific Developmental Disorder of Motor Function [SDDMF]. Note: the latter term is the one that will be used in future by NHS professionals.)

Note:
Comorbidity is the frequency of the incidence of different conditions being seen alongside each other.

As adults it is easy to believe that what is right for us is right for our students. Some students need 'movement breaks' which enable them to find a more comfortable position. Those with Attention Deficits need 'fidget breaks' (a good stretch often helps them to refocus themselves). Adults need to be aware that some students really are far more comfortable lying on the floor when they study and therefore will study better in this position – even with the stereo full on!!!

affect balance, posture and the way that the student reacts/copes with the environment. The combination of Dyscalculia and Dyspraxia can be revealed through the difficulties that can be seen in acquiring skills in numeracy and mathematics. It is important to note that Dyspraxia causes a variety of difficulties depending upon which aspects of it are present. Any, or all, of the following can be present.

POSTURAL DIFFICULTIES

The person may find it difficult to keep in one position for any length of time and be reluctant and/or find it stressful to sit down and read, write etc. for even short amounts of time. Such students need 'movement breaks' where they are enabled to re-settle themselves into a more comfortable position. (Students with Attention Deficits may benefit from such breaks too though they are likely to need to stand up and stretch as well.)

PLANNING AND ORGANISATIONAL DIFFICULTIES

These difficulties are commonly seen in those affected by either Dyslexia or Dyspraxia with the person who is affected by both conditions being at the most disadvantage. This can be seen by a very untidy bedroom/desk/home, or an exceptionally organised one where the individual cannot bear anything being put out of place.

In the long run it is the planning and organisational difficulties (often associated with decision-making problems) which can be the greatest challenge for the adult. (See Planning and Organisation Solutions *by Jan Poustie ISBN 1 901544 81 8 for further details.*)

THE EFFECT OF THE DIFFERENT SUB-GROUPS OF DYSPRAXIA ON THE ACQUISITION OF NUMERACY SKILLS

Occulomotor Dyspraxia

'This is a neurological difficulty in ordering, sequencing and acquiring visual information due to a dysfunction in the control and use of the visual motor system.'[1] This is not recognised as a form of Dyspraxia until the child is about eight years old. Up until that age there may be a 'developmental delay in the control and the use of the visual motor system'[2] which is called 'occulomotor delay'. Students affected by such difficulties may be reluctant to look at text, have frequent headaches-/stomachaches/feelings of nausea (sickness) during term time which noticeably reduce during the holidays.

Students may have considerable problems with learning to read, they may lose their place in the text and/or have difficulties in accurately seeing the text. This causes a variety of problems in the following areas:

▸ Focusing: this affects the ability to copy from the blackboard.

▸ Saccadic eye movements (commonly called 'tracking'): this affects the ability to move the eyes from left to right (or vice versa) in a fluid movement.

This will cause difficulties in maintaining one's place when reading and so the person will omit parts of the sum, or when reading mathematical 'word problems' will omit words, add words, miss lines etc. This difficulty can also cause the letters/words/numerals to move around, overlap, swirl etc. The result will be that the student will tire quickly when reading such problems and may misinterpret the problem.

▸ White spaces between numbers/letters merging together to form a 'river of white' running down the page (this will be worse when the page has a great deal of information on it).

▸ Letters/numerals poorly constructed and work poorly presented.

▸ Letters/words/numerals misaligned when writing in columns, grids, charts etc.

▸ Writing may be poor and reading may be considerably delayed.

▸ Difficulties in drawing and interpreting charts, maps and plans and in doing geometry may be present.

▸ The visual discomfort caused by this condition results in the student being unable to look at sums/text for a

Letters/numerals may be:

▸ written upside down

▸ written back to front

▸ Misread

▸ any number may be written backwards.

Thus 5 may be confused for 2 whilst 6 may be confused for 9.

This can result in the student getting the sum wrong not because s/he could not do it but purely because s/he misread it. (See Chapter 11 Section 4: 'Place Value' for further details.)

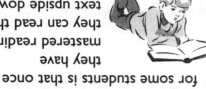

The advantage of this difficulty for some students is that once they have mastered reading they can read the text upside down as easily as they can read it the right way up!

prolonged length of time (for some individuals, even doing the task for a few minutes causes headache, nausea etc.)

(Keith Holland's questionnaire in Appendix 2 can be used to identify those with visual difficulties. Further information on these difficulties plus the perceptual difficulty of Meares-Irlen Syndrome, also known as Scotopic Sensitivity Irlen Syndrome, can be found in Identification Solutions for Specific Learning Difficulties - *see page 171.)*

Some of the individuals affected by these forms of visual difficulty may find it easier to do sums when they are presented on a computer, since the size of the letters and the spacing between the numbers and lines can be enlarged so that there is less overlapping. (The effects of 'glare' can also be reduced by changing the background colour of the screen from white to a colour that the student finds easier to look at.)

Students affected by Occulomotor Delay/Dyspraxia are likely to have difficulties in both writing the sum down correctly from the board and in correctly reading the sum simply because the letters/numerals may not stand still/be in focus long enough for them to remember what they look like! Such students may only have an overall impression of how the sum should be laid out (may especially remember the first and last numerals of a horizontally presented sum) but the exact detail is lost as all the numerals and operation signs may merge together in memory. Such students may also have difficulties in producing neat handwriting and well-presented work with laying out numbers in columns being particularly difficult. Producing and reading maps/plans may also be a problem.

Those with moderate to severe difficulties are likely to need to do eye exercises to train the eyes in correct movements. *Thinking Goes to School* by Furth and Wachs (ISBN 0-19-501927-X) is an American book which is not widely available in the UK but (if it can be accessed via one's local library) does provide some good eye movement games which can help this condition. Some of the Brain Gym exercises may also be helpful.

The student may find it much easier to read enlarged text and so the tutor could enlarge the relevant pages of the textbook (after gaining the publisher's permission) and then allow the student simply to write in the answers. This reduces one of the student's problems but may result in him/her not gaining enough experience of practising the layout of calculations. This situation is a little like the one which arises when in literacy we concentrate on enabling these students to learn to read (and so enable them to access information) and worry much less about them being able to spell. Since most of the visual system has matured by the age of eight years it may be wise to wait until this age before working more on practising the correct setting out of sums. There are many Ann Arbor books which are devoted to various types of tracking exercises and a few of them use numbers for this purpose (see right-hand column for details).

Dyspraxia-based handwriting difficulties (also known as Graphomotor Dyspraxia)

(*Only a few people will actually be affected by this Specific Learning Difficulty but many more are incorrectly referred for it as the various other causes of handwriting difficulties are still not widely known. See Identification Solutions for Specific Learning Difficulties; Part A for further details.*)

This is a difficulty in fine (small movement) motor planning and organisation, and control relating to the hand. Other indicators of Dyspraxia can also be present including difficulties relating to arm/shoulder, gross motor control, posture and difficulties in accurately representing the spatial relations of letters/words/numbers. Each aspect of it causes a different set of problems such as difficulties in forming numerals when handwriting, applying the correct pressure, writing on the line, within a box/column and writing with an even slant.

Students may not know how to 'get the best out of their pen'. One secondary-school student was found to be pressing hard with his fountain pen as he thought that this would make the ink come out!

Many people assume that when a student writes a sum incorrectly it is because s/he did not know how to do the sum. What may not be so obvious is that s/he may actually be having more of a problem with remembering all, or any, of the following:

Spectacles of various types can help.

Behavioural optometrists can do an in-depth assessment of eye movement functioning, advise on exercises and provide glasses if necessary. (See Appendix 1 for address.) One's local optometrist can also help by prescribing spectacles fitted with a low-plus lens. This enlarges the text and can enable such students to read much faster and with greater accuracy.

Number Tracking Math 1
(Published by Ann Arbor Publishers Ltd. PO Box 1, Belford, Northumberland NE70 7JX Tel: 01688 214484)
A self-instruction workbook which can help improve visual accuracy.

Mathematics Solutions – An Introduction to Dyscalculia Part A by Jan Poustie et al   ISBN 1 901544 45 1

Using cutlery can be difficult!

Eating food on a tray on one's lap can be particularly difficult. Different cutlery can help. Those affected by 'hyperacusis' (over sensitivity to sound) may not be able to cope with the sound of the utensils scraping against the plate etc. Students may have difficulties with cutting meat. They can try to cut by 'pressing down' rather than by using a 'sawing' action. Such individuals are also likely to need support in all practical tasks which involve tools; e.g. art, sewing, DT and cooking.

▸▸ How to write each numeral

▸▸ Where to put the numerals in the right place in relationship to the writing line

▸▸ Simultaneously processing the information, constructing the numerals and remembering how to lay out the sum.

Early signs of later writing problems can be seen at the pre-school level where there are likely to be difficulties with any tasks where combined hand/eye skills are needed; e.g.

▸▸ jigsaws,

▸▸ using scissors,

▸▸ construction toys,

▸▸ the fastenings of clothes (e.g. shoelaces, zips and buttons,

▸▸ using eating utensils.

Later on such students, when writing, may:

▸▸ press so hard that one can see the imprint several pages down the notebook

▸▸ gradually widen the left-hand margin as they go down the page

▸▸ produce poorly presented written work

▸▸ reverse/invert letters and numerals

▸▸ find it difficult to write in a straight line on a blank piece of paper

▸▸ find it difficult to keep all the numerals and 'x' height letters the same height and/or may write them incorrectly through the line or write them too tall or too small

▸▸ be unable to write numerals/words using fluid movements

▸▸ have spatial relationship difficulties which can cause problems when:

  ▸▸ trying to lay out work,
  ▸▸ draw diagrams and charts,
  ▸▸ organising personal space
  ▸▸ using mathematical apparatus etc.

(Such students are also likely to knock into people/things and will often acquire bruises 'out of nowhere'.)

Mathematics Solutions – An Introduction to Dyscalculia Part A by Jan Poustie et al   ISBN 1 901544 45 1

Graphomotor Dyspraxia can be reduced by altering a variety of factors; e.g.

▸▸ The writing tool
Some stationers allow you to try out a variety of pens and pencils.

▸▸ The penhold
Let the student explore unconventional penholds (as they can reduce the pain and the amount of pressure used). Avoid imposing your own view of what a correct penhold should be.

▸▸ Reduce the stress of handwriting sums
The younger student could use rubber ink stamps (available from shops such as Early Learning) to record sums so that s/he can then focus on actually doing the calculation. Some students may find it easier to use a good quality word-processor. (Note: some may find it easier to use the number keys that are on the right-hand side of the keyboard rather than the keys at the top. Others may find the right-hand keys confusing as they are not laid in the same way as a calculator.) Once again, one could (with permission from the publisher) use the strategy of photocopying a page of sums and getting the student simply to write in the answer. (This strategy also enables the tutor to enlarge the sums, which is likely to make it easier for the student to read them. The sums could also be photocopied (with the publisher's permission) on to coloured paper if the student finds that a particular colour reduces 'glare'.)

When Attention Deficits is also present, enabling the student to do the sums quickly (by writing the answers on the page) has an added bonus, as this group of students likes to get the task over and done with quickly (and may be very reluctant to attempt the task unless such speed can be achieved.)

▸▸ Use computer programs to reinforce processes   Since most sums that an individual does are written to reinforce a process then the wise tutor can make this into a fun task by using one of the many computer software programs mentioned in *Mathematics Solutions – An Introduction to Dyscalculia; Part B.* If a computer is to be used by the

It is important to reduce the student's level of stress in as many areas as possible.

Help the student to relax   (e.g. through laughter, praise and appropriate support) as this will reduce the tension in the hand. *Take off with Number* (see page 175) has been designed to help reduce mathematical anxiety.

The student who has Dyspraxia may take to computers 'like a duck to water' - at last they have a release from the stress of trying to handwrite tasks such as essays. Some students, despite co-ordination difficulties, find that they learn better if they write out by hand information that has to be memorised.

Reduce the amount of stress in the student's life at school by redefining the task so that the student can finish it at the same time as his peers. Reducing the number of sums to be done can be helpful. The *Oxford Mathematics* series of textbooks can be very useful here as it produces both a long and a short version of each book.

Ergonomic chairs are available; e.g. those made by Sebel Design (C2 The Courtyard, Alban Park, St Albans, Herts, AL4 0LA). They also stock matching desks and are available in a variety of sizes to suit different height pupils.

student then training and support for the student will be necessary. Some students will need to use the computer for the bulk of their written work and in such cases both they and their parents will need training to ensure that the computer can be used with ease. Teaching staff need to provide a safe (and easy to access) storage area for when the computer is not in use. Easy access to a printer and a plug are also necessary!

▸▸ The paper
The surface tension between the pen and paper can affect the writing quality in extreme cases and so different types of paper may need to be explored. Some people (such as the author) find rough papers difficult to write on and may need a smooth writing surface. Some people may find that they have less control on very smooth papers as the writing tool slides too easily over the surface.

▸▸ The writing surface
A pad of paper under the writing sheet is more comfortable than a hard desk/table. A slanting surface can be provided in various ways; e.g. by using a little desk that goes on top of the table, by having a sloping desk, or by using an A4 ring binder file as a base for the book/paper.

▸▸ Classroom furniture
The student's difficulties will be worsened if s/he is sitting at a desk/table (and using a chair) which is far too small/large for him/her.

The Sebel desks (see left) can be adjusted so that the writing surface is at an angle or can be laid flat. If mathematical apparatus is being used then it may be best to use an A4 folder (lying on its side) to provide an angled surface for writing and then the rest of the table will provide a flat surface for the apparatus.

▸▸ Posture
Time may need to be spent adjusting the student's posture to one where his/her body weight is taken by a combination of the chair and his/her feet (which are resting flat on the ground). The ideal posture causes the student to use the least amount of energy possible and the least amount of pain when writing.

▸ <u>Adapting the student's writing style</u>
It is best not to impose one's own ideas of a correct model for writing numerals/letters but instead to encourage the student's development of his/her own personalised script.

▸ <u>Improve the location of the student</u>
Do not sit a left-handed student so that his/her writing arm can collide with the writing arm of a right-handed student.

Verbal (Articulatory) dyspraxia – the hidden difficulty?
Part 1 is an original contribution by Mary Nash-Wortham MRCSLT (Reg.), RSA Dip SpLD, edited by Jan Poustie.

Part 1
The soft indicators for Verbal Dyspraxia are those associated with making and co-ordinating the very precise movements of over one hundred muscles which combine to make the speech apparatus work together to create clear articulations (speech).

The speech apparatus includes:

▸ The lips

▸ The tongue tip, blade and back which pushes against the soft part of the palate. *(The palate forms the roof of the mouth and the soft palate at the back is vital for speech clarity as it moves up to close off the nasal airway or down to let air though the nose.)*

▸ The soft palate *(the back of the palate)* closes off the airways within the nose used for blowing, sucking, swallowing and for speaking the 'm'/'n' and 'ng' sounds. It is also used for resonance and tone of voice.

The voice is created in the central neck region of the larynx, which again depends upon the muscles controlling breath. (The breath has to be both sufficient and controlled enough to synchronise the air passing through the vocal folds (vocal cords) in a series of rapid puffs which cause the sound of 'voice' through vibration.

Normal speech is, therefore, entirely dependent upon breath control from the lungs, passing through the vocal folds to make

The student who has Dyspraxia must be observed and treated holistically, as a whole person, because the difficulties are likely to be spread to a wide variety of dysfunctions including gross and fine movements of the feet, legs, body and arms, hands and finger control. Verbal Dyspraxia may be the only problem for the child, or it may be associated with a range of other difficulties including Attention Deficits and general clumsiness.

Verbal (Articulatory) Dyspraxia has a wide range of associated difficulties

The 'swallow reflex' can be affected. Students may be slow eaters, have had feeding difficulties during babyhood and be slow to learn to suck through a straw. They may have difficulties in:

▸ swallowing their own saliva,

▸ swallowing catarrh,

▸ have problems in learning to blow their nose.

sound. This is turned into meaningful speech by:

▸▸ The rapid movements of the soft palate, tongue and lips.

▸▸ The position of the jaws and teeth.

▸▸ The resonance of the whole process in the hollow sinus regions of the neck and head.

These difficulties in planning and organising the movements of the organs of speech may affect various aspects of speech; e.g.

▸▸ correct breathing for speech

▸▸ speed, rhythm and volume of speech ('it may be unusual, distorted or abnormal')

▸▸ the way that the voice rises and falls during speech

▸▸ saying particular sounds; e.g. 'th' and 'thr'

▸▸ mispronunciation of words; e.g. pronouncing the parts of words in the wrong order, omission of sounds, unclear sounds

▸▸ sentences may be unclear and/or incomplete.

The student's pronunciation difficulties may not be observable to the casual listener as some students 'mumble' the middle sounds of long words. Unless one listens carefully, one is not aware that they are saying the wrong sounds. Students may lose a syllable in long words by 'telescoping' the sounds together. They may also reverse sounds; e.g. say 'lots' for 'lost' and so will repeat the error when writing/reading the word. Sometimes the smaller words can be said but not longer words which have many syllables.

The inability to write clearly is closely associated with Verbal Dyspraxia. This writing difficulty can be linked to:

1. The physical difficulty of actually holding and co-ordinating the fine movements of the writing implement. This will affect the writing of numerals, letters, maps, charts etc.

2. The (often overlooked) verbal language problem. This can be seen as difficulty with the actual processing and formation of words into a meaningful flow of ideas and thoughts:

> ▶▶ from the brain to the mouth (where verbalisation takes place)

> ▶▶ to the writing hand, where the composition takes place as written expression.

Children who have Dyspraxia often have a history of:

▶▶ Delayed onset of speech (or the speech may not be delayed but much of it cannot be understood by the listener).

▶▶ A continuing delay in speech (use of words) and language (use of sentences and structure of sentences).

It is not unusual for such children to start single-word talking as late as three or four years. Progress may be slow and grammatical errors may often persist long into junior (and even secondary) school.

Part 2
The other aspects of Dyspraxia (which are also likely to be present) will affect the student in many areas; e.g. the language difficulties that are commonly seen alongside Dyspraxia, poor handling of apparatus and, if the mathematics lesson is timetabled straight after PE then the student's slowness at dressing after PE, may cause him/her to arrive late to the lesson.

The student may be unable to cope with the smell of the cleansers used in the classroom and/or the heat from the nearby radiator.

It is unusual to find a pupil who has difficulty on paper with spelling order, written ideas and order of concepts who does not have an associated, but possibly less evident, verbal language weakness too. Those with excellent visual memories may be able to spell accurately even though they still mispronounce the words and so they are harder to recognise. The student is likely to have problems in spelling words and in 'breaking words down' into their separate sounds and in 'building the sounds up' to read unknown words. Therefore, the effects of this form of Dyspraxia are likely to be noticeable when the student is asked to do the 'number stories' activity (see *Mathematics Solutions – An Introduction to Dyscalculia; Part B*).

Beware the silent, quiet, seldom heard pupil, who covers up his/her Verbal Dyspraxia with a reserved attitude (and even a stammer) to help prevent the necessity of the teacher paying attention to him.

The difficulties of students who have Verbal Dyspraxia are increased if they also have a form of Dyspraxia which affects their writing. Such students can only rely on their visual skills when learning spellings etc.

Verbal Dyspraxia is a good example of how conditions overlap – Dyspraxia and Specific Language Impairment.

'Early speech and language therapy intervention targeted at the child's main difficulty has been shown to be most effective although children starting therapy later will also progress. Some children will require more intensive therapy and the severity of the difficulty and the motivation of the child will determine this. What is of primary importance is the involvement of the parents (and the other main adults in the child's life; e.g. the teacher) in working with the child on programmes to remediate the problems.

Research has shown that children with Verbal Dyspraxia frequently have problems in developing reading, writing and spelling skills. (Spelling is particularly at risk because it relies on the breaking down of words into their parts and on making the links between speech sounds and written letters.)

Many of these children also have motor Dyspraxia affecting their fine (small muscle movements; e.g. the fingers) and gross motor skills (large muscle movements; e.g. the leg).

A number of this group will have related specific difficulties with numeracy skills.'
(Association For All Speech Impaired Children – AFASIC)

Students with severe Verbal Dyspraxia will need speech and language therapist intervention using such tools as 'The Nuffield Centre Dyspraxia Programme', (Tel: 020 7915 1535)while less affected students will benefit from using resources where they record their own voice. Students with this form of Dyspraxia are likely to have to rely on visual and kinaesthetic (movement; e.g. writing) skills to remember how to write sums and words.

In the field of literacy; the practice of students writing from their own dictation has been found very beneficial in some cases. A similar technique can be used for mathematics. Thus the student dictating sums (with their answers) on to a tape recorder and then writing the sums from his/her own dictation may be a useful strategy to help improve both auditory skills and mathematical functioning. This strategy can be used to help students learn their number bonds (pairs of numbers that make 10 or 20; e.g. 7 + 3 = 10) and their times tables too.

OTHER ASPECTS OF DYSPRAXIA WHICH CAN AFFECT NUMERACY SKILLS

Perceptual difficulties

Various perceptual difficulties are highly likely to be present. Visual-perceptual difficulties will affect the way in which the mind processes visual information and so this will affect many aspects of mathematics; e.g. reading word problems, writing out the sum, sum layout, drawing of diagrams, maps, charts etc. It will also affect both the interpretation and drawing of angles. When this is seen alongside Graphomotor Dyspraxia then we are likely to see a student who is slow to complete any written/drawing task and such work is unlikely to be of a good standard. If Attention Deficits is also present then such students are quite likely to throw away their work in disgust which results in teachers/parents nagging them because they think that the work has not been done.

Only seeing the white bits

Some students affected by Dyspraxia have this unusual way of looking at text. It is a problem related to whether their brain is prioritising the foreground or the background of an item. People tend to assume that when we point to a single letter on a card the student is looking at the 'black bits' which make up that letter/numeral. However, some students do not see the 'black bits' but see the 'white bits' instead. As the white background to a letter/numeral changes shape according to its surrounding letters/numerals these students do not usually progress beyond reading a few words until specialist intervention is provided. They may find it easier at first to do numeracy tasks, simply because there are so few components in early sums and each of the components are well spread out on the page. The first stage of intervention is to tell the student which bit to look at! The 'Developmental Test of Visual Perception, 2nd Edition' can be used to determine the extent of the problem. It includes a variety of sub-tests which look at a range of skills such as figure/ground configuration, eye-hand control and spatial relations. (It is available from NFER-Nelson, Tel: 01753 85896.)

Trying out different colours of text may be helpful here and teaching the student to write using white text/numerals on a

Which do you see first, the faces or the vase?

Some of you will find that your eyes keep going from one to the other.

Mathematics Solutions – An Introduction to Dyscalculia Part A by Jan Poustie et al   ISBN 1 901544 45 1

Handwriting and drawing are complex perceptual-motor skills which require the integration of visual and movement (kinaesthetic) information so difficulties in these areas will affect the student's ability to handwrite and to draw shapes, maps, charts etc. and may affect the handling of apparatus.

black background may also be useful. Referral to a paediatric occupational therapist will also be necessary. (*See Dyspraxia chapter in* Identification Solutions for Specific Learning Difficulties.)

Various combinations of these difficulties will cause different sorts of mathematical skill-acquisition problems; e.g. the student:

▸▸ may not be able to interpret and reproduce the angle of a line correctly

▸▸ may produce reversals (seeing/writing things back to front) and inversions (seeing/writing things upside down).

Developmental Dyspraxia by Madeleine Portwood (ISBN 1 85346 573 9) is a widely acclaimed book on Dyspraxia which is aimed at both parents and professionals. It contains remediation activities to develop perceptual and motor skills, lots of practical advice and a Motor Skills Screening assessment, plus an intervention programme which has been used successfully with both children and adults. A textbook for students and professionals called *Understanding Developmental Dyspraxia* is now available from the same author (ISBN 1 85346 573 9).

Sensory sensitivity
The 'fussy' student may be affected by sensory sensitivity. S/he may dislike certain smells, tastes, textures (in the mouth or against the skin). S/he may also overreact in certain temperatures, especially if the environment is also humid (damp); e.g. the changing room at a swimming pool.

Dyspraxia can cause students to over/under react to information that they receive via their senses; e.g. of touch, smell, hearing etc. Students with this difficulty can be distracted by the unpleasant 'feel' of a necktie, the material of their school uniform, the tightness of a waist-band. They may not be able to cope if they are placed too close to a source of heat (e.g. radiator, window on a sunny day) or are too cold. Thus, taking their GCSEs (or other examinations) at the height of summer on a very hot day can cause them to underfunction. They can find the smell of the dinner cooking too unpleasant to concentrate on their work. The teacher's perfume/aftershave may overwhelm them and cause them to feel ill, as can the smell of the cleansers used to clean the classroom.

If the student is over-sensitive to certain levels of sound (hyperacusis) s/he may find the voices of classmates too loud and may find the high pitch of a teacher's voice very unpleasant. (The student can also find the sounds of certain musical instruments such as the recorder very unpleasant.)

DIETARY SUPPLEMENTS AND DYSPRAXIA

Associated movements

Associated movements can be seen when a person is affected by Developmental Dyspraxia (e.g. the leg moves when the child kicks a ball but, without him/her intending it, his/her hand moves as well). It has been suggested by Madeleine Portwood that the reason for these associated movements is that redundant neural pathways in the brain have been retained. Normally, when a baby is learning to hit the mobile in his/her cot s/he will move lots of different parts of his/her body at once as s/he learns to control his/her arm. The repeated efforts to hit the ball programmes the brain to reinforce the neural pathways for moving the arm when wanting to hit the ball. Eventually all the other neural pathways which controlled the extra movements when s/he moved his/her arm will be made weaker and should disappear. The individual with Dyspraxia keeps many of these redundant neural pathways and so the 'message' to tell the arm to move goes along many extra pathways and so takes longer to process and to execute.

Portwood believes that the situation is different in those who have a metabolic disorder. Here the neural pathways are correct but the brain has problems in transmitting messages from one cell to another. In recent years the effects of metabolic functioning upon the brain plus maternal diet and the latter's relationship with significant feeding problems in new-born infants have been investigated. Sixty per cent of the brain is fat and twenty-five per cent of the fat is docosahexonic acid (DHA). DHA is found in breast milk and it is believed to be an essential requirement during the foetal stage and for the first four weeks of life. It is believed that the metabolic problem is caused because the individual is not able to metabolise some long-chain polyunsaturated fatty acids such as Docosahexonic acid (DHA).

There is increasing evidence from research by specialists such as

Those with Dyspraxia are likely to have great difficulties in transferring their mathematical/ numeracy skills from the classroom to any other situation. However, Dr Ian McKinlay's research showed that those affected by mathematical learning difficulties have usually caught up with their peers by the end of secondary school. (However, their level of mathematical functioning may not take into account their intellectual level and the fact that they may have been functioning b

Up until fairly recently baby formula milk, which is used for bottle-fed babies, did not contain DHA but some manufacturers have now included it.) elow their true potential.

Mathematics Solutions – An Introduction to Dyscalculia Part A by Jan Poustie et al   ISBN 1 901544 45 1

In the past it was commonly believed that taking certain oils might increase the number of seizures in those affected by epilepsy. There is now some debate amongst professionals as to whether this intervention is safe for this group. It is therefore very important that the reader seek the latest advice on this issue via his/her GP.

Up-to-date information on metabolic disorder and specific learning difficulties, foods that contain the right oils etc. will be included in *Identification Solutions for Specific Learning Difficulties* by Jan Poustie et al due for publication in 2001. *(Note: as this a two-part title please check with Next Generation to find out which part has this information in it.)*

Madeline Portwood which indicates that a metabolic disorder is responsible for about eighteen per cent of those who have Dyspraxia. Such individuals appear to need supplements added to their diet in the form of a combination of evening primrose oil and fish oil. Portwood has found that some parents have reported immediate improvements in their children's co-ordination and ability to process information once such supplements are used. The author has also had similar reports made to her of improved functioning in some students (and their parents) when taking the supplements, but she has also found that it has no effect on some students. There is talk that, within the next two years, a simple test will be available to determine who is affected by this metabolic dysfunction.

The present recommendation is that if no improvement has been noted within a fortnight then discontinue taking the supplements. If improvement is noted then it is thought that the supplement will need to be taken for life. There are a number of commercially available preparations which appear to contain the right combination of oils but it is cheaper to make your own combination using primrose oil and a fish oil such as cod liver oil. (Directions for daily intake will be on the relevant packaging.)

It has been the author's experience that when Dyspraxia is present the student tends to either hate computers or takes to them 'like a duck to water'. If the latter is the case then there are plenty of computer programs that can be very useful, Sherston's *Crystal Forest 2000* (Tel: 01666 843200, www.sherston.com) is very good for the development of spatial skills and includes work on angles, shape and work using Logo. (Logo is a simple programming system for controlling the way devices can move which is used in UK primary schools.)

Notes:
1 & 2. *Keith Holland in 'Identification Solutions for SpLD' by Jan Poustie et al (ISBN 1 901544 14 1)*

Praxis II, published by the Dyspraxia Foundation, contains a great deal of information on the management of Dyspraxia (for their address see Appendix 1).

Auditory Dysfunctioning
(Including Central Auditory Processing Disorder)

(Full details on the recognition of this condition and its different sub-groups are in Identification Solutions for Specific Learning Difficulties; Part A *by Jan Poustie et al, ISBN 1 901544 14 1.)*

Auditory-based language difficulties were described in the past by speech and language therapists as 'receptive language difficulties' (see Chapter 6) and this term is still currently used. In the second half of the twentieth century the *Aston Index* was published and this assessment tool enabled teachers to assess for certain areas of auditory difficulty; e.g. auditory sequential memory, auditory discrimination, and so such terms tend to be used by teachers. More recently, the term Central Auditory Processing Disorder (CAPD) has emerged. This term is used by audiologists and it seems to cover a broader range of difficulties than the term 'receptive language difficulties'.

CAPD has been divided into four sub-groups and each one causes different problems in learning. Two of these sub-groups, 'Auditory Decoding Deficit' and 'Integration Deficit', make it difficult for the student to learn using the usual multisensory methods.

Those with Integration Deficit need a gradual introduction to multisensory methods whereby a combination of movement and visual memory are trained first; e.g. by mouthing (rather than saying out loud) the name of the operation sign (e.g. +) whilst looking at a correctly written example of it. Once they are used to doing this they can then be encouraged to speak the name of the symbol (or the teacher says it). Finally, the student progresses to saying the name of the symbol etc. whilst looking at it or writing it.

The main cause of Integration Deficit appears to be delayed neuromaturation (also known as Neuro-Developmental Delay (*see pages 45-46*). Neuro-Developmental Delay can produce a range of auditory difficulties. The maturing of auditory

CAPD can affect the student's ability to deal with information that is presented to him/her auditorally and/or his/her ability to understand written text (comprehension).

What will work for one student will not work for another! Those with Auditory Decoding Deficit are likely to suit visual/kinaesthetic techniques; e.g. where they trace over the numerals as a way of remembering how to write them.

A multisensory method enables the student to learn because they are using as many senses as possible simultaneously when doing a task. Usually the senses of movement (kinaesthetic, e.g. hand-writing, speaking), listening (auditory, e.g. hearing one's own speech) and seeing (visual) are used together.

REA: The right ear usually receives language-based auditory input better than the left until the child is about ten years old.

It may well help the learning ability of some SpLD Profile students if they are moved to locations within the classroom so that their dominant ear faces the main conversation/discussion areas.

Use of Aston Index Sub-test 9.
(Available from LDA, Tel: 01945 463441.)

It should be noted that the Aston Index test advice is that, when conducting this test, the student should listen to a transistor radio, or a watch. Only if language-based auditory input is used, is this test likely to indicate the dominant ear for received language; e.g. the radio is tuned to a conversation.

functioning is related to the development of the part of the brain called the corpus callosum. Research has shown that this part of the brain may not work efficiently in those who are affected by Dyslexia. The development of the corpus callosum can be speeded up if the student learns to sing and play a musical instrument.

RIGHT EAR ADVANTAGE (REA)

Whenever possible the tutor should explain mathematical concepts/give instructions by talking towards the student's dominant ear. Some students may find it easier to listen to music with one ear but may find it easier to listen to speech with the other. Generally speaking, an individual is right ear, leg and hand dominant; e.g. they use the right leg to kick, the right hand to write and find it easier to listen using the right ear (so most of us put the phone to our right ears). However, the SpLD Profile student may have mixed dominance; e.g. left hand and right leg. (Non-audiologist professionals can use *Sub-test 9 of the Aston Index* to gain an indication as to which ear is dominant.)

STAGGERED SPONDAIC DIFFICULTIES

Listening difficulties can occur when one ear hears better than the other (or there is an assymetry in hearing ability between the two ears). Specialists in this field do not agree on appropriate remediation for such difficulties. One suggested strategy is to aid amplification of the poor ear (using a hearing aid with only minimal amplification and only worn at school). This strategy does not work for all children and some specialists are against its use because it increases the noise level of the speech organ. Some strategies are agreed by all; e.g. that preferential seating is always beneficial (with the student's good ear close to the centre of the classroom's activities/area of discussion and away from noise coming through windows and hallway doors etc.).

ENVIRONMENT

Central Auditory Processing Disorder can cause problems for the individual in the busy/noisy classroom and such students may benefit from small teaching groups. Individuals are likely to experience greater listening difficulties in places like older classrooms with tall ceilings. Such students suit an environment where they are not taught by lecturing but this may be difficult to achieve in a college/university setting. However, some lectures in such environments are now being televised. Students would find it helpful if they were enabled to watch a video recording of the lecture. They could then play it several times until the language was understood. A glossary of terms used in topics, given out several weeks before the topic is started, would also help individuals familiarise themselves with the vocabulary prior to having to listen to the words being used.

Sometimes these students can be told off for poor concentration, daydreaming, or copying from the student next to them. The individual should sit as close to the tutor/lecturer/ therapist as possible. It is best if the adult speaks slowly and simply whilst facing the student (or his/her dominant ear).

AUDITORY STIMULATION

Lack of stimulation

This appears to cause the unstimulated auditory pathways to atrophy (reduce their functional activity). Research has shown that auditory stimulation and training will improve the auditory processing abilities of the individual; for example, Jira, in 1992, used an intervention programme which focused on intensive listening exercises. These emphasised auditory memory and language comprehension. At the end of the programme the children showed improvement on selected auditory tasks, and both teachers and parents reported an improvement in overall school performance.

Learning to play a musical instrument

Learning to play an instrument by ear (e.g. via the Suzuki method) can be beneficial to students with auditory processing difficulties but they will take a long time to develop the skill, and a good deal of patience and understanding is required of their music teachers and parents. Such students can take a very long time to go through the grades; e.g. five years to gain Grade I even for a very bright student. Towards the end of that time they may need to combine the strategies of both learning by ear

Students can be helped if the environment is made as quiet as possible (carpets are best for floor coverings). Classroom environments (and swimming pools and churches) tend to be acoustically poor as the many hard surfaces reflect sound. Difficulties in processing are therefore likely to occur in rooms without carpets (students are also likely to experience problems in pubs and cars.)

Learning to play a musical instrument will help to improve auditory processing skills although those students who are affected by both Dyspraxia and auditory processing difficulties may find it difficult to learn to play an instrument. (For further information see *Music Solutions for Specific Learning Difficulties* by Jan Poustie et al ISBN 1 901544 73 7.)

and learning to read music. If the Suzuki method is adopted, teachers and parents will need to ensure that the child does not feel out of place in the group lessons (which are part of such tuition) as his/her peers are likely to progress much faster than they do.

Management of auditory processing disorders

It is important to remember that each student will be different and each will have a different range of difficulties – what will work for one, will not work for another. Therefore, great care must be taken to suit the intervention programme to the particular student's needs. Intervention to help the student overcome his/her auditory difficulties should occur as soon as they are noticed. Bellis in *Assessment and Management of Central Auditory Processing Disorders in the Educational Setting* provides very good information on the management of auditory processing disorders. She recommends that intervention is multidisciplinary (e.g. involves professionals across a wide range of disciplines including teachers and speech and language therapists). Two of the key elements of intervention are that:

▸▸ The classroom environment be adapted to the student's difficulties so that little auditory effort is needed to learn academic tasks. The remediation environment however, should be gradually enriched with auditory information at a rate that is appropriate to the student's level of processing.

▸▸ The student's auditory difficulties are overcome by remediation activities and compensatory strategies. (A FM Radio Link system is very effective- either a personal one or with a speaker which gives consistent access to the speaker's/teacher's voice.) The student's local education authority will have Hearing Support Service which can advise on equipment, strategies etc. for students affected by listening difficulties.

Auditory strategies

Auditory Processes by P. Gillet ISBN 0 87879 094 2 R (published by Academic Therapy Publications, USA) provides a huge number of simple strategies to overcome difficulties in each of the different auditory skills. Although it is aimed at classroom use, many of the activities would also be suitable for home use.

The *Early Communication Skills* pack by Lynch and Cooper (ISBN 0 86388 096 7)provides a wide range of activities (including auditory-based ones). The activities are designed to be carried out in the home environment for pre-school children under the supervision of a speech and language therapist. The pack is published by Winslow Press, Bicester, UK.

Care does, however, need to be taken that the activity chosen is appropriate to the student. Thus, in the auditory memory section the activity requiring the student to name objects in his/her environment may be too hard for some students with word-finding/labelling difficulties. (Word-finding difficulties cause the student to have difficulties in accessing a word from memory, word-labelling difficulties occur when the student forgets the name of even common items; e.g. ruler.)

For some time now we have been able to improve literacy listening skills through the use of the *Listening skills* books. The author has recently learnt that a similar set of materials called *Listening Skills* (Maths Key Stage 1 and 2, published by The Questions Publishing Company Ltd, 27 Frederick Street, Hockley, Birmingham B1 3HH.) They have been published to help students improve their mathematical listening and mental calculation ability and they may be useful for some students. The tasks require the student to listen to some instructions and most of them require that the student then performs a mental calculation. As the student may have both difficulties in listening and in working out calculations it would be best if the tutor worked out the sums with the student first and then does the relevant listening exercise with the student. Depending upon the task, some students will need equipment (e.g. Cuisenaire Rods, plastic coins etc.) to help them to do the calculations.

Tutors working with students who have moderate to severe listening/mathematical difficulties may well need to do the following for each task when using the *Listening Skills Maths Keystage 1 and 2* books:

▸▸ Make sure that the appropriate mathematical concept is understood before starting the task. If the concept is not understood then either omit the task or thoroughly teach the concept prior to doing it.

▸▸ Explain the meanings of all the mathematical words and other main words that are used in the task. This will be especially necessary when Specific Language Impairment/poor mathematical vocabulary is present.

▸▸ Break the instruction into phrases.

▸▸ Say the first phrase and ask the student to process it (e.g.

When auditory skills are weak the tutor will need to use a variety of visual aids to help the student understand both the vocabulary and the information being taught. Worksheets (with plenty of relevant diagrams/pictures) videos, television programmes and computer programs can help the individual to understand key points. (These strategies may be essential if the individual also has considerable problems in reading.) The Mind Mapping strategy of showing the connections between pieces of information can also be useful here (see Appendix 3 of *Planning and Organisation Solutions by Jan Poustie*).

A useful strategy is to train the student to use contextual clues to work out what is likely to have been the missing number/ word. It is best to use mathematical information that s/ he is familiar with to teach this skill and initially miss out the final number/word of a line; e.g.

1, 2, 3, 4, 5,
once I caught a fish ……….

6, 7, 8, 9, 10
then I threw him back …...

John has 3 cars.

He gives one car to Sam.

?   How many cars does John have now?

by pointing to the relevant part of the picture, doing that part of the calculation).

▸▸   Then do as above with the next phrase and so on.

Auditory closure activities

Auditory closure is the ability of the listener to fill in the missing spaces in what s/he hears to work out the words/sounds which make up the sentences. The listener has a greater chance of achieving auditory closure if the topic and the vocabulary/ grammar used are familiar to him/her. Some individuals will be able to understand speech in an ideal listening environment but will have major problems when listening to unfamiliar speakers and listening through background noise. Such individuals may well find initial attendance at playgroup/school very stressful, confusing and traumatic.

Strategies for making it easier for the student to understand instructions

Difficulties in word finding (accessing the word they want from memory) and processing difficulties relating to the information that they hear can cause problems with understanding the teacher's explanations. CAPD students can have frequent episodes of 'glue ear' and this will cause difficulties in hearing the teacher. (It is known that each episode of 'glue ear' results in the student failing to acquire vocabulary at the same rate as his/her peers of similar age and intellectual ability.)

It is essential that student and teacher have a good relationship and are in harmony. The teacher will need to attract the student's attention before giving instructions. (This can be achieved by saying the student's name and then giving the instruction while physically demonstrating the task. This strategy may also help to reduce any word-finding/labelling difficulties that may be present.) The teacher should ask the student to explain what s/he has to do before expecting him/her to do the task. Some students will only be able to remember the instruction/mental arithmetic task if they draw a picture of it and/or write down the task as shown in the example on the left using the simplest drawing techniques possible such as 'stick men'.

Specific Language Impairment

Sections of this chapter have been contributed by the Association For All Speech Impaired Children (AFASIC), edited by Jan Poustie. Further information on Language Impairments can be obtained from AFASIC – see Appendix I.

TERMS USED TO DESCRIBE LANGUAGE DIFFICULTIES

Aphasia = no speech
Dysphasia = impaired speech
These are the oldest terms for describing speech and language difficulties. These terms are usually used to describe acquired impairments of speech and language in adults. (This means that the impairments occurred after the person was born.) Children's difficulties are more usually described as expressive or receptive language difficulties.

SPECIFIC LANGUAGE IMPAIRMENT CAUSES DIFFICULTIES IN:

▸▸ Word-finding (accessing words from memory); e.g. the student may not be able to access the word 'fraction' from memory though s/he will be able to describe what a fraction is to the teacher.

▸▸ Word-labelling (remembering the names of objects etc.). The student can forget the names of common items around him/her.

▸▸ Organising words into correct sentence order and organising one's thoughts. This will create problems when the student has to write a mathematics assignment (e.g. for GCSE work) or a 'number story' (see *Mathematics Solutions – An Introduction to Dyscalculia; Part B* by Jan Poustie et al).

▸▸ Using grammar correctly (see pages 82-85).

▸▸ Learning vocabulary (mathematical vocabulary may be weaker than literacy-based vocabulary). Being taught the vocabulary at the beginning of the lesson before the topic is introduced will make it easier for the student to learn the concept/process which is being taught.

EXPRESSIVE DIFFICULTIES

Difficulties in speaking (articulation) or using language. There can also be difficulties in using appropriate body language.

Speaking and writing

RECEPTIVE DIFFICULTIES

Problems in understanding the spoken or written word. There can also be difficulties in understanding other people's body language.

Listening and reading

Most children with speech and language impairments will have difficulties in both areas, but will have a main difficulty in one area.

Some of the student's difficulties are obvious because the child has speech difficulties. Other difficulties are hidden because we have  either not recognised the problem or the child and the adults around the child, have instinctively put in place strategies to accommodate their difficulties.

Example 1
'six divided by two' (6 ÷ 2)

'two into six' (2$\overline{)6}$)

In these two sums we actually have to do the same calculation and will obtain the same answer (3). However, the order in which we say and record the sums is very different which is why some students are not sure how to read the first example and so say 'six into two' for both sums.

▸▸ Expressing what is known and understood (expressive language). This can cause the student to have difficulties in explaining what it is that is not understood and what is known.

▸▸ Understanding what is heard or read (receptive language). The student may have difficulties with understanding the teacher when s/he is explaining concepts and so on.

▸▸ Use of prepositions (words that tell us the position of a thing in space). The student is likely to take longer to learn when to use the 'position' words (e.g. before, beside, under etc.) and is likely to need to use concrete apparatus when doing a task involving such words; e.g Lego™ characters and objects. The Stile 'Maths Language' pack can be very useful here for the primary school-aged child. The early-years child would benefit from regularly watching the television programme *Sesame Street* (which at the time of going to press was on Channel at 6 a.m.). This excellent programme also covers the numbers 1-20 and simple classification work.

Grammar

Mathematics has its own grammar and if the student does not understand how it is used then there will be difficulties in interpreting word problems/textbooks and the teacher's examples. Grammar relates to the order in which information is recorded or spoken. Knowing the grammar rules is very important as Example 1 shows.

In word problems we may be asked for an item in a complex manner; e.g. *'What is the product of two times six add five?'* The product is of course the answer but it appears in the first part of the question. However, we usually record the product (answer) at the end of the sum. Many students with mathematical learning difficulties will feel quite threatened if the sum is recorded in the way that we say it; e.g. with the answer first even though, as shown in Example 2, the sum can be recorded in either way.

Students with classification, vocabulary and grammar difficulties may find it difficult to cope with a questions such as: *'Find the lowest common factor of six and twelve'*. We can enable the student to understand this sentence if we use the strategy of relating the information to the real world whilst at the same time establishing the order in which we need to attack the question. The terms 'lowest' and 'common' describe something; e.g. the noun (which in this case is the word 'factor'). The following example, derived from Professor Sharma's question strategy for teaching grammar, shows one way in which we can adapt his method for use with students with language difficulties. The starting point has to be the student (his/her features, pets, etc.);

A. Training the student to understand a complex sentence
Question: *'Are you a girl?'* (Ans: Yes)
Question: *'Do you have dark hair?'* (Ans: Yes)
Question: *'Do you have a cat called Sasha?'* (Ans: Yes)
Revise the questions; e.g.
> *'Do you have a cat called Sasha and are you a girl?'*
> (Ans: Yes)
Question: *'Can you tell me the name of a dark-haired girl who has a pet cat called Sasha?'* (Ans: Student says his/her own name.)

B. Introducing the terms 'lower' and 'lowest'
We start to explain the mathematical terms in our phrase the 'lowest common factor'. We can explain what lowest means by using items on the wall or parts of the student's body when s/he is sitting or standing; e.g.
'You have to bend down to reach your feet.
(The tutor and the student bend down and touch their feet.)
So, your feet are lower than your hands.
(The tutor demonstrates the word 'lower' at the same time as s/he says it by moving his/her hand towards the floor. The student repeats the word and the tutor's actions.)
Which is lower, your hands or your feet? (Ans: my feet.)
Enable the student to understand the word low when it has the 'est' suffix at the end (e.g. lowest) by putting three things in height order and whilst pointing to the correct item say the word 'lowest'.

C. Introducing the term 'common'
We have to explain the term 'common' as being something that we can see a lot of; e.g.

Example 2
A: 2 + 6 + 5
B: 2 x 6 + 5 = 17
C: 17 = 2 x 6 + 5

The order of recording and doing the sums in Example 2 is important. When calculating Sum A the order in which we do the sum does not matter. (This can be very useful as it enables the student with Dyscalculia to deal first with the pairs of numbers that s/he finds easiest to manipulate.) No matter what the order in which s/he tackles the numbers s/he should always end up with the answer 13; e.g.
2 + 5 = 7 and 7 + 6 = 13
or
2 + 6 = 8 and 8 + 5 = 13

However, if s/he calculated Sums B and C in Example 2 by adding the 5 to the 2 first and then multiplying by 6 s/he would get a different answer.
(5 + 2 = 7 then 7 x 6 = 42)

Mathematics Solutions – An Introduction to Dyscalculia Part A by Jan Poustie et al ISBN 1 901544 45 1

Language difficulties can cause problems when recording sums and difficulties in understanding mathematical phrases.

'We see *lots of students in a classroom. We can say that it is common to find students in a classroom. Is it common to find students in a classroom?'* (Ans: Yes.)

'Is it common to see cars on the road?' (Ans: Yes.)

D. <u>Extending the meaning of the word 'common'</u>

We explain that things can be common to two items:

1. Show the student a chair which has arms, and say that sometimes we call parts of two different things the same names.

2. Point to student's arm: *'What do we call this?'* (Ans: An arm.) Point to the student's leg: *'What do we call this?*

3. Then the tutor points to the arm of the chair and says *'We call this part of the chair an arm.'* The tutor points to the chair legs and says *'We call this part of the chair the legs.'*

4. Say: *'When a chair and a body have the same things we can say that they have these things in common.'* Provide lots of examples of two things that have things 'in common' until the student understands the term; e.g. bikes and cars have seats and wheels in common etc.

5. Then go back to the chair and the student's body and repeat 1-3 above. Ask: *'What does your body and this chair have in common?'* (Ans: They both have arms and legs.)

6. After revising section B (on page 83) we then progress to comparing the position of two identical groups of things (e.g. a calendar, a poster and a clock). Put one group of things on a wall and the other group on a desk. Ask: *'Which things do the wall and desk have in common?' 'Which is the highest thing on the wall?' 'Which is the lowest thing on the desk ?'*

7. Repeat the question: *'What do the wall and desk have in common?'* Then ask *'Which is the lowest common thing on the desk and the wall?'*

We need to think very carefully before we teach a mathematical phrase, so that we can ensure that the meaning is properly understood. All too often a teacher will:

➥ start at stage D8 in the example on the right,

➥ will not use Cuisenaire Rods to determine the factors (but will use the times tables instead) and so will leave the student who experiences mathematical language difficulties totally confused.

8. Explain what 'factors' are. (A factor is a whole number which will divide exactly into another whole number. Numbers which are multiplied together are factors of the answer; e.g. in the sum 2 x 3 = 6 the factors are 2 and 3.) Our task is to find the lowest common factor of six and twelve. First of all

we need to find the numbers that will divide into both 6 and 12 (we can use Cuisenaire Rods to find this out). We find that:

➤ 3 and 2 both divide into 6

➤ 2, 3, 4 and 6 will divide into 12.

We now know that two numbers (2 and 3) can be divided into both 12 and 6. Therefore 2 and 3 are common factors of 12 and 6. As 2 is a lower number than 3 it is the lowest common factor of six and twelve.

THE RANGE OF LANGUAGE DIFFICULTIES

Children with speech and language impairments, delays or disorders have a range of difficulties. They will almost certainly find their ability to read and write affected in some way and the following provides an overview of the range of difficulties that some children face.

Articulatory and expressive difficulties
The following can be present:

➤ Verbal (Articulatory) Dyspraxia (*see Chapter 4*).

➤ Phonological difficulties where the child has difficulty in pronouncing a number of sounds.

➤ Cluttering: where the child's speech can be so rapid and muddled that the listener cannot understand the child. (The speaker may be unconcerned, or unaware, of his/her difficulty.)

➤ Dysarthria: which affects speech production. The result is slurred speech due to weak, or incorrect, movements of the speech organs. Such difficulties can range from mild to severe and, in most cases, the speech is slow and limited in range.

Receptive or comprehension difficulties
This is where the child's ability to understand spoken and written language is impaired. For these children it is important to consider listening and speaking skills separately, as the two will not be working together effectively. Language comprehension is the understanding of what words and phrases mean in sentences.

Always check that the student is listening and has focused His/her attention on you before giving verbal information. You can do this by saying the student's name and gaining eye contact.

Mathematics Solutions – An Introduction to Dyscalculia Part A by Jan Poustie et al   ISBN 1 901544 45 1

Difficulties in understanding the speech of the child can cause great distress and frustration to both the child and the listener.

Breakdown in any, or a number, of these areas will affect the student's ability to understand and will impair his/her ability to interact with (and understand) the world s/he lives in. His/her ability to read and write will be affected in a number of ways and there may be difficulties in accessing the National Curriculum.

It involves the following skills, each of which will impact upon the student's ability to understand the explanation of concepts and processes either through reading a textbook or by listening to the teacher's explanation:

1   Hearing
2   Paying attention to the sounds in speech (Attention Deficits can affect this).
3   Distinguishing or discriminating between speech sounds (this is known as Auditory Discrimination).
4   The ability to process language
5   The ability to remember the sequence of sounds (this is known as Auditory Sequential Memory)
6   Knowing word meanings (semantics)
7   Understanding sentence structure (grammar)
8   Making sense of language in and out of context
9   Seeing the text clearly.
10 Knowing how, and when, to question the information read or listened to.

The presence of Central Auditory Processing Disorder can affect 1, 2, 3, 4.

If receptive language difficulties (e.g. slow auditory processing and reduced short-term memory difficulties) and/or Central Auditory Processing Disorder are present then the speaker may become frustrated with the listener. The listener may be accused of:

➼   Not paying attention and/or misbehaving

➼   Giving up trying and/or being slow to carry out the instruction

➼   Doing the exact opposite of what she was told to do

➼   Carrying out the instruction incorrectly (or not carrying it out at all!)

The *Listening Skills* materials mentioned in Chapter 5 may help these students.

Auditory sequential memory
This is the ability to hear a sequence of sounds, words or sentences, and being able to hold them in memory for sufficient time as to be able to:

➼   gain information from them

➡ process and organise that information

➡ respond to that information.

Memory difficulties can often be mistaken for laziness and it is important that both the child and those around him/her are aware of the problem and that strategies to address the problem are in place; e.g.

➡ Train the student to cluster (group) information. So, instead of learning the telephone number 289559 as 'two - eight - nine - five - five - nine' the student remembers it as 'twenty-eight, ninety-five, fifty-nine' or as two groups of three digits – 289, 559.

➡ Use auditory games to train the student to remember events and the correct sequence of the days of the week etc. Thus the tutor and the student can take turns to add one more event, action, person, description etc., with the items that are added being included at any point in the story; e.g.

➡ On Monday evening I went to a meeting.

➡ On Monday evening I went with my Mum to a meeting and on Tuesday I took a tulip to school.

The use of alliteration (making the words have the same first letter; e.g. Monday and Mum) plus having different items in each sentence (e.g. meeting in the first one and a tulip in the second one) uses elaborate memory to help the child learn the order of the days.

➡ Do not talk for too long and do not assume that everything that you have said has been processed/ understood/heard.

➡ Provide visual memory hooks for the information that you are presenting e.g. single sums in different colours on the board, or better still pictures, BUT the tutor must allow the student to look at each sum/picture and process the information from it before carrying on talking.

Semantic-Pragmatic Disorder
'Semantics' is the meaning of words and 'pragmatics' is the social use of language. Some students who have difficulties in these areas will appear to have good mechanical reading skills. They

Many children with a history of late speaking and early speech and language difficulties find that, although these difficulties resolve, there are residual problems (problems that are still present) that only parents and teachers can detect. The key factor in this is limited auditory sequential memory span which is apparent in the child's difficulties with reading and writing. By the time that the student has reached secondary age, it is unlikely that the memory span will improve significantly. However, auditory memory training activities/ strategies combined with teaching the student to use a multisensory approach which favours his natural learning style can improve the student's ability to function in the classroom.

may have age-appropriate grammatical skills and 'on the surface' may appear to use appropriate language. Although some might demonstrate mild Verbal (Articulatory) Dyspraxia, most have fluent speech. However, closer examination of their understanding shows that they have particular difficulties with the conceptual aspects of language, particularly with regard to language relating to 'time' (temporal) and that relating to 'space' i.e. location (spatial), and this will impact upon their ability to learn these areas of mathematics.

These students may be unaware of categorisation – for example, that knives and forks are 'cutlery' – which will cause them to have difficulties in coping with 'sets' in mathematics and in other classification tasks. There can be a failure to understand language associated with a topic. These students tend to take language at a literal level and so do not understand irony and sarcasm.

When mixing with others, these students often do not know how to start or maintain a conversation. Their social skills, body language and facial expression may be impaired and they may fail to recognise these signals in others. Students affected by Attention Deficits may need to be taught some of these skills too; e.g. understanding body language. These skills have to be taught by strategies such as:

▸▸ Modelling body language – the tutor shows the student how the face looks when s/he is angry, slightly annoyed, worried, sad, happy etc. and the student with the help of a mirror creates the same face. Then the tutor and the student take turns to model the face whilst the other person guesses the emotion. However, such students do need to be able to recognise the emotion within themselves first and so the tutor should discuss prior to the modelling how one feels when one is angry, happy and so on.

Specialist intervention; e.g. from a speech and language therapist, is likely to be needed if the student is unable to recognise his/her own emotions. It is absolutely essential that children from as young an age as possible (e.g. pre-school) are taught these skills. If this does not occur it can appear to the child that adults suddenly 'lose their tempers' without warning. Such children do not recognise

3 days	☀		🌧
2 days	☀	☀	🌧
1 day	☀	☀🌧	☀🌧
	Week 1	Week 2	

The student can understand information at a basic level and label things; e.g. *sun* in this block-chart of weather. However, s/he may not be able to explain or understand *sunshine*.

the facial and body signs of the adult slowly losing patience with the child. This can make the student feel very insecure, especially in the school environment. An American computer programme called 'Gaining Face' might be of use here as it has been designed to teach students facial expressions (see http://www.ccoder.com/GainingFace for further information).

▶▶ Role plays of social situations.

▶▶ Use of materials such as *SULP (Social Use of Language Programme*, by Wendy Rinaldi (secondary school version from NFER-Nelson, Tel: 01753 858961, primary school version from Child Communication and Learning, Tel: 01483 458411).

Higher Level Language Impairment (HLL)

This book has already discussed the 'grey area' between the behavioural conditions (Dyspraxia, Autistic Spectrum Disorder and Attention Deficits). The existence of Higher Level Language Impairment appears to be another 'grey area'. Such students can appear to be complete contradictions – at one moment there can appear to be little wrong with their use of (and understanding of language), the next moment there can be a lack of comprehension or totally inappropriate use of language. Difficulties that can be seen include:

▶▶ Not taking turns during conversation (this will affect group work)

▶▶ Failure to keep the conversation flowing and/or being unclear about what they are saying. (This may be partly due to word-finding and word-labelling difficulties and difficulties with the organisation of language.) The result can be a somewhat frustrated student who is unable to explain clearly either what s/he needs to know and what s/he does not understand.

▶▶ Behaviours associated with Autistic Spectrum Disorder may be apparent; e.g. liking their room to be set out in a certain way, idiosyncratic behaviours and limited interests.

Such students may find the transition between one type of provision and another difficult. Thus, the transition from playgroup to school may be difficult, though the difficulties are

A student may have semantic difficulties without pragmatic problems. However, a student with pragmatic problems will always have semantic difficulties. This latter group may be viewed by some professionals as being within the autistic spectrum, although they may merit a diagnosis of autism. However, there is still much academic debate concerning this matter.

Limited social development may be apparent when Higher Level Language Disorder is present.

Mathematics Solutions – An Introduction to Dyscalculia Part A by Jan Poustie et al   ISBN 1 901544 45 1

Times of transition; e.g. moving house, changing schools, classes) can be a problem for children affected by language impairment.

likely to be more obvious when in transition from infant to junior school (Year 2 to Year 3) in the primary school and then again when the child enters secondary school. The infant/junior transition is made more difficult because the infant curriculum is usually fairly concrete (lots of handing of objects in order to learn concepts and processes). Therefore, HLL does not start to show significantly (to the uninitiated) until top infants. The difficulties in transition from playgroup to primary school can be present because such children:

▸▸   Can no longer base their interactions with other children on physical play and physical activities.

▸▸   No longer have a high ratio of adults/pupils within their environment and so do not have an adult 'at hand' to help them socialise and relate to others. This ratio of staff to children is a major problem when our children are entering school at four years of age rather than attending a pre-school establishment where the adult/child ratio is much higher.

▸▸   Once they attend school they also have less time to play with objects/toy people which enable them to model and role-play situations. Such activities can be very important to this group as they may not be able to explain their problem (nor understand it themselves). The modelling and role-playing with objects and toys also enable such students to communicate their worries etc. to the adults around them.

It is generally recognised that those affected by Dyspraxia, Dyslexia and Dyscalculia are also likely to be affected by a language impairment of some type which will vary in severity from mild to severe and with either, or both, expressive and receptive language being affected. Sometimes one of the parents of the student is also affected by a language impairment too. Parents may often feel very concerned that their child will fail to achieve qualifications and will fail to cope in social situations etc.

All students affected by Asperger Syndrome are also affected by Higher Level Language Impairment.

Some parents assume that the child who can make their views known at home but who talks little in the classroom and other social settings is just 'shy'. Sometimes teachers do not make the connection between advanced reading skills (or oral work) and written work that is of a lower standard. It is also easy for

Mathematics Solutions – An Introduction to Dyscalculia Part A by Jan Poustie et al   ISBN 1 901544 45 1

teachers to underestimate such students and their abilities. Educational psychologists, too, may not see the warning signs of the presence of a language impairment. One sign is a student who has good to excellent written comprehension skills but performs poorly during the aural (listening) comprehension tasks within an assessment of intellectual ability; e.g. a WISC or BAS assessment. Such a situation can occur when there are language and/or auditory processing difficulties.

The child who is affected by Specific Language Impairment is at risk of having a very unhappy time at school (both within the classroom and in the playground) with the situation being far worse if their problems are undiagnosed and unprovided for. (Such problems may carry on into adulthood with the adult having only a very small circle of social contacts.) Even those who are highly intelligent can be badly affected in the school situation if they are not supported, as the following case studies show. However, some of these cases also show that such students (when supported) can achieve a great deal, and our expectation should be that we will enable them to achieve their potential rather than see their language difficulties limiting them throughout their lives.

A language impairment can be confused with shyness.

Oh, he doesn't like talking to strangers.

CASE STUDIES

Case Study 1 – Child A

Language impairment may cause even highly intelligent students to be forced into unusual behaviours. The less supported the child, the more stress s/he will be under and so there are more likely to be such behaviours. One such pupil happily attended a pre-school playgroup and a nursery. However, she would hide under the dining-room table and refuse to get dressed prior to going to school in the morning. She would then spend part of the school day sitting in a corner of the reception classroom with her thumb in her mouth. Her teacher failed to recognise that this child was in distress. The child's behaviours occurred because both her academic and social needs were not being met, with the school failing to recognise that they had a highly intelligent pupil who could already read before she attended school.

This child's situation could have been markedly improved if the

Even very young children may learn to mask their feelings when at school and so their teachers do not realise that they are in distress because of a language problem.

school had accepted the information on the child's skills which had been provided by her pre-school playgroup and her mother prior to her attending school. Instead they relied on a test administered by the school during the girl's first term which was designed to find out whether the child was ready to read. As this test showed that the child was **not** 'ready to read', the fact that she could already do so was ignored!!

(Even with the assessment of pupils upon entry to the reception class that now occurs in state schools, liaison between pre-school groups and the child's school must be more than just a visit to the group by the reception teacher. Pre-school playgroup leaders and nursery staff are professionals and should be regarded as such. Their input to health visitors and teachers can be invaluable and if they indicate concerns regarding a child's functioning, or state that the child has achieved 'such and such' a skill level, then they should be believed. If, once the child enters the school, that skill level is not apparent then that in itself is cause for concern as it is likely to indicate that the child is not functioning appropriately in the school environment.)

In Child A's case, the transition between playgroup/nursery and school had been slightly eased because the school had a policy of children attending for only part of the day for the first part of the reception term. However, although the mother realised that the child was not thriving in the school setting the school did not. Teachers may see a child that 'clings' and is then 'perfectly happy during the day', or see a child who leaves his/her mother with no hesitation and then shows no obvious signs of distress.

Child A found the transition from primary school to secondary school equally difficult and actually became hysterical during her second week of secondary school and refused to attend. It took a great deal of persuasion on the part of the mother plus a flexible attitude on the part of the school (in allowing the child to attend for just a lesson a day for a short while) to solve this problem.

Children, like adults, learn to mask their feelings and some learn this very early for fear of being teased by their peer group or, in unfortunate cases, by the adults around them. Just as an adult would not show his/her distress whilst in the company of non-family members, these children may not show their distress by crying or, by being angry. Instead they may become very passive and insecure, may misbehave or have far more illnesses because of the stress that they are under. There may also be a noticeable change in behaviour between holidays/weekends and during the school term. After a long period in school (e.g. by Year 4 and above) there may be little difference between school and nonschool behaviour as by that time the child is under so much stress that s/he cannot 'unwind' even during the long summer holiday.

Her difficulties with mathematics started to be really noticeable when she was seven years old. She came home from school and told her mother that she had had a bad day because she did not know how to do a sum and the teacher was so busy that she had not been able to come to help her. The next day the mother arranged with the teacher for her daughter to bring her maths book home so that she could do a little catching up at home.

At five years old this child could read at 150 words a minute (the speed at which many adults read). By now the mother was very concerned when she realised that this exceptionally bright child who could read with understanding at an exceptionally fast speed was struggling with mathematical word problems. It was soon realised by the mother that the child was floundering in other areas of mathematics too and that she had just learnt processes rather than concepts. This resulted in her recording mathematical information in odd ways (which only confused her still more) not being able to explain what she was doing and what she did not understand. Her difficulties in mathematics became apparent in music as well for she found it difficult to learn aspects of music which required mathematical skills; e.g. learn rhythms, count the beats in a bar etc.

By the age of eleven years Child A gained a SAT Level 6 in reading (only two per cent of the population gain such a high level and this puts her into the gifted/superior intellectual ability category). Her mathematics skills have never reached the same high level as her literacy skills but, fortunately, this student did receive the help she needed and went on to be in the top maths set of her secondary school for Years 7–9 and then was placed in a set suitable for Intermediate level for her GCSE work.

This student's auditory processing difficulties were identified when she was quite young, they were first suspected when she was two years old. Episodes of 'glue ear' were common in early childhood and continued until well into her teens, though they occurred with less frequency by the age of fifteen years. Her

More than one condition can be present, so the student with language impairment may also be affected by other conditions within the SpLD Profile. This particular student had noticeable receptive language difficulties, auditory processing difficulties and was also affected by Articulatory (Verbal) Dyspraxia and Developmental Dyscalculia.

Learning to play a musical instrument/to sing in tune speeds up the maturation of the corpus callosum part of the brain thus improving many areas of functioning. What a pity that the amount of music in our primary schools has been much reduced over the years.

Mathematics Solutions – An Introduction to Dyscalculia Part A by Jan Poustie et al   ISBN 1 901544 45 1

At age fifteen this student still occasionally mispronounces words usually by:

▶▶   putting the wrong emphasis on a word,

▶▶   not knowing how to read unusual sound patterns (e.g. 'tian'),

▶▶   not knowing whether the vowel sound is long (e.g. 'a' as in 'cape') or short (e.g. 'a' as in 'cap').

Language impaired children and adults may have few friends. They may find it difficult to start and maintain conversations.

receptive language and auditory processing difficulties were overcome, to a certain extent, by her receiving specialist music tuition from the age of five. First she learnt to play an instrument via the Suzuki method which traditionally concentrates on auditory skills. Then she joined a music appreciation class where she learnt the recorder and was introduced to the reading of music via a recorder book in which the notes were colour coded. Later she joined school choirs and a strings orchestra.

Discussion with an audiologist when she was fifteen revealed that the auditory processing difficulties present at that time will remain throughout her life. Perhaps one of the most frustrating aspects of this is that she still finds it difficult to process information against a busy auditory background (e.g. other people talking whilst she is trying to listen to the teacher etc.) and unfortunately there appears to be at present no means of improving this area of functioning and so this difficulty will continue on into adulthood.

She still finds some social situations difficult. Understanding the expectations of the different teachers at secondary school and when 'rules can be bent' has been difficult for her to learn and she still can find 'handling' people of her own age 'tricky', especially when they are not close friends. She can still find both initiating (and maintaining the flow of) conversation difficult and, especially when tired or stressed, will repeat the same question/ initiate the conversation by saying the same thing/ask the same question and then later on in the conversation (or perhaps a little later in the day) ask a similar question again. This can occur even though she has thoroughly understood the previous conversation.

The combination of her Dyspraxia and her language impairment makes this student much more vulnerable and easily distressed than her peer group. She becomes very upset when she has to face mixing with a new group of students; e.g. when she found herself separated from all of her friends at the start of her GCSE work. By the end of Year 10, despite being on a slightly reduced timetable (she was taking one less GCSE than her peers), she was absolutely exhausted and very stressed – the exhaustion not being helped by the fact that she always grows extremely fast during the summer which further tires her.

The combination of the SpLD conditions, and associated stress and exhaustion means that she can become highly emotional over incidents that peers of similar chronological age and intellectual ability would easily take in their stride. What many teachers would find hard to realise is that this extremely intelligent student (she gained the best report for her year at the end of Year 10) was so unable emotionally to cope with her parents arriving late to an event that she became extremely distressed. Like so many students with such difficulties she puts on a brave face to the world and her teachers, and, like so many others, the real extent of her problems are little realised by those who teach her.

Stress and the presence of language impairment can cause students to be easily distressed.

Case Study 2 – Girl B

This student had severe expressive and receptive language difficulties as did her mother. Her brother was also affected by expressive written language difficulties. Girl B's receptive language difficulties were so severe that she had difficulties in understanding the teacher and so tended to switch off. Her language difficulties resulted in her having virtually no friends at school, being unable to read more than a few words and being unable to express her thoughts either orally, or, in writing.

Her difficulties were also affecting her acquisition of mathematical skills. She started to receive specialist support from the author when she was seven years old. Many areas of mathematics were affected by her language difficulties with fractions being particularly hard for her to learn.

It took a lot of work for her to accept the correct method of recording fractions, this being finally achieved by dividing several bars of chocolate into different fractions – which of course she ate as we went along! The support she received enabled this student to develop social skills (though she still had problems when she wanted to put her point of view across to her friends). Students such as Girl B are not likely to do well in the educational setting without specialist support from a speech and language therapist and from a specialist teacher. A 'whole school' approach to language difficulties is likely to be necessary for those with moderate to severe impairment. In such an environment all teaching staff are aware and have an understanding of the impact of language difficulties upon learning.

One of her biggest stumbling blocks was in accepting how we record fractions. She believed that the way to write two halves etc. was by writing:

$$\tfrac{1}{2} \ \tfrac{1}{2} \quad \text{instead of} \ \tfrac{2}{2}$$

Mathematics Solutions – An Introduction to Dyscalculia Part A by Jan Poustie et al   ISBN 1 901544 45 1

Clock Language (published by Next Generation) is based upon the information that it was necessary to teach her so that she both understood the concept of time and acquired the concepts and vocabulary that she needed in order to read the time.

She had great difficulties in learning to tell the time. Time is a very difficult concept to understand – it is like the wind but much more intangible. One can see, hear and feel the wind but one cannot see, hear and feel 'time', one can only measure its passing by the passage of the sun or by using instruments which measure time. One can see time passing by seeing the increase in height of a young child or the wrinkles on the face of the elderly. However, these effects happen so slowly that they are not a very useful way for a child to understand the concept of the smaller units of time; e.g. seconds, minutes and hours, or for them to have a true understanding of the passing of time. The passing of the sun is not reliable as a measuring device as although the passing of twenty-four hours in a day is constant we in fact see that days (i.e. daylight) are longer during the summer and shorter during the winter. Time is therefore a very abstract concept and it is difficult for the student to grasp it if both language and mathematical learning difficulties are present. Students can have huge problems in learning to tell the time as so many skills are involved; e.g.

▸   spatial skills,

▸   the ability to read both Arabic and Roman numerals,

▸   an understanding of the twenty-four-hour clock,

▸   interpretation of the data (the time looks very different on a digital clock than it does on an analogue clock which has two or more hands.

BULLYING

Language impairments can make a student more vulnerable, especially when they are present alongside another condition which can cause the student to have problems in interacting/ playing with others (e.g. Dyspraxia, Attention Deficits, Autistic Spectrum Disorder, etc.) or which cause them to have low self-esteem because they do not obtain good grades in their work no matter how hard they try. This vulnerability makes them an easy target for being bullied by their peer group, physically or verbally. Verbal bullying by members of their family and even in some cases by their teachers can also occur. Some professionals can also be responsible for verbally bullying the parent, especially if s/he lacks good language skills him/herself and/or has low self-esteem. S/he may be at his/her 'wits end' because s/he does not know how to communicate his/her great concerns for his/her child and explain the problems the child is experiencing. Fathers, as much as mothers, can find it difficult to explain their concerns, especially since, unlike most women, a number of men prefer 'action rather than words' and find discussion difficult. (One of the parents may just 'hide' from the problems by believing that if they are ignored then they will just go away.)

Unless the child is at boarding school s/he will spend more time with his/her family than at school. If the teacher, or other professional, is finding it difficult/stressful to cope with the situation and to find solutions for the child's problems then how much more stressful is the parent's situation? We cannot support the child effectively if we do not support the parents. This means that we must communicate and liase with the parents on a regular basis and regard them as being part of a true partnership rather than just the token one that can occur in some educational establishments.

LITERACY SKILLS MAY INTERFERE WITH MATHEMATICAL SKILLS

Many children with speech and language difficulties experience problems with the acquisition of literacy skills. For some of them this will be a result of their speech and language impairment, for others Dyslexia will be an additional difficulty over and above their speech and language difficulty.

Sometimes the person may have good to excellent literacy skills. These can 'get in the way' of understanding the language of mathematics because the individual may always first think of the meaning of the word as it is used in literacy (e.g. in a story) rather than as it is used in mathematics. This sort of difficulty can cause major problems in understanding written problems or when listening to the teacher explaining how to do an operation. An example of this sort of problem can be found in the use of the word 'by'; e.g. *'The piece of wood is 5cms by 5cms. 'What is its area?'*

In this case 'by' is requiring the individual to multiply the relevant numbers. However, when reading the word 'by' in a novel it can be used as a word relating to:

If one of the parents is also affected by a language difficulty then professionals must take great care to ensure that information is understood and that the parent is enabled to put his/her point of view across. In meetings with these parents it is important for the professionals to remember that the person in the room with the most experience and understanding of the impact of language impairment is likely to be the parent – not the professional!

Mathematics is a foreign language. A student who is learning a new language (e.g. German) thinks first in his/her native language and then thinks in the second language. The student with superior literacy skills (as compared with mathematical language skills) can become very confused as s/he is likely to try to access the word from memory by:

1. Thinking in his/her native language (the meaning of the word as it is used in stories and in the real world around him/her)

2. Then thinking about how the word is used mathematically.

(Sometimes the student will not be able to progress to the second stage as the real world usually dominates the thought processes.)

Eventually the student may be so embarrassed that s/he will tell the teacher that s/he understands even though s/he does not.

▸▸ sequence or a line of items; e.g. the animals went into the ark one 'by' one,

▸▸ position; e.g. the duck went by the house,

▸▸ 'to a visit'; e.g. I'll drop by your house tomorrow.

Both sequence and position are concepts that are used in mathematics so the individual may 'try' those first. The individual cannot pay attention to the rest of the teacher's explanation/information in the question etc. until the use of the word is understood. The student has to work out which meaning the teacher is referring to whilst listening to the explanation of the concept, process etc. Thus s/he can miss out on understanding it. S/he can be helped by an initial discussion of the various meanings of the word followed by the meaning of it in the present mathematical context.

When the teacher is aware that the student has become confused s/he may take time to explain the concept etc. to the student. When this occurs in the middle of a group/class session and is conducted in front of the whole class the student can become extremely embarrassed because everyone is looking at her/him. The embarrassment causes the student to be under greater stress and so increases the confusion.

LACK OF HIGHER LEVEL LANGUAGE EXPERIENCE

Problems can occur because higher level language may not have been introduced at the beginning; e.g. 'sum' and 'take away' were used but not the term 'equation' and 'minus'. Such individuals spend a lot of time 'translating' the teacher's vocabulary into their own (and vice-versa) and so can 'miss' vital parts of the explanation.

WORD CONFUSION

The student may have word confusion problems due to:

▸▸ word-finding difficulties (cannot access the word from memory),

▸▸ failure to internalise vocabulary/understand the concept, (a simple concrete example plus explanation does not help the student).

Mathematics Solutions – An Introduction to Dyscalculia Part A by Jan Poustie et al   ISBN 1 901544 45 1

There are many other areas of language which need to be considered when teaching mathematics and this area is so complex that it requires a book of its own – *An Introduction to Mathematics and Language* (ISBN 1 901544 96 6). There are relatively few computer programs at present which are really helpful to the student with language difficulties. The two 'Maths Circus' computer programs are very good and they provide a fun way of improving aspects of mathematical language functioning. An added advantage of these programs is that they can read the text on the screen if necessary; e.g. if the student has Dyslexia. (They are available from 4Mation, 14 Castle Park Road, Barnstaple, Devon EX32 8PA, Tel: 01271 325353).

LANGUAGE SKILLS ARE VITAL – WE CANNOT IGNORE THEM!!

Language difficulties create a vicious circle.

Many children with speech and language impairments will also have a range of other difficulties which might include learning difficulties, motor problems, listening and attention difficulties. Memory problems and organisational difficulties can also be present. This wide range of difficulties can affect many areas of both the student's academic life and his/her career.

▸▸ In order to process information we need to think.

▸▸ We use language in order to think, create a 'schema' of mathematics and to build the 'model' through which we understand a topic. The model incorporates appropriate elements of language plus an understanding of the concept involved and the process by which the calculation is achieved.

▸▸ In order to communicate our thoughts we need to use oral or written language.

▸▸ In order to understand those around us, and to learn information, we need to be able to understand and process the language that we hear and read.

▸▸ In order to learn language and thus gain a good command of it (e.g. grammar, vocabulary etc.) we need to speak, and hear it, and, later on, to write and read it.

Both professionals and parents can miss the signs of language difficulties in students, especially when the student is of above average, or high, intelligence, as their intellectual ability can mask the condition. We gauge people by their language (their ability to both understand and provide information via spoken and written language). Thus, when a student has language difficulties we are likely to under-estimate their true intellectual ability. Language impairment will depress the scores of all of the verbal sub-tests in an intelligence test. It should be noted that the main IQ tests used in the UK (the WISC III[UK] and the BAS II) are administered orally so students with receptive language difficulties are at a disadvantage.

▶▶ If we cannot speak, hear (and process) our native language to a standard appropriate to our age and intellectual ability then we have less language skills than our peers and will have greater difficulties in both understanding mathematical language and in using our native language than our peers. Consequently, our language difficulties will cause us to have problems in processing information when we think, write, speak, hear or read and so on … and so on…

The only way that those affected by these problems can break out of this vicious circle is for us to enable them to overcome their difficulties and support them so that they can succeed in their academic and life goals. Such individuals require:

1. early identification,

2. specific targeted provision through speech and language programmes,

3. appropriate multisensory teaching that targets their natural learning style,

4. specialist teaching and speech and language therapy,

5. effective liaison between the various professionals involved with the student and liaison between the professionals, the parents and the student.

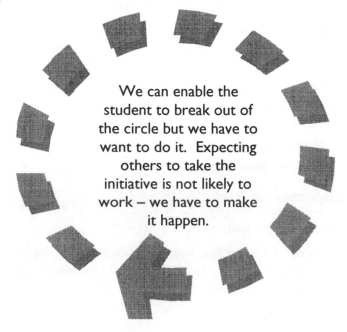

We can enable the student to break out of the circle but we have to want to do it. Expecting others to take the initiative is not likely to work – we have to make it happen.

Mathematics Solutions – An Introduction to Dyscalculia Part A by Jan Poustie et al   ISBN 1 901544 45 1

Dyslexia

The British Dyslexia Association's definition of Dyslexia as published in *The Dyslexia Handbook 2000* is:

> 'Dyslexia is best described as a combination of abilities and difficulties which affect the learning process in one or more of reading, spelling, writing and sometimes numeracy/language. Accompanying weaknesses may be identified in areas of speed of processing, short-term memory, sequencing, auditory and/or visual perception, spoken language and motor skills.
>
> Some children have outstanding creative skills, others have strong oral skills. Whilst others have no outstanding talents they all have strengths. Dyslexia occurs despite normal intellectual ability and conventional teaching; it is independent of socio-economic or language background.'

THE FORMS OF DYSLEXIA

Broadly speaking, there are two main types of Dyslexia – that which is acquired and that which is developmental.

Acquired Dyslexia
This is usually found in adults (e.g. through injury to the brain etc.) but can also be found in children through such conditions as ME (also known as Chronic Fatigue Syndrome/Post Viral Fatigue Syndrome) and Childhood Hemiplegia. This form of Dyslexia has many sub-groups ranging from Phonological Dyslexia (difficulties with the analysis of sounds and an inability to read irregular and nonsense words) to Direct Dyslexia (also known as 'hyperlexia') where the words can be read but the understanding of what is read is poor.

Developmental Dyslexia
This is always present from birth. Again, various sub-groups have been described; e.g. Dysphonetic Dyslexia (where the student has problems in building up and breaking apart the sounds in words). Some people have doubts as to the validity of the use of some of the sub-groups to describe the student's difficulties.

The identification of Dyslexia relates to an individual's abilities with regard to the reading and spelling of symbolic language. In the case of mathematics this relates to symbolic language representations; e.g. numerals, operations signs (+, x) etc.

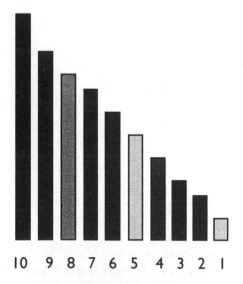

The student affected by Dyslexia may become tired after reading or writing only a few paragraphs or pages. By the end of an examination s/he can be exhausted and barely functioning, no matter how high a reading age s/he has managed to achieve.

10 9 8 7 6 5 4 3 2 1

Cuisenaire Rods
Available in the UK from Educational Solutions, Tel: 0118 987 3101. An invaluable tool when teaching students who have any form of mathematical learning difficulties.

THE CHARACTERISTICS OF DYSLEXIA

There is usually a family history of Dyslexia/reading difficulties/ other SpLD Profile conditions being present plus we will see:

▸▸ Difficulties in using, understanding and acquiring phonological skills (the sounds that letters make when seen singly or together)

and/or

▸▸ Difficulties in being able to remember what a word looks like (and so a word read accurately one minute may not be recognised the next).

Alongside these difficulties there are likely to be found difficulties in any of the following areas:

▸▸ Short-term memory.

▸▸ Sequencing skills.

▸▸ Speed of processing information in certain areas; e.g. speed of reading comprehension.

▸▸ Planning and organisation.

▸▸ Directional confusion (confusing left and right is common, but other directional opposites can also be confused; e.g. up/down and in/out).

▸▸ 'Good' and 'bad' days with regard to literacy and numeracy functioning (this can lead to adults saying that s/he is 'not trying' as s/he can do it one minute and therefore should be able to do it the next).

Sequencing Difficulties
Forming a 'staircase' from Cuisenaire Rods (see left) can help the student learn the sequence of numbers from 10-1. It should be built by the student at the beginning of the lesson and kept on display at all times. (The staircase can also be built in reverse order so that it starts at 1 and ends at 10.) The first task is to teach the student the value of each rod. This can be done by the tutor holding up different rods (from the box) and asking the student to use the staircase to work out their values. Once the value of each rod is known automatically then the rods can be an exceptionally useful tool when teaching students of all ages affected by any form of mathematical learning difficulty.

Mathematics Solutions – An Introduction to Dyscalculia Part A by Jan Poustie et al   ISBN 1 901544 45 1

Memory difficulties

These can be found as part of several of the conditions within the SpLD Profile; e.g. Dyslexia, Attention Deficits and Autistic Spectrum Disorder. Combined sequencing and short-term memory problems can result in mathematical processes not staying in the memory. As a result the student may be able to do the sum at the start of a page but have forgotten how to do it later on in the page and when doing homework. Working memory difficulties may also be present where the student is unable to manipulate/process the information that has just been received.

Memory can be trained to a certain extent, as can sequential skill development. LDA (Tel: 01945 463441), Taskmaster (Tel: 0116 270 4286) and CALSC (Tel: 020 8642 4663) stock materials to help with these skills but the basic difficulty in these areas will remain.

Auditory short-term memory difficulties

Frequently, an auditory working memory difficulty is seen. Such difficulties cause problems with functioning in the classroom; e.g. following the teacher's talk on a topic, processing the teacher's instructions.

Classification skills can be taught and improved by using games such as the number version of Rummikub™ (available from Next Generation and toy shops) and practical activities relating to the classification of shape, size and colour with regard to numbers can also help. Ultimately this process must be taken to the point where the student is able to classify such information using the appropriate ways of recording it. This can be achieved by using Carroll, Venn diagrams and alternative organisational formats; e.g. Mind Maps®, Shape/Picture Maps, Grids and Lists dependent upon the learning style of the student. These recording techniques help to connect the individual pieces of information within the brain and so make them more accessible to the student. (These formats can be found in *Planning and Organisation Solutions* ISBN 1 901544 81 8.) This title also includes strategies for teaching classification skills.) Once the information is organised in the mind there is at least a chance that the student will be able to access the information when required.

Classification skills

Memory is dependent upon access and access is dependent upon the organisation of the information. Students affected by Dyslexia do not appear to have a natural organisational system for words. They may also lack planning and organisational skills in many other areas. The greater the stress that they are under the more likely these planning and organisational skills will deteriorate.

Technology has made incredible advances in recent years and for many students it is the technology of the present, and the future, that will provide some of the support that they need in school and much of the support that they need in adulthood.

This chapter has been kept short deliberately as many books have been written about Dyslexia and mathematics and how to overcome the difficulties that this group of students experience. For details of some of these titles see Appendix 3.

THE COMBINATION OF SHORT-TERM MEMORY AND SEQUENCING DIFFICULTIES

Short-term memory and sequencing difficulties may be found because of the difference in functioning that exists when Dyslexia is present and/or because of the presence of attention and co-ordination difficulties. Short-term memory and sequencing problems are the cause of many of the problems of those who have Dyslexia, and they carry on causing problems in adulthood. On top of all this, what can loosely be described as a 'word-finding' receptive language difficulty may also be present. This difficulty, combined with short-term memory and classification difficulties, causes the student to have problems with accessing from memory the word which s/he wants to use. A similar difficulty can occur when listening, where the student cannot remember the meaning of a word that the teacher uses and so loses the 'thread' of the discussion/explanation.

UNDERSTANDING MATHEMATICAL CONCEPTS

As part of Dyslexia we can see difficulties in understanding and remembering symbols. The presence of Dyslexia may cause the student to fail to learn the concepts because s/he cannot read the workbook. However, the student may have no problems with understanding the concepts once the information is read to him/her. Difficulties with remembering sequences is likely to affect the student's ability to remember the times tables and to remember the stages of the process (and their correct order) when doing a sum.

We know from Richard Ashcroft (Head of Mathematics at Mark College – a specialist school for those affected by Dyslexia) that seventy-five per cent of those affected by moderate to severe Dyslexia also have mathematical learning difficulties. The fact that pupils from his school achieve passes in mathematics at GCSE level shows that such difficulties can be overcome. Once introduced to concepts in a more visual and kinaesthetic (movement-based) way students who have Dyslexia may find mathematics much easier to understand and may be able to go on to gain a 'C' grade or higher at GCSE level.

Mathematics Solutions – An Introduction to Dyscalculia Part A by Jan Poustie et al   ISBN 1 901544 45 1

Attention Deficits

The presence of Attention Deficits can cause students to have major difficulties in functioning within the classroom and in achieving tasks that require mental effort. Both sexes can have Attention Deficits. Although both twins and non-twins may have the condition, twins (particularly boys) are especially likely to have difficulties in concentrating and staying on task. *(Contact TAMBA for further information – their address is in Appendix 1.)*

Difficulties in learning mathematics are commonly associated with the presence of Dyslexia and Dyspraxia. Attention Deficits can often be seen alongside both of these conditions. These combinations of difficulties are not always recognised for several reasons:

1. UADD may be present. This is the non-hyperactive form where the person is a daydreamer and usually shows signs of anxiety.

2. The 'Not as Specified' (NOS) form of Attention Deficits may be present. This is where the person meets most, but not all, of the criteria for Attention Deficits. The problems of such students are often ignored as a diagnosis of ADHD or UADD is not given.

3. When the hyperactivity in ADHD takes the form of fidgeting with fingers/hair etc. and restlessness (rather than the form of ADHD where students are frequently out of their seats/ moving round the room). Hyperactivity may also be seen as 'verbal diarrhoea' where the person talks 'too much'.

CAUSES OF ATTENTION DEFICIT BEHAVIOURS

Working out the cause of the ADD behaviours enables us to work out the best ways in which we can help the student. There is increasing evidence that ADD behaviours can be caused by a variety of factors; it appears that each of these factors can result in any of the forms of ADD being present.

▸▸ A chemical imbalance
Normally the cortex of the brain dampens the limbic

The term Attention Deficit Disorder (ADD) is also used. There are various forms of Attention Deficits; e.g. UADD = Undifferentiated Attention Deficit Disorder and ADHD = Attention Deficit Hyperactivity Disorder.

Complementary therapies such as homeopathy and cranial osteopathy can help in some cases.

Attention Deficit behaviours in the listening environment can be found when Central Auditory Processing Disorder is present. Once the auditory processing has improved and the student's difficulties are compensated for, the behaviour is likely to improve. (See Chapter 5.)

system of the brain. The limbic system is closely involved in emotional behaviour. A chemical imbalance in the brain decreases the dampening effect of the cortex and causes difficulties in controlling one's actions/thoughts.

This group appears to respond to chemical interventions (e.g. Ritalin, combinations of various drugs) in order to enable them to focus on academic work and reduce unwanted behaviours.

▸▸ A metabolic disorder
The reduced number of reinforced neural connections in the brain (that are believed to occur when Dyspraxia is present) result in the limbic system of the brain not being dampened enough by the cortex.

The individuals in this group may respond to the use of dietary supplements; e.g. omega fatty acids (see pages 73 and 74 in this book and Portwood's *Developmental Dyspraxia* ISBN 1 85346 573 9).

▸▸ A lack of 'cranial moulding' during birth
The cranium (skull) consists of various bones which at birth can move a small amount to allow the baby to pass through the birth canal. This passage through the canal causes 'moulding of the cranium' to occur. If this moulding does not occur (e.g. through a very fast second stage of labour, a Caesarean birth) then ADD behaviours can result.

The ADD can be reduced by the use of cranial osteopathy. This treatment can be carried out no matter what the age of the student though it should be noted that older students are likely to require more sessions. One needs to contact one's local osteopath (see Yellow Pages telephone book) to find out which ones have a speciality in this field.

▸▸ Hyperactivity caused by items within the diet
Elements in the diet appear to cause hyperactivity in some students. (A variety of foods, including oranges, certain colourings, chocolate, coke etc., can all contribute to such problems.)

An unbalanced sugar level can also occur. The student has 'sugar highs' just after taking sugar-laden foods (sweets etc.), then does not eat enough or does not eat mixed carbohydrate foods and so hits a 'sugar low'. Very uneven behaviours can result from this.

Modifying the diet can modify the behaviour. However some ADD students eat only a small range of foods and may be very resistant to trying new foods/changing their routines. Interestingly enough, the author noted that in one child the behaviours were increased when the child had milk chocolate but were not increased when the child ate white chocolate.

▸▸ <u>The student being intellectually superior</u>
The gifted student can appear to show behaviours similar to those of the ADD student.

Both gifted and ADD students need a modification of various factors such as the environment/task if they are to be anything other than 'square pegs in round holes'. The importance of changing the environment and/or the task cannot be underestimated and so these are discussed further in Chapter 9.

No matter what the cause of the ADD behaviours, homeopathy can be helpful (contact the Society of Homeopaths, Tel; 01604 21400 for local professionals) and an understanding adult who can help the student to talk through the situations that stress him/her may be essential.

Of course some students may be affected by many of the causal factors mentioned above; e.g. when giftedness, Dyspraxia and CAPD are all present. In such cases, strategies for each aspect of functioning will need to be put into place if better behaviours are to occur.

LEARNING AND ATTENTION DEFICITS

When Attention Deficits is present, students often fail to give close attention to detail and may make careless mistakes. Thus, they are not likely to learn to spell with any ease and may make careless errors when writing sums.

Those affected by ADHD (and Dyspraxia) often need to fidget/

The Attention Deficit student may be so disgusted with his/her work that s/he tears it up in temper/ disgust, or damages the tool that is being used to record the information!

move around. These difficulties, plus their problems in sustaining their attention, mean that it is less likely that they will sit at a task for very long unless it really interests them. Their problems with starting and finishing work, and being distracted from their task, mean that if, one is lucky, they will sit down and start the task – and, if one is even luckier, they may actually complete it! Often they are likely to concentrate only on one part of a project and ignore the rest. The completion of the whole task may be beyond them without someone encouraging, coaching and guiding them. Students who are global/qualitative learners (who see things 'as wholes') are likely to find completion of projects etc. especially difficult to achieve without support.

Qualitative learners are like grasshoppers who move from one aspect of a task to another in random order. They prefer to work on the 'whole' rather the elements of the task/project. Some will find it very difficult to see the individual elements/steps which make up the task. Others find it very difficult to maintain motivation once they have gone beyond the initial 'whole concept/idea'. They can distinctly dislike (i.e.find frustrating, boring, tiring and difficult to focus on) the 'petty' parts of the task; e.g. proof-reading, or, the fiddly bits of creating an index; and so never complete the task.

When a qualitative style is present alongside Attention Deficits then one may see a student with plenty of ideas but lacking the ability to follow a task through to its conclusion. This is not through laziness but simply because the final part of any task involves checking layout, checking each step of the process of a calculation etc. Those of you who spot the printing and layout errors that, no doubt, will escape the eye of the author (who hates the final 'fiddly' stage of writing a book) will not be surprised to learn that she has Attention Deficits!

The Attention Deficits student's common dislike/avoidance of tasks which involve sustained mental effort makes all numeracy tasks hard work. However, once these difficulties have been reduced/overcome and a motivating force has appeared there is a chance that these students will work intensively to overcome their problems. Motivating forces include developing a strong interest in a subject or the acquisition of a certain level/aspect of

Their teachers (parents and spouses) find ADD students very frustrating as their tendency to lose things and be forgetful results in them appearing for lessons/activities without pen,

Mathematics Solutions – An Introduction to Dyscalculia Part A by Jan Poustie et al   ISBN 1 901544 45 1

mathematical functioning in order to obtain a particular life goal. These students' distractibility and forgetfulness can cause problems in and out of lessons. If one is very unlucky, such students will become distracted on the way to a lesson and this, combined with a poor time sense, may mean that they never appear for it!

The endless restlessness/fidgeting/desk-tapping etc. of the ADHD student angers many of those adults around him/her especially when repeated requests/instructions to stop it have no effect. Encouraging the student to gently tap his/her leg instead at least reduces the noise of the 'desk-tapper'. The frequent verbal and physical interruptions of such students in the lesson, the need for them to say their piece (before they forget it) and the need to have their turn NOW are also frustrating for all concerned. The frustration can be further increased (and the student can further waste class time) when the teacher 'loses the thread' of what s/he is discussing because the student interrupts once too often.

Frustration can be very great when the student's profile includes Attention Deficits, Specific Language Impairment and Central Auditory Processing Disorder. This particular combination can cause great problems for the student when listening and can also cause great difficulties when s/he wants to explain the problems that s/he is experiencing.

The effects of Attention Deficits on others can be great but perhaps the worst aspect of it for the ADD individual is poor memory and the huge effort that is usually needed to put things into long-term memory.

Unless the information really appeals to the student (or has an impact on him/her) it can be incredibly difficult to learn it. Thus the author can find it exceptionally difficult to remember dates. However, she can remember (with apparent ease) single fascinating facts; e.g. Wall Street in New York was named because it was sited where the original wall to keep out the Red Indians stood. Unfortunately, such facts are not much use unless one is playing Trivial Pursuit!

This is not the student that one tries to talk through problems with unless one has some concrete objects/diagrams/pictures etc. to help him/her focus on, and better understand, the subject of the conversation.

Mathematics Solutions – An Introduction to Dyscalculia Part A by Jan Poustie et al   ISBN 1 901544 45 1

Strategies that suit these student's natural learning style must be used when revising for examinations. For six years after the author gained her degree she had recurrent nightmares where she dreamed that she had failed her exams. These nightmares were caused as a result of the stress of having to overwork to the extent of only having two hours sleep a night for over six months in order to push enough information into memory. Even then she could only put about half her course into memory. (While studying for her GCE 'O' level examinations, equivalent to today's GCSE examinations, the author had realised that some types of questions came up more than others and so had only revised part of the course.) During her revision for her degree she had to use the same strategy as she knew that it was impossible for her to memorise the whole course. If only she had known about Mind Mapping® as a revision technique then! (See *Planning and Organisation Solutions* by Jan Poustie, ISBN 1 901544 81 8 and *Get Ahead* by Vanda North and Tony Buzan, ISBN 1 874374 00 7 for further details of Mind Mapping® strategies.)

Those affected by Attention Deficits are likely to have short-term memory difficulties too and these affect many classroom activities; e.g. copying from the blackboard (a task which can take them much longer than their peers and their work is likely to contain errors).

It is very much a trial and error process to find a suitable method for teaching numeracy and other mathematical skills to this group of students. Finding a responsive tutor that the student likes (and using a system of coaching strategies) is likely to be of the most benefit. The ADHD Family Support Group UK produce a leaflet on coaching (see Appendix 1).

Some students within this group may never develop the patience and motivation to be consistently accurate when writing and working out sums. Equally, they may be much keener on working the sum out in their head and may find it frustrating to have to learn a particular written process. At GCSE level, marks can be given when the student shows how s/he worked out the sum (even if the answer is wrong). This, of course, can cause problems for the Attention Deficit student for, unless we

If the needs of ADD students are not met they can become frustrated and can lack motivation to work in the subject.

can persuade them to show their 'working out', they stand to lose valuable marks. Of course the Attention Deficit student who is a qualitative learner, with Developmental Dyscalculia also present, may well have no idea of how s/he arrived at the answer and so will not be able to write down any 'working out' at all!

Attention Deficit students are under a great deal of stress and, often, so are those around them! They need to have:

▸▸ a meaningful relationship with their work (so it needs to relate to them and their interests/goals)

▸▸ the work has to be seen as valid; e.g. it is not some pointless question that could never happen in real life.

▸▸ Their high levels of stress, and their dislike of mental tasks, mean that they also have to find their work pleasurable. Here a computer can be a very useful way of providing them with the necessary reinforcement for the basic four rules of number (addition, subtraction, multiplication, division). There are plenty of computer programs around and many of them are themed; e.g. Davison's 'Maths Blaster' series of programs which are set in outer space.

Parents and teachers need to look for programs that have themes/layouts that are likely to appeal to the student. For the younger child 'Count and Add' (published by Lander Software and available from REM, Great Western House, Langport, Somerset TA10 9YU) is good fun. However, before using the program the tutor has to make sure that the child is not upset by the spiders in one of the games.

Generally speaking, the less boring the material/activity the more likely that ADD students will learn the information.

It is easy to assume that ADD students are not trying. What is forgotten is that for these students just settling down to a numeracy task may require much greater self-discipline and concentration than the rest of their peer group ever have to use except perhaps in an examination situation.

The 'Maths Blaster' programs are available from: Knowledge Adventure, 2 Beacontree Plaza, Gillette Way, Reading RG2 0BS.

They are suitable for PC/MAC. Although they are designed for the age range 4-12 years, the author has found that some older teenagers enjoy using them, especially for tasks such as learning times tables.

Behavioural Problems

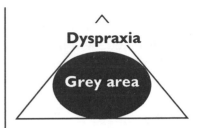

Attention Deficits

Autistic Spectrum Disorder

A person can have any combination of these conditions and some will have all three of them.

There are many aspects to behaviour and several of the Specific Learning Difficulties Profile conditions have large behavioural elements; e.g. Autistic Spectrum Disorder (ASD) and Attention Deficits (ADD). Behavioural differences also accompany Dyspraxia which are often associated with the presence of hyperactivity with Attention Deficits (ADHD). A level of social immaturity compared with the individual's peer group is commonly seen alongside Dyspraxia. Each is a distinct condition but there is believed to be a large 'grey area' linking them. Students affected by Dyspraxia and Attention Deficits can also have elements of ASD; e.g. Autistic Tendencies. The different combinations which are possible plus the many sub-groups of each condition make identification difficult unless you are able to recognise all three of them. *(See Identification Solutions for Specific Learning Difficulties; Part A published by Next Generation for further information on these conditions.)*

The 'grey area' is the subject of research being conducted by various people at present, including Madeleine Portwood (senior educational psychologist based at Durham County Council). This research is being carried out because many of those working in the field of SpLD have noted that we are seeing behaviours that we would expect to see in one or more of these behavioural conditions but that the rest of the student's profile does not match the condition. Certainly, part of this can be explained by the functioning of the brain when in an overload situation; e.g. in stressful situations first the mammalian and then the reptilian brain becomes dominant and so alters our behaviour.

The mammalian brain controls sleeping and eating patterns plus our emotions. The reptilian brain controls our fight/flight response (so when we feel threatened or stressed we either avoid the task (by removing ourselves from the task; e.g. by daydreaming, being sent out of the room) or we fight the task (become aggressive etc.). These behaviours are 'automatic'; i.e. the student has no control over them.

The effects on mathematics of Attention Deficits and Dyspraxia

It is important to remember that each student is unique and has a unique set of difficulties, weaknesses and strengths. We have to use the strengths to overcome the student's difficulties.

have already been dealt with in Chapters 4 and 8. This chapter has been included to give the reader some idea of the behavioural problems that occur when an element of ASD or ADD (with or without hyperactivity) is present and to offer some strategies that can be tried.

The strategies in this section are not meant to replace specialist advice but they may be found useful while the adults involved with the student are in the process of finding out information from specialist agencies mentioned in Appendix 1. Professionals can also find out information via their Local Education Authority's (LEA) special advisors on students with behavioural/ communication difficulties. In more enlightened authorities, parents have access to these advisors too (they can be accessed via the LEA's Education Department at the county's headquarters which is often called County Hall).

Each of the behavioural conditions requires different management, with Autistic Spectrum Disorder requiring the most change both in teaching environment and practice. The closer we 'fit' the environment and the work to these students the less likely we are to have to cope with behavioural difficulties. This chapter deals with simple yet effective ways of achieving this 'better fit'. The adjustments and changes mentioned in this chapter do not cost money, they just show that a 'better understanding' of our students will enable us to achieve a 'better fit' for them.

UNUSUAL SENSITIVITIES TO SENSORY INFORMATION

These are associated with the presence of Dyspraxia and Autistic Spectrum Disorder. Students can be hypersensitive to texture, smell, taste, noise etc. They may become distressed when touching wax crayons or a plastic desk or some of the objects used when weighing. They may find the smell of the teacher's aftershave, perfume or the cleansers used in the classroom unpleasant.

The sound of the fire alarm can be particularly frightening and they may become confused, refusing to leave the building along a route not normally used; e.g. through the fire door.

ASD students may become fascinated by the gentle movements of a streamer hanging from the ceiling and watch it for hours; lights, a moving part of machinery or the sound of a pen scratching on paper can be equally riveting.

MANAGING THE STUDENT IN THE CLASSROOM

It is important to remember that what will work with one student will not work with another. Adults faced with dealing with such students may realise that they need to prevent the difficulties occurring but feel that specialist knowledge is needed in order to do so. Specialist advice may not be that easy to obtain.

Case Study – seven-year-old boy

The author recently learnt of a case in which a little boy became very distressed within a day of entering his local junior school. Although a combination of conditions were present; i.e. Asperger Syndrome, Attention Deficits and Dyspraxia,his difficulties were not regarded as extensive enough by his LEA to award him a Statement of Special Education Needs.

At the end of the first day of junior school he was very distressed because the teacher had been shouting at him a lot (because he was not listening – never an easy task for a student affected by this pattern of difficulties). He was kept in at break because he had not finished his work. His mother was worried sick, as her son had become aggressive in a previous school when he was unable to cope with the teacher's management of him. On his second day, she had a great struggle to get him into school and feared that by the end of the next week she would not be able to get him into school at all.

When the mother raised her concerns with the headteacher, she was told that a meeting between the Special Educational Needs Co-ordinator (SENCO, also sometimes known as AENCO), the class teacher and the parent could not be arranged for a fortnight. This delay only made the situation worse and heightened the mother's concerns.

This child's assessment history is typical of those with a complex SpLD Profile. Just before going to print the author was advised that a further assessment had altered the diagnosis to that of Tourette Syndrome, obsessional behaviours and ADD. (Tourette Syndrome is characterised by the individual making repetitive and involuntary movements and vocal sounds over

The ADD student can find it difficult to stay on task (especially when mental effort is required).

The presence of ADD or ASD is likely to result in students finding it difficult to cope with the teacher shouting at them or shouting at other children in the class. They may find it so distressing that they refuse to go to school or feel ill before going to school in the morning. (Note: the presence of any of the other SpLD Profile conditions can also cause students to find such situations distressing.)

which s/he has no control. Readers who require inforamtion on this condition should contact Tourettes Syndrome UK Association, PO Box 26149, Dunfermline, Fife KY12 0WT.)

Some professionals can find changes in diagnosis difficult to deal with (or even difficult to believe). However, once the various factors involved in assessment are noted it then becomes easier to see why diagnoses may change, or be added to.

▸▸   It is the nature of the behavioural conditions of the SpLD Profile that behaviours change as the student develops, and so diagnoses may well alter.

▸▸   We have the perennial problem that each assessor's experience, background and qualifications are different, and therefore the focus of the assessment will also alter.

▸▸   We have the problem that the 'grey area' between the conditions can make assessment difficult.

▸▸   Assessments conducted before specialists realised that it is common for a student to have more than one condition present may well have found only 'part of the picture'.

▸▸   There is only 'so much time' that any professional can devote to assessment and the writing of the report.

▸▸   The student may be unco-operative during a particular assessment.

When ASD and ADD are present, there can be great difficulties in staying motivated long enough to finish (and sometimes even to start) tasks. Some students (due to decision-making difficulties) may find it exceptionally difficult to find the starting point of the task. Attention Deficit students find it particularly difficult to stay on task when mental effort is required. Dyspraxia can cause the student to write very slowly and this too can make task completion difficult.

This student's set of difficulties meant that finishing his work would have been an unusual achievement rather than the normal one for him! Keeping him in to finish his work was not a solution. Instead the task itself needed to be changed, so enabling him to complete it. Thus, towards the end of the task he could have been asked to complete it orally, or he could have

Mathematics Solutions – An Introduction to Dyscalculia Part A by Jan Poustie et al   ISBN 1 901544 45 1

been asked to complete the whole task (or part of it) in a more practical manner, using pictures etc.

This parent tried to access her local authority's Special Educational Needs Support Team but was instead transferred to her LEA's Parent Partnership Officer. This professional can be helpful in some cases but, where a school is not being co-operative in the management of/provision for a student, s/he lack any powers to make them be so. The LEA advisor for children with communication difficulties was eventually accessed via another professional. He informed the parent that he could not become involved because her son did not have a Statement of Special Education Needs. This raises a serious issue. There are indicators at present that Statements are going to be even less common in the future than they are at present. if LEAs do not want the vast expense of parent's attempting to obtain a Statement for their child as the only way of gaining appropriate support for them, then students without Statements will need to be appropriately provided for and their parents enabled to have access to the appropriate support staff. This problem does not cease once the student moves on to Further and Higher education, as there too it is the Statement that determines the level of provision.

It is important for adults to be aware that there may be little awareness of social hierarchy, especially when ASD is present. When this occurs, the teacher (or any other adult) is no more important than any other human being (including even young children). Therefore there is no reason to obey the adult!!!

The whole premise that only two per cent of the population require Statements appears to be based on very much out-of-date information as to how many students were recognised as having severe difficulties in the mid-twentieth century. Many students in the past would have gone unrecognised. This is especially the case where Dyscalculia is concerned as relatively few professionals had in the past (and have now) the expertise needed to make assessments.

Topic/task choice and strategies

ASD students, in particular, have difficulties in producing written work/taking on information etc. which is not related to their own areas of interest. (ADD students may also have such difficulties.) The importance of relating information that has to be known/learnt to the ASD student's areas of interest and favoured way of learning cannot be understated (and this also applies to students where ADD is present). Homework

Mathematics Solutions – An Introduction to Dyscalculia Part A by Jan Poustie et al   ISBN 1 901544 45 1

If the teacher is to avoid being totally frustrated by the student (and the stress that this causes) then the student's needs will have to be accommodated.

instructions may be disregarded when they are being given out unless the student is enabled to relate to the information homework may also not be done.

Making the work relevant to the student can be helpful when trying to overcome this difficulty; e.g. if the student likes Star Wars then the tutor can relate topics to it. So, if the class is doing a topic on dimensions then the student could be allowed to measure Star Wars characters, space vehicles etc. rather than measure the desk etc. Similarly, if the student has an obsession with the Second World War then we can relate his/her work to that topic when first introducing it. For example, if the topic is long addition and long subtraction then we can ask the student to look up statistical details relevant to different wars and compare them; e.g.

➤ The number of mules killed during two different campaigns in the 1st World War

➤ The dimensions of the Battle of the Bulge memorial in Belgium.

Teachers may feel that they have neither the time to look up the relevant facts for obsessional students nor have easy access to the relevant reference books. Fortunately, students who have obsessional interests are also likely to possess the reference books needed and both parents (and the students themselves) can either be co-opted to find out the information required or can provide us with the books so that we have a better chance of teaching the student!

The Theory of Mind relates to the student's perception of emotions, pretend play and how other people may be perceiving the world. Practical strategies to enable the student to have a better understanding of these areas can be found in *Teaching Children with Autism to Mind-Read* by Howlin, Baron-Cohen and Hadwin, ISBN 0 471 97623 7.

Calendar and numerical information is often of great interest; e.g. dimensions of UK cathedrals, the dates of every Manchester United football match. When this is the case, we can enable the student to achieve success by directing his/her work towards this aspect of learning. Thus, if the student likes a particular football team, we can use the scores of the team during the past or present season as the basis for calculations.

Points to note
1. <u>Difficulties with making inferences</u>
   Abstract thinking may be well developed in the ASD student

but making inferences may not be – this is linked to an inability to imagine a situation and what is called the Theory of Mind. (Other language-impaired students may also have a similar difficulty.) This may be a problem once GCSE assignment work is required, as the student may happily do all the calculations required but then have difficulty in (or not see the relevance of) putting the information into assignment form. This is also likely to be a problem in class especially when the teachers fail to specify exactly what they want the student to do but instead leave it to be inferred from a statement that they make. Thus, the teacher may say 'I will be really glad when you stop talking John.' As far as ASD (and some ADD) students are concerned, such a comment may be regarded as just a statement of fact and not require a modification of their own behaviour.

Difficulties with making inferences, and in achieving tasks which require imagination, can occur, especially when ASD is present. Some ADD students also find this difficult. Some students may have limited skills in certain areas but may not be able to transfer those skills to other areas of their lives.

2. Difficulties with understanding the feelings of others
    Some ASD and ADD students may be able to put themselves into 'other people's shoes' and may be able to develop some understanding of the feelings of other people. (Alternatively, they may be able to develop an acknowledgement that other people have feelings which will be different from their own). However, for many students such skills are weak (or in some cases may not exist at all) and this can cause problems when they fail to acknowledge the feelings of the teacher and their peer group.

    This awareness of the feelings of others may develop in ADD students once the 'executive function' in the frontal lobe of the brain matures; e.g. at the end of puberty, or when this functioning is supported via medication.

    Puberty usually occurs later for boys than for girls. This later maturing of the 'executive function' in the ADD male, plus the fact that the body of a teenage boy is giving him an hourly boost of testosterone, means that his ability to concentrate is further limited. He is therefore, likely to be distracted by his body's need to attract/react to the opposite sex. These factors can put the ADD boy at a severe disadvantage during the key years of his schooling.

3. Comprehension difficulties
    Verbal skills may be highly advanced in the ASD student, so s/

The student affected by ASD may be quite egocentric and so appear self-centred. S/he is likely to have lots of needs rather than wants.

ASD can be present alongside a condition called Tuberous Sclerosis which results in various problems including the growth of cysts on the kidneys. One teenage girl (who had both these conditions) spent several hours one night rocking the toilet off the floor!!!! This behaviour occurred because one of the screws was loose – so it really does pay to keep the general maintenance of the student's environment up to scratch!

ASD students do not like to be distracted from their own thoughts and so directing their attention to the topic under class discussion etc. may not be easy.

he may have a very good vocabulary. However, auditory comprehension in such students may be very weak and allowance will need to be made for this in conversation/ teaching etc. Weak comprehension skills will affect the student's ability to deal with word problems.

4. Disorganised sensory information
   The student is likely to find it difficult to cope with disorganised sensory information; e.g. people moving around in a random way, items not displayed in a uniform way (according to their concept of what uniformity and randomness mean etc.). Bizarre behaviours can result from this; e.g. being unable to cope with the change of texture where a carpet edging strip joins two pieces of carpet.

5. The problem of ritualistic behaviours
   Ritualistic behaviours are common in the ASD population and need to be fulfilled by the student in order for him/her to feel secure. Trying to change (or stop) the ritual merely results in another ritual taking its place. Rituals can be very frustrating for the student's carer as the student can sometimes take a very long time to complete the whole ritual before any meaningful work can be started. (Interrupting the ritual is only likely to make the student start from the beginning again!)

6. Difficulties in doing group work
   ASD is characterised by difficulties in establishing normal effective relationships with people (including teachers and peer group). One consequence of this is that group work may be impossible for the student as s/he may just be an 'onlooker' or may wander off and do his/her 'own thing'.

7. The problem of the student being on a different 'wavelength'
   ASD (and ADD) students may be thinking of concepts/areas of information that are far beyond the interests of their peer group and their originality of thought enables them to form their own theories. This originality, level of thinking and different approach to life etc. may make such students appear eccentric and this in turn increases their difficulties in relating to their peers and vice versa.

8. The teacher's need for control
   Teachers can feel overwhelmed when dealing with an ASD

Mathematics Solutions – An Introduction to Dyscalculia Part A by Jan Poustie et al   ISBN 1 901544 45 1

(or an ADD) student. The teacher's need to control and the student's inability to meet the teacher's needs can result in frequent conflict between teacher and student (and the student's parents) which further worsens the situation. The answering back (or the muttering under his/her breath) which can occur when the student does not want to do a task, can increase this level of conflict.

9. <u>The need for routine and 'sameness'</u>
Routines and the need for 'sameness' (e.g. an unchanging environment and unchanging tasks) are exceptionally important to some students. Although some ADD individuals (such as the author) detest anything which appears to be of a routine nature, most ASD and ADD students do not cope well without routine.

ASD students, in particular, require their world to be unchanging. Such students are likely to find it very difficult to cope when a supply teacher has to cover for their own teacher. Special events that change routine; e.g. sports day, may cause stress and unwanted behaviours. Therefore, both ADD and ASD students tend to function better when events happen at expected times and the requirements of the tasks do not change. When ASD is present it is necessary to inform students even of changes in lesson structure before they occur.

Both ASD and ADD students need to be warned well in advance of changes and pictorial reminders on an easy-to-understand calendar can be useful here. (It should be noted that ASD students may have difficulties in understanding terms such as yesterday, today, tomorrow, before, after, etc. and so the reminder of the change will also have to occur the morning of the event and just before the event as well.)

The need for 'sameness' affects the ASD student's handling of changes in the environment. Thus, even different types of methods of gaining entrance to a building can be a problem for these students; e.g. automatic doors, going down escalators,using lifts and different types of door handle (e.g. lever or knob).

10. <u>Stress</u>
It is often not realised that stress is a major cause of

Handwritten work may be poorly presented. If this is the case the student should be enabled to produce the bulk of his/her work via a computer program.

Mathematics Solutions – An Introduction to Dyscalculia Part A by Jan Poustie et al   ISBN 1 901544 45 1

behavioural difficulties and this is especially the case when the student's needs have not been provided for adequately.

Stress causes the student to function less well academically and to require 'sameness' in the environment and tasks. Thus any student whose needs are not being met is likely to function better when in a structured environment and when s/he knows what to expect in a lesson/task.

11. Problems resulting from having to do tasks in a set way
ASD (and ADD) students are likely to produce their best work when they produce the work in their own way. They are likely to perform badly when the task has to be done in a set way. A successful strategy with the ADD student is to do the following:

▸▸ Enable him/her to do the task in his/her own way.

▸▸ Use a check list so that s/he can see which parts have been omitted. (This enables the student to see the areas that s/he tends to miss out and provides an opportunity to discuss the problems that s/he has with particular tasks.)

▸▸ Enable him/her to add on elements to their work so that the whole task is completed – the use of a computer is invaluable here.

12. The problems of tests and examinations
ASD students, in particular, (and some ADD students) are likely to perform badly if they have to produce work using knowledge that has been learnt; e.g. in tests/examinations. There are various causes of this; e.g. memory difficulties, difficulties in motivation because the subject does not interest them, difficulties in settling down to revision and so on.

13. The ASD and ADD students' difficulty in learning from (and co-operating with) others
Unfortunately for us, ASD (and some ADD) students appear only to be able to experience the world (and the information that we present to them) in their own original way. Groupwork-based tasks with their need for co-operation, acknowledgement of other people's needs/ideas and the ability to work together as part of a team may be impossible for these students to achieve. ASD students are likely to find

Perhaps, it is useful to note here that teachers may well also be affected by stress, especially in our ever-changing world of education in the UK. They, too, may need 'sameness' and so may well find the challenging behaviour of some ASD and ADD students very difficult to deal with. Being able to predict the situations which are likely to cause the behaviours will be of great help here (see conducting a risk assessment on page 130).

learning from others (including the teacher) difficult. Therefore, teachers who believe that their function is to impart knowledge (rather than to enable students to learn knowledge in their own way) are immediately in a conflict situation.

14. <u>The parent's perception of the student may be different from that of the teacher</u>
The perception of the student from the point of view of the parents and the teacher may be very different. Thus when ADD or ASD (including Asperger Syndrome) are present, the parent may see a student who is not living up to his/her expectations. The teacher expects the student to sit still, pay attention, answer questions, learn the subject s/he is teaching and score well in examinations. However, a student who has these conditions may be unable to meet such expectations, or at least will find it very difficult to do so.

In a similar way we could group students according to their learning style. Thus, those who need to use practical apparatus in order to learn could be in one group whilst those who prefer to listen to the teacher could be in another.

In an educational setting, Asperger Syndrome students may need to interact with those around them in order to feel secure and to acquire knowledge. (Anxious students and those affected by auditory processing/receptive language difficulties may also need to do the same.) Such students will need to be involved in an interactive way with the individuals around them via constant questioning of peer group and adults. However, the teacher wants his/her students to acquire knowledge in a more passive way; e.g. through reading instructions and then doing the calculations etc.

A way of overcoming this problem, and enabling this group of students to learn, might be to put them together in a small group at the end of the classroom so that discussions can take place without distracting the rest of the class. This group of students would need to include the 'global/ qualititative learners' who also need to use questions as a means of learning.

15. <u>Exceptional achievement and the ASD student</u>
ASD affects both the learning process and what the student is prepared to learn. The student may easily grasp abstract concepts. As long as intellectual functioning is normal, or above average, there may be a good intellectual grasp of the world, but, whereas the rest of the class will follow the lead of the teacher, the ASD student has to follow his/her own

The ASD (and the ADD) student may distract others unless in a very organised and structured environment. Staying at his/her desk may also be very difficult for him/her.

Mathematics Solutions – An Introduction to Dyscalculia Part A by Jan Poustie et al   ISBN 1 901544 45 1

Connecting information is vital if the student is to build his/her own 'schema' of mathematics. The various planning and organisational techniques that can be found in *Planning and Organisation Solutions* by Jan Poustie (ISBN 1 901544 81 8, published by Next Generation) could be explored for ways in which the student might organise each new piece of information into a 'whole' which includes all previously learnt information.

£ $ + <

Difficulties in learning symbolic language (e.g. numerals, mathematical signs etc.) may be found when ASD or Specific Language Impairment is present.

path. The blinkered attitude and interests which results from this can, in some cases, lead to exceptional achievement in the chosen area of study. This can occur because, unlike the rest of us, such students may not be distracted from studying because of a need to socialise with peers etc.

16. The problems of copying
Adults need to be aware that what we expect to happen with ASD students may not necessarily occur. Thus, for most students, copying sums from a blackboard (which uses short-term memory) is easier than writing the sums from dictation (which is a long-term memory retrieval task). However, Hans Asperger (whose name has been given to Asperger Syndrome) noted that the opposite can be true of Asperger Syndrome students.

Copying from the blackboard (or a book) can also be a difficult task because of visual-perceptual difficulties which may be present when Dyspraxia or Autistic Spectrum Disorder is present or because visual difficulties are present due to the presence of CFS/ME. The ADD student may make careless errors when copying due to attention difficulties. (On top of all this if Dyslexia is present too then the student may lose his/her place when copying and copy words/letters in the wrong order.) The end result, whenever any of these difficulties are present, is that attention will wander and the student will have difficulties in staying on task. The solutions to all of these difficulties is to reduce copying to an absolute minimum by providing sheets on which the student simply has to enter his/her answers. We do need to ensure that the student gains experience of laying out the sum and this can be achieved by the student writing his/her own sums based on the number stories already mentioned in this book.

17. The problems of mechanical methods of learning
ASD students need to create everything out of their own thoughts and experience, and so mechanical methods of learning are unlikely to work for them. (ADD students may have similar needs.) The ADD student may lack the motivation to learn by rote and both types of student, along with those affected by Dyslexia and Dyscalculia, may have such great memory difficulties in relation to numbers that

Mathematics Solutions – An Introduction to Dyscalculia Part A by Jan Poustie et al   ISBN 1 901544 45 1

learning tables by rote may be an impossible task. 'Tablesgraphics Set 1, (published by Next Generation) provides a non-rote learning method for learning times tables which may be effective in such cases.

18. Memory difficulties

If Autistic Spectrum Disorder is present there may be substantial difficulties in memory function though some students may be able to remember figures by rote if they are of interest to them. Lesson structure and tasks need to utilise the student's interest as a way of enabling him/her to relate to the information being taught and so be able to learn it. However, there is a group of students affected by this condition who are known as 'savants' and such students may be gifted mathematically. Memory difficulties are also associated with ADD.

Long-term rewards (e.g. praise at the end of the lesson) are not likely to work, especially for young children. However, short-term rewards of praise for staying on task by placing a counter in a beaker (well attached to the desk and well away from the student's arm) every time the tutor walks by may be more successful.

SUCCESSFUL STUDENT MANAGEMENT

This is more likely to be achieved if the tutor remains calm - no easy task at times! The adult also needs to be in control of the student in an environment where there is the least amount of sensory stimulation. Just telling the student 'to concentrate' is not going to be effective. Unfortunately, telling the student off for not concentrating is also unlikely to be effective as it is likely to merely result in a stressed student, teacher and parent. Strategies need to be found to help the student to concentrate and here the independent study carrel can be useful when a task requiring written work is required. (A study carrell is constructed so that the student's view is screened off on three sides of the desk. It is best not to decorate the inside of the screens as the posters etc. can also distract the student.)

Care will be needed in the placement of the carrel; e.g. place it away from moving children, away from the teacher talking, away from door-ways and away from windows. However, some ASD students panic if they are too far away from a doorway as they feel trapped. Such students could either be placed by the firedoor (and shown how it operates) or be placed to one side of the door where there will be the least amount of traffic. A placement with perhaps one desk between them and the door may be suitable, for then they do not see the movement of

Some of Asperger's strategies for dealing with conflict are:

▸ Verbally agree with the student and just continue with the task as though the conversation had never occurred.

▸ Use the same voice tone and pitch that the student uses as there appears to be less resistance to doing the work/following the instructions if the teacher does this.

▸ Issue commands instead of making polite requests of the student. Thus, *'I would like you to ...'* may not result in the required action but *'Now you will do ...'* is more likely to be effective.

people travelling through the door out of corner of their eye as they work. It should be noted that ASD (and ADD) students may be distracted by sounds etc. that the rest of us do not notice; e.g. the sound of water passing through a radiator.

Adults can find it very difficult to resolve the conflict when a student says that s/he no longer wants to do a task. Hans Asperger (in his original paper translated in *Autism and Asperger Syndrome* edited by Uta Frith, ISBN 0 52138608 X, published by Cambridge University Press, UK) suggested that a variety of strategies can work.

Case Study: Girl A (ASD present)

The mother of Girl A found the following strategy worked with her child. She said to the child: 'Imagine that we as a family need to push a boulder across the road. The rest of the family are pushing the boulder from the back but you are pushing it from the side or the front.' (A concrete demonstration at this point can help the student to see that the boulder is going to have problems in moving forward when people are pushing it from different directions.) The mum went on to tell her child that 'We need you to help us push the boulder from the same direction that we are pushing it from.'

This case study also shows how the rest of the class can help the student achieve success if they co-operate with the teacher and the child. Thus the class was told by the teacher that Girl A was going to try to work independently. All the members of the class tried really hard not to fidget and to be quiet so that they helped the child concentrate on the task. She managed to concentrate for fifteen minutes and received a round of applause from her classmates for doing so.

GULLIBILITY AND SEXUALITY

When ASD, ADD or Dyspraxia are present, students are vulnerable to having their behaviour being misinterpreted. Their gullibility may result in them becoming the stooge for a gang and failing to see where the gang's actions are leading them and thus they may do whatever they are told to do by the members of the gang.

If the behavioural conditions found within the SpLD Profile are present students may have various difficulties relating to sex. Some of these difficulties can be seen quite young and others will carry on into adulthood. Some individuals may have difficulties with understanding and accepting their own sexuality – their first sexual experience (with or without intercourse) may frighten them. Others may greet headlong their emergent sexuality at puberty and thus be at risk of getting themselves into a situation of intimacy beyond that with which they feel comfortable.

ASD students may demonstrate inappropriate and unconventional ways of satisfying their sexual needs which may often not involve other people. Students can form a sexual attachment to a physical object – fortunately, as their behaviour may not be recognisably sexual to the onlooker, it may have little impact upon the other students.

Any object within the student's environment can be the focus for such attachment and attention; e.g. the plastic cover of their reading book which can be stroked or rubbed against their skin. Such behaviours may continue to occur or they may die down of their own accord. If such behaviours continue to occur, the peer group may be happily oblivious to the implications of what is happening near them. However, the adult in charge of the student may find such behaviours rather disturbing and so may wish to access specialist advice.

STRATEGIES FOR HELPING THE STUDENT WHO HAS REACHED AN 'OVERLOAD' SITUATION

Overload situations need to be handled in different ways according to the individual student and the SpLD Profile conditions present. ASD students are likely to need pictorial/ written reminders which show them how they need to behave in certain situations which can occur regularly e.g.   s/he wants the radio turned off as the sound of it has become distressing. Students who have gone into an overload situation may exhibit one of several behaviours; e.g.

▸▸ Withdraw.

▸▸ Become frozen.

▸▸ Behave in such a way that the adult is forced to take

Mark Segar (an adult who has Asperger Syndrome) has written a book called A *Guide to Coping Specifically for People with Asperger Syndrome*. It contains do's and don'ts for sexual behaviour and relationships and can be obtained from: The Early Years Centre, Publications Department, 272 Longdale Lane, Ravenshead, Nottingham NG15 9AH.

Impulsive Attention Deficit individuals may:

▸▸   Rush into relationships.

▸▸   Find controlling their sexual urges difficult.

▸▸   Explore their sexuality early. Their impulsivity and forgetfulness may also result in a failure to use contraceptives.

Cards could be kept in school in a special container which is attached to the desk with blutak. At home, cards could be kept in a bag which is worn around the student's waist or they could be attached to a key ring on a belt etc.

Attaching the cards together is likely to be sensible as it will stop the student becoming frustrated if the cards are dropped when showing them to the adult. If the student is not located in one classroom then a set of these cards should be in every classroom. Every teacher in the school should know the location of the cards as this will then help the teacher who has to 'cover' for the usual teacher when illness occurs etc.

control of the situation. In the ASD student this behaviour may take the form of 'screaming' and other unusual behaviours whilst both ASD and ADD students may interfere with their brother's/sister's/peer's toys etc. Carers mistakenly tend to respond to the behaviour itself rather than the trigger which caused the behaviour. Thus the carer may try, usually without much success, to control (or ignore) the behaviour and expect this to resolve the problem.

Students need to be taught ways to tell the carer/her brothers/sisters etc. that they are overwhelmed. Initially this may be done by using a three-stage strategy which uses coloured cards based on the colours of traffic-lights.

Stage 1

▸▸ Red indicates 'I am very overwhelmed, can't cope – I'm at a stop'.

▸▸ Yellow indicates 'I'm feeling upset and going to stop soon.'

▸▸ Green indicates that all is well.

Stage 2
We want to progress the student to communicating their problems in a more adult and socially acceptable way, which means via language, as soon as possible. So we write words on the cards and the adult states these words to the student when s/he shows a card; e.g.:

▸▸ red – 'very upset',

▸▸ yellow – 'starting to feel upset',

▸▸ green – 'okay'.

When the student is not upset the adult could explain that these are the words that she wants the student to use when s/he is upset; e.g. 'I am very upset.' The adult now encourages the student to show the card and/or read the words.

Note: some ASD students cannot talk, or elect not to do so. When this occurs there will be a need for the student, and those working with him/her, to learn an alternative communication system. Contact the National Autistic Society for further information – see Appendix 1 for details.

Stage 3

Some students may progress to this stage. Here they are encouraged to explain the problem in greater detail. The student could have a series of red and yellow cards which have a picture/ word on the front each explaining a problem. Eventually the student may be able to tell the carer the problem rather than showing the appropriate card.

The Picture Exchange Communication System (PECS) can be used in a similar way to the traffic-lights cards to produce an individualised communication package for any age. It is suitable for a variety of situations; e.g. displaying the timetable for the day and providing the student with an individualised package (via an individual folder which the student takes from classroom to classroom etc.). It uses words and picture symbols which are attached via velcro to a board etc. The use of this system can result in the student making tremendous strides in communication, increasing their vocabulary and the amount of speech used as well as leading to an improvement in behaviour.

The PECS system is available from Pyramid Educational Consultants Inc., 226 West Park Place, Suite 1, Newark, DE 19711, USA Tel: 00 888 732 7462 (website: www.pecs.com).

HAVING A GREATER UNDERSTANDING OF THE STUDENT'S DIFFICULTIES

We tend to understand better if we can have some personal experience of the problem. Thus all those who deal with students at home (and in the educational setting.) may benefit from a demonstration of what it is like to be overloaded by sensory information; e.g.

▸ the radio turned up really loud while someone is shouting an instruction,

▸ the television and the radio turned up really loud with the group trying to follow what is on the television while someone is moving in front of it etc.

(Be very careful that you do not use flickering lights as part of any such demonstration as this can cause problems for students affected by epilepsy. Care will also need to be taken to ensure

Computer clipart could be used for the pictures; e.g.

noise

other children/ students

too hot

Mathematics Solutions – An Introduction to Dyscalculia Part A by Jan Poustie et al   ISBN 1 901544 45 1

A 'risk assessment' with the parent prior to the student being introduced to any new situation may be worth its weight in gold.

Only by being aware of how the student is likely to react can the carer devise strategies that may be successful in overcoming the problem. Professionals have to accept that the 'expert' here, to whom they can turn for a great deal of useful information, (including strategies that might work) is likely to be the mum and dad!

that no student/adult is present who is hypersensitive to high levels of the sensory information being used in the demonstration. The demonstration should obviously occur when the ASD student is not in the room.)

CONDUCTING A 'RISK ASSESSMENT'

It is obviously better to avoid problems before they start and so the teacher/learning support assistant will want to know what situations are likely to cause the student to have difficulties and what the student's interests are etc. before s/he enters the classroom. The wise carer will conduct a 'risk assessment' to reduce the student's behavioural difficulties/stress before introducing him/her to the new situation.

REFERRALS AND SUPPORTIVE AGENCIES

When behavioural difficulties are present and advice on management is required then the student should be referred via his/her GP to the appropriate specialists; e.g. to one of the following local agencies/specialists:

▸▸   Child development Centre,

▸▸   Community paediatrician,

▸▸   Communication Disorder clinic,

▸▸   A specialist centre such as the Newcomen Centre at Guy's Hospital, London.

Diagnosis for Dyspraxia, Attention Deficits and Autistic Spectrum Disorder is made via the medical sector but it is the teachers, special needs support assistants etc. who have to cope in the educational setting with the problems that such conditions can cause in learning and in the classroom. Effective management of these students requires good and frequent liaison between the educational and medical professionals and between educational establishments and specialist local education authority advisors. Unfortunately this does not always occur.

The author learned recently of a headmaster who was admitting a student with Asperger Syndrome into his school without bringing in any support/providing a knowledge base for the teacher. When the teacher requested such support she was told that she was a good teacher and 'would cope'. Such a failure to provide appropriate support is just setting up possible failure/stress for the teacher, student and parents.

SUPPORT

Professionals need to be aware that the behaviours caused by the presence of Attention Deficits and Autistic Spectrum Disorder can make even the best of parents appear unable to cope. These parents, and those of the student who has Dyspraxia, can pass from one embarrassing moment to the next on a frequent basis (daily if they are lucky, hourly if they are not). Parent's suffer from temper tantrums in Marks and Spencers (with onlookers saying 'Tut, tut – I never let my children behave like that'). They can have mother-in-laws telling them that they must be firmer and that they are spoiling the child.

Parents may dread receiving the phone call from school for yet another meeting where they are taken to task for their child's behaviour. If the school does not understand the conditions then staff can feel threatened. The parent may have learnt a great deal about the condition and how to manage it but fears upsetting the professionals. This fear can be present throughout every meeting between parents and professionals.

Parents may fear rejection when asking for their child to be treated differently from the other children even though that differentiation is both their child's right and 'their need'. They watch their child become less and less happy at school and, because of the stress of the academic environment, the child becomes more and more difficult to handle at home.

The final straw for many parents is when they are viewed by professionals as being incompetent, lacking in discipline, demanding or having unrealistic academic goals for their child. (Professionals can easily assume the latter when the SpLD Profile conditions mask average or superior intelligence.)

When any of the conditions mentioned in this chapter are present, students can be 'testing' for the most competent, knowledgeable and able professional. All those involved

Parents face the embarrassment of the odd full glass of ice-cold coke cascading down the businessman's suit at the Little Chef, followed by the fork and the food landing on the floor. (All these behaviours are due to poor co-ordination skills and nervousness in a new situation.)

Behavioural difficulties require that we all work together to help each other cope with them. Support can be obtained from a variety of sources; e.g. the local group of the relevant UK national charity can provide support for both parents and professionals – see Appendix 1 for details.

(whether parent, professional or other carer) need to support each other. When the student's behaviours are particularly difficult to manage there should be, whenever possible, 'time out breaks' where the adult is enabled to be away from the student for a period of time. Such breaks may be essential when the teacher has the student for the whole of the school day as can occur in primary schools.

Various agencies offer family guidance which can help the whole family to cope with the presence of behavioural strategies, e.g.

▸▸   Social services.

▸▸   The NSPCC.

▸▸   Family guidance can provide parents with someone to talk to on a regular basis and can provide feedback and support.

▸▸   The presence of any of the SpLD Profile conditions can have an impact upon other family members and here 'Contact-a-family' is also a useful organisation as it provides support meetings for the brothers and sisters of the child affected by the conditions within the Specific Learning Difficulties Profile.

The telephone numbers of all these organisations will be in the family's local telephone directory. The family's public library will also have a list of them.

Assessment

HOW DO WE ASSESS FOR MATHEMATICAL LEARNING DIFFICULTIES?

'One should consider the possibility of assessment for Dyscalculia if the individual's performance is significantly below the level expected given their age and intellectual/cognitive ability' and [they have a] 'difference in achievement and expected level of performance [of] at least two years.' [1]

It should be noted that some student's mathematical learning difficulties are masked by their high intelligence. Such students may perform at an age-appropriate level and teachers may not be aware of their intelligence unless an assessment of intellectual functioning is made.

WHAT SHOULD AN ASSESSMENT INCLUDE?

The structure of this assessment (steps 1– 4) is derived from the course *Diagnosis and Remediation of Learning Problems in Mathematics*, Professor Mahesh Sharma.

The five-step assessment procedure

1. The learning style of the individual; e.g. qualitative/ grasshopper or quantitative/inchworm.[2]
    A particular method of using the Rey-Osterrieth Complex Figure Test can be used to determine learning style (natural and learnt), difficulties relating to visual perception and the degree of maths anxiety present. Information on this will be in Sharma's diagnosis and assessment handbook for learning problems in mathematics which is due for publication late 2001. Note: If visual-perceptual difficulties are found, then an assessment for Dyspraxia is needed; see page 136 and Chapter 4.

2. An assessment of the individual's mathematical level This can be assessed via standardised tests such as the 'Wide Range Achievement Test' (commonly known as the WRAT) and 'The Profile of Mathematical Skills'.[3] Once the student has completed the test, the strategy of *Mathematics Communication* should be used. Here the student should be asked to 'talk through' each calculation to the assessor. This is an invaluable assessment procedure as it provides a 'window

The five-step assessment procedure
Those interested in training courses should contact Jan Poustie (see page 176 for contact details).

Notes
1. Professor Sharma, during his Certificate Course in the UK, 1995.
2. For information on Learning Styles see the Sharma notebooks, Chapter 2 of Mathematics for Dyslexics: A Teaching Handbook *by Dr Steve Chinn and Richard Ashcroft (pub. Whurr Publishers Ltd.) and Alistair Smith's book* Accelerated Learning in the Classroom *(ISBN 1 85539 034 5).*
3. The Profile of Mathematical Skills *is available from NFER-Nelson Publishing Co. Ltd., Darville House, 2 Oxford Road East, Windsor, Berkshire SL4 1DF and the* Wide Range Achievement Test (WRAT) *is available from the Dyslexia Institute, 133 Gresham Rd, Staines, Middlesex. TW18, 2AJ.*

Mathematical Language Assessment tip

The assessor can just pick every tenth word from the appropriate list and ask the student to explain its meaning. If twenty-five words are selected it is then easier to convert the final score into a percentage (e.g. by multiplying by 4). Teachers in England and Wales could pick one or two words out of each section from the age-appropriate list of *The National Numeracy Strategy: Mathematical Vocabulary*, ISBN 0855229551. (Anyone can obtain a free copy of this book – Tel: 0845 6022260). Information on the National Numeracy Strategy can be downloaded from the following sites: www.qca.org.uk www.standards.dfee.gov.uk/ The latter site also includes a mathematical dictionary.

Notes
4. Prof. Sharma's 'The Diagnostic Assessment of Mathematics Potential and Achievement' will identify some of the main areas of sub-skill dysfunctioning which prevent the individual from acquiring mathematical skills. This test is only available to those who hold his 'Diagnosis and Remediation of Learning Problems in Mathematics Certificate. At the time of printing, this Certificate was held by relatively few people in the UK.

into the mind of the student'. Through this window can be seen the types of internal processing errors that occur, whether self-correcting skills are present and whether expressive language difficulties are hindering the student's mathematical processing. Sometimes this strategy reveals the extraordinarily complex way in which some students arrive at the answer!

3. Mathematical language level
   This needs to cover vocabulary level plus word-finding/word-labelling difficulties which affect the acquisition of language and understanding of instructions etc.). A useful tool for this purpose can be found in *Mathematics as a Second Language – Part Two Mathematics Word Problems* by Mahesh Sharma. This is one of the Math Notebook booklets published by the Center for Teaching/Learning Mathematics (see page 171 for details). During this task the assessor should look out for expressive language difficulties (see Chapter 6 for details).

4. The prerequisite skills for learning mathematics[4]
   (Brief details of these can be found on page 26). At present only holders of Professor Sharma's *Diagnosis and Remediation of Learning Problems in Mathematics Certificate* have access to an appropriate assessment tool. Full details of the pre-requisite skills and their remediation can be found in *Mathematics Solutions - An Introduction to Dyscalculia, Part B How to teach students who have specific learning difficulties in mathematics*, by Jan Poustie et al ISBN 1 901544 72 9.)

5. An assessment/screening for the presence of the other conditions that are found within or alongside the Specific Learning Difficulties Profile.
   See pages 136 – 138 for details.

The use of the four tests mentioned in steps 1– 4 are covered in the Professor Mahesh Sharma courses leading to a Certificate in the Diagnosis and Remediation of Mathematical Learning Difficulties but relatively few people in the UK have gained his certificate. Some professionals also favour an assessment of times tables knowledge. (Including this in an assessment can show whether the individual can learn information by rote and whether sequencing difficulties are present. The assessor can then see if the individual can use his/her tables knowledge in the questions that form part of the standardised test above. In a one-to-one situation the assessor can also see whether the individual has to count from the beginning of the table to get to the answer s/he requires.)

Other aspects of number functioning can also be assessed. The Number Triangle test favoured by Kosc looks at the student's ability to:

▸▸   stay on task (whilst maintaining accuracy),

▸▸   process simple numerical information for a prolonged simple addition task.

This test can be found in *Focus on Learning Problems in Mathematics – Dyscalculia* see page 171. (The student has a column of fifteen single-digit numbers dictated to him/her and s/he is required to add pairs of numbers together and write the answer in the next column. Once the next column has been created, the student has to add a further group of pairs of numbers and so on until fifteen columns of numbers have been completed. By the end of the task a triangle of numbers will have been created on the sheet of paper, e.g.

```
7
            9
2       + }=   1
            2
                        }=      6
0       + }=   5
            3
3
```

The task is made more complex when the answer is higher than 9 for the student has to write the units number and omit the tens number. Thus the student has to work out mentally the answer to the sum, retain in memory the original answer and then select the units digit prior to writing it down. As the student has to use a blank sheet of paper for this task difficulties in alignment, visual-perception, spatial skills and numeral construction can be observed. Difficulties in staying on task (and memory difficulties) may indicate the presence of Attention Deficits and this should be explored if appropriate (see *Identification Solutions for Specific Learning Difficulties*, page 172). Such difficulties can also be associated with Autistic Spectrum

The Number Triangle Test

The procedure changes when two numbers are added that come to more than 9; e.g. 9+2 = 11. In such cases the number in the tens column is ignored and just the number in the units column (in this case 1) is written.

The final form of this part of the Number Triangle test will look similar to this:

```
7
        9
2               1
            2               6
0               5
        3
3
```

Mathematics Solutions – An Introduction to Dyscalculia Part A by Jan Poustie et al   ISBN 1 901544 45 1

If any of the conditions that can be found within the SpLD Profile are found to be present in an individual then their mathematical ability should also be checked and   appropriate provision made for any difficulties that they may be having.

Children as young as four years of age can be identified as having difficulties that come within the Specific Learning Difficulties Profile. However, identifying the exact condition which is causing the problems may not always be possible at this age. Assessment of pre-school, or early years, children is likely to require a very specialist assessment by an assessor who has a broad knowledge of the whole field. (Madeleine Portwood's *Developmental Dyspraxia* includes lists of indicators of motor difficulties in the early years.)

Disorder (see Chapter 9). Difficulties with processing the information when the group of numbers are first dictated may indicate an auditory processing/receptive language difficulty (see Chapters 5 and 6.)

It is quite useful to use this type of prolonged simple addition task as it can give the assessor an idea of how demanding even the simplest of maths tasks are for the student and the amount of time even such simple computations will take. It is also useful to note the number of errors students make, including the need to backtrack when they suddenly realise that they have made an error earlier on or need to check the reliability of previous calculations. From such a task we can see how confident the student is when faced with a maths task and how quickly their computational ability becomes insecure. It should be noted that some students can become completely 'lost and disorientated' in the task (and do not know which pairs of digits to add next) whilst others may become very anxious during it as their mathematical skills become unreliable.

Assessment/screening tests for SpLD Profile conditions

Having read this section it will have become apparent to the reader that we can no longer look purely at mathematical functioning when assessing for mathematical learning difficulties/ Dyscalculia. Instead a much broader assessment and provision base is needed if we are to help such students overcome their difficulties. As it is apparent that mathematical learning difficulties are commonly seen alongside Dyspraxia (and the moderate/ severe form of Dyslexia) then it is important to screen for these conditions too via suitable assessment tools; e.g.

▸▸   The Portwood Motor Screening Test: age suitability seven years to adult. (It is part of the book *Developmental Dyspraxia* by Madeleine Portwood, published by David Fulton).

▸▸   Movement Assessment Battery for Children by Henderson and Sugden: age suitability six to ten years (published by The Psychological Association, who are part of Harcourt Publishers, Tel: 020 83085 700).

Auditory Sequential Memory should also be assessed via what is commonly known as the 'Digit Test' and this test can also be found as a sub-test of the following tests:

1. The Aston Index
    (available from LDA, Duke Street, Wisbech, Cambs. PE13 2AE). As part of this sub-test an assessment of times tables knowledge is also made. This test has been available for some years and includes a battery of sub-tests which look at sub-skill functioning for literacy (and for some aspects of motor skills). It can be administered by teachers.

2. The Dyslexia Early Screening Test (DEST) or Dyslexia Screening Test (DST)
    (Both are published by The Psychological Association, Tel: 020 83085 700 and between them they cover the age range 4.6 years up to 16.5 years.) These tests (which are comparatively new on the educational scene) contain an audio tape of the digit test which makes it easier to administer. They can be administered by teachers.

3. WISC III^{UK} or BAS II tests
    These are administered by educational psychologists or by specialist teachers under the supervision of an educational psychologist. There are various versions of these tests appropriate to different ages. Each have many sub-tests and a group of them are administered to assess intellectual functioning. The battery of tests includes ones that assess literacy and numeracy functioning.

The Digit Test has two parts:

▸▸ Part 1 assesses Auditory Sequential Memory. (The assessor says a string of digits at one-second intervals which the student then has to repeat.)

▸▸ Part 2 is administered by the assessor in a similar way but this time the student has to listen to the assessor saying them and then has to manipulate the information and say the digits in reverse order without grouping them. Thus the assessor may say 4, 2, 5, 6 and the student must reply 6, 5, 2 4 (but cannot group the digits by saying six-five or two-four, or sixty-five, twenty-four). Grouping makes the task easier and Part 2 of the task is designed to see if the student has working memory difficulties.

A low Reverse Digits score is of concern. If the student also scores low on the working memory aspect of the Rey-Osterrieth Complex Figure Test then the student has a major problem as both auditory and visual working memory are poor. Such students will have great difficulties in manipulating information in their heads. This will  affect mental calculations plus mathematical tasks which require the student to manipulate information; e.g. tasks involving transivity skills (see *Mathematic Solutions – An Introduction to Dyscalculia; Part B*).

Students with a low score in Part 2 of the Digit Test will need special provision when doing the mental arithmetic section of the UK's daily Numeracy lesson which occurs in all state primary schools.

If working memory difficulties are present then, at a later date, one does need to teach the student to use the grouping strategies mentioned above. Even after being taught such strategies the student's scoring on subsequent Reverse Digits tests may not alter very much (because the student is not allowed to group items whilst doing it). However, the strategy will help the student to overcome some of his/her difficulties in his/her studies and in life.

A low score in Part 2 of the Digit Test indicates that the student is likely to have difficulties in doing mental calculations. The student will need extra time to process the calculation. Some students will not be able to achieve the task at all or will only be able to achieve it if they have some visual reminders of the elements of the question. Such students will need special provision when doing the mental arithmetic tasks.

Who assesses for mathematical learning difficulties?
Teachers and educational psychologists will be able to assess the individual's mathematical age and areas of weakness but unless they also know how to assess the particular sub-skill difficulties they will not be able to gain a whole picture of the individual's difficulties and may well not be able to identify the presence of Dyscalculia.[5] There are two main forms of assessment available in the UK at present:

1. Mathematical assessments which may include the use of Sharma assessment tools
    A sub-skill (prerequisite skill) assessment is part of every Professor Sharma course but there are relatively few Sharma-trained teachers in the UK at present. At the time of printing, the author plus some private schools, offer this type of assessment to pupils other than their own as detailed below:

    ▸▸ The author of this book assesses for mathematical learning difficulties as well as screening and/or assessing for other difficulties caused by the conditions within the Specific Learning Difficulties Profile. Jan Poustie can be contacted on: Tel: 01823 289559.

    ▸▸ Edington and Shapwick School (Somerset), Tel: 01278 722012.

    ▸▸ Appleford School (Wiltshire), Tel: 01980 621020

Note
5. Sub-skill assessment is part of Professor Sharma's courses.

➤➤ Steve Chinn, (Mark College, Somerset) Tel: 01278 641632.

2. <u>Some organisations which offer a different form of mathematical assessment</u>

➤➤ The Dyslexia Institute (has many training centres throughout the UK), Tel: 01784 463 851.

➤➤ The Helen Arkell Centre (Surrey), Tel: 01252 792 400.

WHAT DO DIFFERENT TESTS ASSESS?

It is very important that those making assessments/looking at reports made by educational psychologists (and other specialists) are aware of what different tests of mathematical functioning actually assess. Tests can assess very different areas of functioning, as the following information on three commonly used tests for one-to-one assessment show.

WISC III^UK Arithmetic

Almost all the questions are read to the child and they are embedded in text. The student is asked oral word problems that contain simple mathematical terms; e.g. 'dozen'. This test is therefore assessing verbal comprehension and problem-solving using mathematical word problems. The book *Intelligence Testing with WISC III* by Kaufman ISBN 0158002504 (published 1994 by The Psychological Corporation, Tel: 020 83085700) explains that this test is closely related to the verbal sub-tests within the WISC. It would therefore reveal difficulties with:

➤➤ the acquisition and use of mathematical vocabulary

➤➤ the understanding of the language of mathematics,

➤➤ the ability to use the language of mathematics.

There is a time limit on each of the questions, with those appearing early on having a time limit of thirty seconds. Students who have both mathematical learning difficulties and language and/or auditory processing problems are at a great disadvantage in this test.

A student who can do the mathematical process must be able to produce the result in an ordered written manner which is achieved by working in a step-by-step manner. However, a student may not understand the concept but still be able to memorise the procedure (and so achieve the correct answer). If the culture in the classroom is one where the 'ticks count' and maths discussion does not occur then staff may not realise that the student does not understand the concept.

Professor Sharma usually comes to the UK several times a year to give lectures, and once a year to run his course. Information on these can be obtained from Mrs Patricia Brazil, Tel: 01189 474864, Fax: 01189 461574.

Mathematics Solutions – An Introduction to Dyscalculia Part A by Jan Poustie et al   ISBN 1 901544 45 1

Basically, the BAS II Number Skills Worksheet, at the Block B and C level, is looking at competency in the processes of mathematics covering the four operations (+, −, x, ÷). It does not require mathematical language to be used and a student of, for example, nine years can obtain a score within the average range without having successfully calculated with either decimals or fractions.

BAS II Number Skills Worksheet
This test is divided into blocks; e.g.

<u>Block B</u>: This contains simple items; e.g.
➤➤ the child is asked to say different numbers aloud (thus showing an understanding of the significance of place value; e.g. 201

➤➤ some slightly complicated two-column vertically presented sums; e.g. 26
39 +

<u>Block C</u>: This contains harder items, and moves into multiplication and division using the easier tables of 3x and 5x.

The test is administered so that although the student may have failed on one or two of the harder items (e.g. when adding simple decimals) s/he would not have been stopped from moving on to the harder items. It is not until the student reaches Block D that s/he progresses to more complex tasks.

WRAT 3 – Arithmetic
The WRAT 3 – Arithmetic has two forms -Tan and Blue so that the interval between testing can be shorter. It is a timed test (15 minutes) which is divided into two sections. The first section is administered orally and is not usually given to a student aged eight years or above unless s/he fails the early items of the second section.

<u>First Section</u>: This includes the student counting items, being asked to say simple numbers out loud (e.g. 4) and a couple of more complex numbers (e.g. 52). Other tasks include simple mental arithmetic (e.g. 2 + 4).

WRAT 3 – Arithmetic
Theoretically, it does not matter whether the Tan or the Blue form is administered but in fact the tables knowledge required in the early stages of the Blue form (similar to Block C level of the BAS II) is harder than that of the Tan form. However, at the same stage of the Tan form the student has to deal with multiplication of a three-digit number by a single-digit number.

<u>Second Section</u>: The first four items are very simple. The fourth item involves the addition of two-digit numbers which are presented vertically. Quite quickly, the student has to cope with the harder tables (e.g. 7 x 6) which may well cause problems for students who have difficulties in remembering numbers. Unlike the BAS II, there are no simple box-division sums so the student has to divide two-digit numbers by single-digit numbers (e.g. 24 ÷ 6) and then has to cope with much harder sums involving long division. The rest of the test involves much harder sums; e.g. four-column addition, long-multiplication sums, fractions, decimals, percentages, and algebra.

Quite early in the test the WRAT 3 – Arithmetic assesses more than just the four operations at a simple level and requires the student to be able to know and use the harder tables. WRAT 3 – Arithmetic assesses the student's ability to apply the processes of mathematics. In its early stages it uses simple numbers and it gradually progresses in complexity of sum (e.g. more numbers to add etc. in any one sum).

The block system of the BAS II causes the test to be discontinued when a certain number of errors have been made. In WRAT 3 – Arithmetic this does not occur and so there is nothing to stop the student going on to meet some very hard calculations where s/he has to perform the four operations using fractions, decimals, percentages, averages, until its final elements which contain complex algebra and compound interest etc.

Students working through the A, B and C sections of the BAS II Number Skills Worksheet are presented with sums using the easier tables and sums involving two-digit numbers. The hardest tables the student has to know in Block C are the 3x and 5x. In the section of the WRAT 3 – Arithmetic that corresponds to Section C of the BAS II Number Skills Worksheet the student has to know the 6, 7, 8, 9x tables if using the Blue form or 2, 3, 5 and 6x tables if using the Tan form. In the latter s/he also has to be able to add a group of three three-digit numbers presented vertically.

Once students achieve four or more of the items in Block C in the BAS II Number Skills Worksheet they progress to Block D. Block D contains more complex items such as converting fractions to decimals, dividing a three-digit number by a two-digit number and multiplying two two-digit numbers. The corresponding section of the WRAT 3 – Arithmetic is again different. In the Tan form the student has to be able to cope with subtraction using decimal numbers whilst in the Blue form the student has to be able to cope with the addition of four rows of numbers (with two to four numbers in each row).

Having examined these three tests some facts become obvious:

▸ The three tests are not assessing the same areas of mathematical functioning.

▸ The WISC III^UK Arithmetic makes the greatest demands upon both working memory and auditory memory skills.

If we wish to fully understand the student's functioning then, once one has looked at the differences between the tests that have been used with him/her, we must look at the strengths, weaknesses and errors etc. that the use of the *Mathematics Communication* strategy (see page 133) has highlighted. This strategy will also highlight the student's problems with understanding the concepts of mathematics and the use of mathematical language.

Notes:
The WRAT 3 covers the widest student age range.

Mathematics Solutions – An Introduction to Dyscalculia Part A by Jan Poustie et al   ISBN 1 901544 45 1

A student may have a high percentile score in the other Verbal IQ sub-tests (so the language for literacy is intact) but a low Arithmetic sub-test score because s/he has a problem in acquiring and using mathematical language.

▶▶ The WRAT 3 – Arithmetic and the BAS II Number Skills Worksheet are both assessing the student's ability to do calculations based on the four operations (+. x, ÷, –) but their method of administration and their differences in types of questions asked mean that a student may well gain a different score of mathematical competency on each test.

▶▶ WRAT 3 – Arithmetic Tan and Blue versions are very similar up until item No. 4 of the second section. After this, although the type of calculation usually remains the same (e.g. addition, subtraction) the number of digits involved in each sum differs in each form.

▶▶ We cannot say that a score within the average band in the WRAT 3 – Arithmetic or the BAS II Number Skills Worksheet means that mathematical functioning is satisfactory if the student achieves a below average score in either the WISC III^{UK} Arithmetic sub-test or in a test of mathematical language.

▶▶ A score within the average range in the BAS II Number Skills Worksheet or WRAT 3 – Arithmetic does not necessarily mean that the student understands the concepts behind the calculations s/he may merely be able to remember the process by which to do the sum.

▶▶ A low WISC III^{UK} Arithmetic sub-test score (as compared with chronological age and other areas of the student's known intellectual functioning) indicates a language and/or auditory processing difficulty. This will affect his/her ability to acquire and use mathematical skills.

DOES ASSESSMENT MEAN THAT APPROPRIATE PROVISION WILL OCCUR?

Once one understands the differences between these tests then it becomes obvious that professionals should not use the result of a high score on one test as a reason for not providing specialist provision. Instead, they must look at:

When deciding upon the provision for a student with mathematical learning difficulties we must ensure that we know what the tests used have assessed. Only then can we have an idea of the students strengths and weaknesses and make appropriate provision for them.

▶▶ A whole set of results of tests of mathematical functioning,

▶▶ Observations made during assessment,

▶▶ Discussion with the student and his/her teachers/parents as to how s/he does different calculations.

Only in this way can we fully understand the student's

mathematical functioning and the difficulties that s/he is having in acquiring and using mathematical skills and language. Even when a thorough assessment has taken place there can still be difficulties in gaining provision as the following case study shows.

Case study A – girl aged 11 years in final term of primary school.

This student had severe difficulties with Dyslexia, language impairment and auditory processing difficulties being present. The combination of SpLD Profile conditions was causing this student major problems in the acquisition and use of both the concepts and the language of mathematics.

At seven years:
She scored at the 97th-99th percentile for three BAS II spatial skill sub-tests.

At age 9 years 6/7 months:
She scored 10 years 3 months on the BAS II Number Skills Worksheet. (This showed that she could do simple calculations using small numbers and the easier times tables.)

At eleven years:
Her Total Language Score (using the Celf-R language assessment tool) was at the 4th percentile (only three children out of a hundred would be worse than her.)
The WRAT 3 – Arithmetic score was at the 5th percentile for arithmetic functioning (only four students out of a hundred would be worse than her).

Evidence provided by an assessment made in 1998 (using the WISC IIIUK Arithmetic sub-test) and another one made by the author in 2000 showed that the student had considerable problems with:

➤ understanding and using mathematical language,

➤ understanding the concepts behind the processes (thus she may be able to do a calculation but she does not always understand the concept within it).

Her difficulties affected both spoken and written language with her problems being compounded when mathematical language was used. During the last term at primary school her Individual Education Plan (IEP) showed that she needed the following help in mathematics:

➤ a reader to help with written problem solving,

The assessment of this student included:

➤ an assessment of Receptive Mathematical Language based on Sharma's Mathematical Language Lists,

➤ WRAT 3 Arithmetic

➤ the use of the *Mathematics Communication* strategy

(The prerequisite skills had already been assessed at an earlier date.)

Test results
WRAT 3 – Arithmetic
Arithmetic IQ
= 5th percentile

BAS II
Spatial Sub-test results
= 97th-99th percentile.

There was a large discrepancy between the individual BAS II sub-tests; this alone reduces the validity of an overall IQ score Her score on the WRAT 3 – Arithmetic provides further evidence that an overall IQ score is likely to be unreliable.

Just as when weighing a mixture of ingredients on a pair of scales it is a combination of problems that tips the balance towards students having major problems within the academic environment. When severe language problems exist alongside other difficulties, education at secondary school can be 'sheer hell' as students are less and less able to cope as they progress through the school. They can become disruptive or the totally passive, quiet student that sits in the corner of the classroom, their difficulties not being recognised because they are not disruptive.

▶▶　help with the understanding of maths vocabulary

▶▶　she was receiving ten minutes of support at the beginning of each maths lesson.

Under the 'future provision' section of the Individual Education Plan (IEP) was written 'Same IEP'. Other information provided by the LEA revealed the breadth of her learning needs. She had been provided with booster lessons (in a small group) for both numeracy and literacy during the lead up to the Year 6 SAT examinations plus one-to-two Learning Support Assistant (LSA) provision for the Literacy Hour and history and geography.

This student was about to transfer to secondary school and within that environment she would be expected to process, acquire and use, mathematical language at a much higher level. The IEP indicates that this student would need considerable support in maths (and therefore would need this support in all mathematically based tasks no matter where they were in the curriculum. Thus would help would be needed for statistics in History and calculations in Science, DT and other practical subjects plus considerable support in mathematics lessons. On top of all this her auditory processing and language difficulties meant that she would also have greater problems in all subjects where the teachers explain concepts and ideas verbally rather than use diagrams and practical work.

This student had little chance of succeeding in the more demanding verbally oriented secondary-school classroom unless she received a huge amount of support which (in her case) required a Statement of Education Needs naming a specialist private school and stating (within Part 3 of it) specialist speech and language provision. This student falls into the classification that, at the time of the production of the original Code of Practice, had been little thought of: that of comorbid conditions. The Draft of the UK's new Code of Practice (available just before this book went to press) draws attention to comorbidity (i.e. more than one condition being present).

'In deciding whether to make a statutory assessment the critical question is whether there is convincing evidence that, despite the school, with the help of external specialists, taking relevant and purposeful action to meet the child's learning difficulties, those difficulties remain or have not been remedied sufficiently. ...LEAs should recognise that there is a wide

spectrum of special educational needs that are frequently inter-related ... The impact of these combinations on the child's ability to function, learn and succeed should be taken into account.' (Draft Code of Practice, paragraph 7.10)

Many years ago the figure given of students needing Statements was two per cent. This figure of two per cent is still being used but it does not seem to be based on modern educational realities, especially the fact that we are now much better at identifying students with learning difficulties than we were in the past. When one condition is so severe that a student is within the 2nd percentile, it is usually accepted by the school etc. that this student needs both help and a Statement. The problem of students who perform at only a slightly higher level than the 2nd percentile in several areas is often overlooked.

At the time of finishing this book, this student's LEA had refused even to make a multidisciplinary assessment of her, let alone provide her with a Statement of Special Education Need. This case shows the real problems that students, and their parents, have when trying to obtain vitally needed provision for specific learning difficulties in mathematics. The whole issue of gaining provision, and the distress that it can cause all parties, is dealt with in great detail, from the points of view of the student, teacher and parent, in *Identification Solutions for Specific Learning Difficulties by Jan Poustie et al*. However, we all need to be aware that the difficulties in gaining provision applies to adults too and may even apply to students in teacher training establishments.

Case study B: Joanne, Middle-aged lady who had taken a Bachelor of Education degree at a teacher training college in Scotland.

Despite her Dyslexia Joanne had passed, with flying colours, all aspects of her teacher training course except for maths. She had passed her first year mathematics examination but despite re-sitting it several times was unable to pass the third year mathematics examination.

April 1999: Because of her inability to achieve the mathematics requirements for the course, Joanne's studies were terminated in accordance with course regulations. Joanne appealed against this decision. Further assessment in July 1999, funded by the College as part of the appeal case, showed that both Dyscalculia

Statements:
Specialist speech and language provision must always be provided in Part 3 of a Statement. (If it is entered in Part 6 instead then there is no obligation to provide it.)

It is very easy for people involved with SpLD students to be unaware of the difficulties faced by those who are trying to gain provision for the student. Thus, parents may be unaware that the child's teacher may also realise the need for specialist intervention but s/he too may be prevented from enabling the student to access it because of the limitations imposed upon him/her by the LEA or senior teaching staff.

Mathematics Solutions – An Introduction to Dyscalculia Part A by Jan Poustie et al   ISBN 1 901544 45 1

That two years have elapsed without this college resolving Joanne's situation must be a cause for concern for all those involved in the Scottish education system. Those who wish to follow this case can access information on it via the author at the following e-mail address: jan.poustie@virgin.net

The General Teaching Council of Scotland is in the process of creating an e-mail forum for their teachers who have disabilities (including specific learning difficulties). For details contact the GTC:
Tel: 0131 314 6000

People who have specific learning difficulties in mathematics can be an invaluable asset to the teaching profession. These individual's life and educational experiences enable them to provide the emotional and educational support that our specific learning difficulties students require.

and Dyspraxia were present and that her difficulties required that she receive an alternative form of assessment.

Summer 1999: The Appeal Committee decided that
'her appeal should be upheld and her case referred back to the Board of Examiners for re-consideration based on new evidence brought by Joanne.'

Summer 2000: The Board of Examiners agreed that a group of external specialists be identified to determine the best way forward. Once they had familiarised themselves with the course regulations and with the background to the case, two of the group of three external specialists met with Joanne. Their recommendations included the following:
'We would recommend an assessment process ...that focuses upon the act of teaching, her ability actually to teach mathematics, rather than answer questions about how mathematics should be taught.'

Mid-September 2000: Joanne's case was reconsidered by the Board of Examiners and alternative assessment arrangements are currently being made which will allow Joanne to demonstrate competence in teaching Mathematics in the elements where competence has not yet been shown through previous Maths assessment based on the recommendations made by the external specialists.

Our teacher trainers train our teachers. If they lack knowledge on specific learning difficulties in mathematics then we cannot expect there to be an appropriate climate of understanding of (and a knowledge of how to deal appropriately with) such difficulties within the body of our teachers. Our trainers should be able to provide appropriately for those student teachers who have the SpLD Profile conditions. They should provide appropriate training so that all of our student teachers:

▸▸   have an understanding of (and an ability to identify) the range of specific learning difficulties that are found within (or associated with) the SpLD Profile and know of their impact upon mathematics,

▸▸   are able to provide appropriately for their future students who have these conditions.

Mathematics Solutions – An Introduction to Dyscalculia Part A by Jan Poustie et al   ISBN 1 901544 45 1

Living with Dyscalculia

WHAT ARE THE EFFECTS OF MATHEMATICAL LEARNING DIFFICULTIES ON THE INDIVIDUAL'S LIFE?

Numbers are all around us, so individual's affected by moderate to severe number difficulties have to cope with stress and frustration being part of their normal day. As with all the other conditions found within the SpLD Profile, one can have good and bad days. Many individuals may struggle at home, at school and in the workplace, but for individuals with Dyscalculia the situation will be worse, as they can exist in a world of total mathematical confusion.

At school

A working knowledge and understanding of number and mathematics are necessary for many subjects; e.g. working out calculations in science, statistics in history, map-reading, co-ordinates and graphs in geography, reading tables in English. If the student is bright, concerns may not be noted until s/he is seven years, or older, when the demands of the secondary mathematics curriculum become too much for the pupil's weak mathematical skills.

Everyday tasks

The individual affected by Dyscalculia may have an inability to remember any numbers for any length of time, even those which have great meaning for them. This lack of retention of numbers can make for an interesting life. When individuals are travelling across country they can forget which road they are meant to be following! If individuals are unlucky enough to live in a town where all the roundabout turn-offs and intersection signposts do not have place names on them but just use numbers instead they may rarely get to their destination at the first attempt.

A continuous source of embarrassment can be the individual failing to give their phone number accurately during a telephone conversation despite the fact that they are looking at it at the time. People do regard individuals as being a little odd when they

In all lessons, the individual with poor mathematical language will have to translate common terms said as part of instructions; e.g. 'You have *quarter of an hour* to finish this task,' and 'This should be a *right angle*.'

Dyscalculia affects many areas of one's life, which range from remembering one's 'pin number' so that money can be taken out of the 'hole in the wall' at the bank, to being able to work out a simple calculation. Remembering numbers accurately can pose quite a challenge when using a 'PIN' number and a bankcard to withdraw money. Failure can result in no money for that weekend!

Fortunately some problems can be solved by passing on the responsibility for the timing of events to others. Thus, repeated failures to send birthday cards/ presents can be solved by sending them when they are bought, even if it is two months before the event. (This strategy also solves the problem of the individual losing the present because they put it in a 'safe place' prior to sending it!)

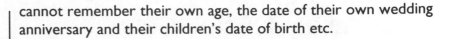

cannot remember their own age, the date of their own wedding anniversary and their children's date of birth etc.

Many everyday tasks involve number, spatial skills and time; e.g. setting the video manually, writing appointments at the correct date on the calendar, using clock-reading skills to get children to school on time. The individual may fail to get to meetings on time because a totally different date and time were entered into the diary and/or because clock-/watch- reading skills may be totally unreliable no matter whether digital or analogue systems are used.

Sometimes using a kitchen timer can help one know what time one has to leave. However, if the individual's number skills are unreliable then there is no way of being certain that it has been set correctly. Thus the mother who has Dyscalculia can find it totally humiliating and frustrating when the teacher rings her up to ask her to collect her children as school finished over half an hour ago. Of course she had set the kitchen timer but poor number skills mean that it says that she still has a half hour spare before she needs to pick them up!

Cooking can be very stressful! In order to cook a meal one has to:

▸▸ correctly interpret the numerals in the recipe,

▸▸ proportionately increase the ingredients according to the number that one is catering for,

▸▸ measure the ingredients accurately, set the oven/hob at the correct numbers (some knobs have numbers whilst others rely upon the individual's spatial skills instead; e.g. turning the knob to a particular point between a picture of two flames),

▸▸ plan the operations involved,

▸▸ time both the preparation and the cooking so that all the elements of the meal are ready at the same time.

At work
On a bad day it can become an art to obtain the right number when using the phone or calculator. The individual thinks s/he is pressing the right number but s/he is not.

A talking calculator helps – at least it tells you what you have done even if you have forgotten the correct operation to do the sum! It is often 'third time lucky', or even 'tenth time lucky' on a very bad day. (Talking calculators are available from the High Street store Tandy.)

The likelihood is that the individual's job entails using reasonable (or even exceedingly good) reading skills throughout the day so s/he cannot even use the 'I've forgotten my glasses' trick that the individual with severe literacy difficulties sometimes uses to avoid the task.

Budgeting

It is best if children are encouraged to budget when young and have experience of changing money. Some children find changing a group of low denomination coins (e.g. those with a value of less than £1) for a £1 coin very confusing and threatening. The parent/tutor may know that the value stays the same but the student sees that the quantity is now much smaller. (Smaller equals less, so s/he must have less money! Even highly intelligent students may find it very confusing because although part of them realises that the value stays the same the evidence of their eyes says the amount is smaller.) Thus, even when the adult counts out the money, such students are still not able to accept that they have the same amount of money especially when it is their pocket money that they are changing in this way! (The computer program Number Shark which is suitable for all ages contains a game which involves changing money, available from White Space Ltd, Tel: 0208 748 5927.)

Accounts

Those in business would be wise to talk to their accountant and inform him/her that their Dyscalculia affects their ability to calculate and explain the sort of errors that they are likely to make. The accountant can then keep a watchful eye and make sure that simple errors do not become major problems. If your accountant is not sympathetic to your problems then it may well be best to find another one.

The presence of Dyscalculia should not be used as an excuse for letting the accounts look after themselves! Accurate

The person affected by Dyscalculia should not just 'grin and bear it'. Some people feel that they must attempt to use their weak number skills for all tasks. It is far more sensible to allow themselves to give in to the temptation of following an easier path for some aspects of their lives. Computer-based accounts packages can be an absolute boon.

There are a host of budgeting software programs around which are suitable for `older teenagers and adults but some lack the flexibility to be an effective tool for these individuals. Quicken (published by Intuit) is one that is easy to use.

The author has Attention Deficits so perhaps it is not such a surprise to the reader to find that she delayed attending to her accounts this year. The result was that she ended up paying her income tax on the very last day that she could do so without incurring a fine!

maintenance of the accounts; e.g. keeping all receipts in date order and numbered and doing the same with all invoices and/or till receipts will save a vast expense at the accountants. Though many of us will find ourselves doing such tasks only at end of the financial year it is much better if a date each month or week can be set aside for such activities.

Most of us with these problems are likely to be safer employing a bookkeeper to manage our everyday accounts or using a computer program to manage them for us. Many accounts programs use what is called 'double entry bookkeeping' as the way of organising and keeping the accounts. This can be very confusing for those of us with mathematical difficulties. A safer option is to use a program such as Quickbooks (produced by Intuit). This is a relatively easy to understand program though the individual should be prepared to use their technical help line for the first few transactions. (Fortunately this help line is free for the first sixty days!)

Those with Attention Deficits and Dyscalculia are likely to become easily distracted from task and are likely to find mathematical-based tasks so frustrating, difficult, boring and unrewarding (even with the use of a computer) that adopting sensible regular book-keeping habits is very difficult for them. However, the taxman and national insurance can never be ignored. The author was once contacted by a man who had owned his own business which had collapsed because of his numeracy difficulties. He employed staff but was not able to work out the calculations needed to be able to deduct their tax and national insurance contributions. He ended up paying the bill for them, his business could not support the cost and so it collapsed.

A person needs to be able to read Roman numerals in order to read some clocks. Some clocks have more than one 'clock face' display and so can show Roman numerals, a twenty-four hour face, as well as the normal twelve hour face, Polydron produce a sturdy working clock of this type, Tel: 01285 770055.

Clocks and watches

In order to read the time we have to have a concept of it and understand the language used. As our sense of time can be distorted, it is best to either be very laid back and not care about time (though you will end up missing some meetings etc.) or have a clock in every room. The types of clocks that you have will depend upon the types of specific learning difficulties which are present in the different members of your family. If there are young members of the family then a working teaching clock is useful to have in one room; e.g. the kitchen. Such a clock will show 'past' and 'to' and will have all the minutes displayed. (Argos usually stocks watches which show 'past' and 'to'). It is important to make sure that the clock shows the minutes as two groups of thirty minutes; e.g. starting at the o'clock 0–30 minutes on the 'past' side of the clock and starting at half past '30–0 minutes on the 'to' side of the clock. The child cannot read the clock properly using the terms 'to' and 'past' if the minutes are shown from 0–60 as, in such cases, quarter to ten would be read as forty-five minutes to ten rather than fifteen minutes to ten.

Language difficulties are a major cause of problems in acquiring numeracy skills. Students with such problems may find it difficult to learn to read the time. Next Generation's 'Clock Language' has been designed to teach the concept of time, plus the vocabulary and fractions needed to read it.

Watches

Some of us can find digital watches particularly difficult to set – even when we do read the instructions! Remembering the sequence of buttons to press on a digital watch can be very hard. Once one has found out how to do a particular operation (e.g. set the stopwatch) it can help to write it down in one's own words. Alternatively, you can do as the author keeps on doing which is to fight with the watch every time that she wants to use the stopwatch function and press every button several times until it works!

Fortunately, for those of us who find reading the time an almost impossible art, help is at hand via Argos and the RNIB. Argos stock a talking watch and the RNIB (Tel: 0845 702 3153) stock both talking watches and clocks.

Calendars and diaries

Like everyone else we can have a tendency to avoid time related issues but it is important that we are well organised with regard to them as otherwise our whole lives can be very disorganised, as the author knows to her cost!!! Diaries that show a week at a time (and have a month-at-a-glance sheet, seem to be best. Always choose ones that have the half hours shown at the side of each day so that appointments can be easily entered without worrying as to whether you have written the correct numeral.

Collins produce some good diaries, with the *Elite Manager Week* being particularly good for those in business. This particular

Analogue or digital

Individuals affected by Occulomotor Dyspraxia/Delay may find it easier to read the time on an analogue clock because the position of the numerals will tell them which number they are looking at. Those affected by these difficulties can reverse numerals (turn them back-to-front) and invert them (turn them upside down) when they read them. However, in order to read an analogue clock one needs good spatial skills and the ability to understand fractions (i.e. $\frac{1}{4}$, $\frac{1}{2}$, $\frac{3}{4}$).

Buy some coloured stickers of various shapes and use them to mark special days on your calendar and in your diary. It is best to attach a pencil with a rubber at one end to your diary or a dry-wipe pen to your wall planner so that:

▸▸   you have something to write with at hand,

▸▸   entries can be easily changed.

Sasco produce a wide range of wall planners including academic year ones for students.

diary also has a pen-holder at the front – a feature which is so necessary for those of us who spend all of our time hunting for something to write with!

Wall calendars

Here we have a need for space as well as organisation. Again, the 'A week at a time' format provides enough space to write on clearly. Boots produce a five-column one that is particularly good. In the author's house we have one column for each family member with the final column being used for the weekly shopping list.

If in business, a large wall calendar can be useful. The layout of some of these can be very visually distracting. Look for one where different weeks are in different colours and where the columns are headed by days of the week rather than the days of the month; e.g. 1, 2 etc. The latter layout can be very confusing. Also look at whether the layout is vertical or horizontal, the author finds she is much more comfortable with one that is set out vertically. The amount of space to write on each day can be very limited.

Some planners, like the Sasco Year Planner (available from stationers such as Office World) come complete with coloured stickers which can be used to indicate that something special is occurring on that day. Thus the author might use the blue stars in her calendar pack to show which days she is due to be lecturing away from home and she can then look to the diary to find out the details of the event. Alternative shapes available with the calendar could be used for other important dates; e.g. appointments with the accountant! Family events of special significance; e.g. birthday parties and parent's evenings, can be shown by using different coloured shapes. This particular calendar comes complete with a dry-wipe pen so that entry errors can be easily corrected without making a complete visual mess of the whole thing.

Cooking

Cooking is an area of particular difficulty for those of us affected by number difficulties. A range of problems range can be present including:

Mathematics Solutions – An Introduction to Dyscalculia Part A by Jan Poustie et al   ISBN 1 901544 45 1

> ➤ poor spatial skills which affect our ability to judge the height of the gas flame and to set the controls correctly,
> ➤ problems in calculating when the different elements of a meal will need to be put into the oven and when they will be ready. (Kitchen timers are invaluable here.)

The author usually has several timers on the go when cooking a complex meal (e.g. Xmas dinner). Writing down a schedule of when each part of a complex meal has to go in the oven, on the hob or in the microwave can make cooking such a complex meal bearable – and ensure that everything is cooked all at the same time! Besides writing a schedule such as the one below the author finds it very helpful if she uses a microwave to cook and reheat parts of the meal as this ensures that the whole of the meal is hot when everyone sits down to the table.

It is much better to do all the preparation for a complex meal the night before, especially if Dyspraxia is also present which causes difficulties when using cooking tools; e.g. potato peelers.

Time	Preparation	Hob	Oven	Microwave
10.30		Par-boil potatoes and parsnips 15 mins		
10.40		Cook cauliflower 12 mins		Make cheese sauce
11.00		Put turkey breast joint in oven		
12.45				Reheat cauliflower cheese
1.00	**DINNER IS SERVED!**			

One year the author found a wonderful solution to her stress when preparing vegetables. She broke her right arm just before Christmas. (It was actually broken during a pickled-onion-and-spoon race at her local dog-training club when her rather boisterous border-collie-cross puppy decided to get his lead entangled with the other contestant!) The other members of the family decided that they did not want to spend Christmas morning preparing vegetables and so they prepared them on Christmas Eve. A new Christmas tradition has started – the Poustie family will definitely be preparing the vegetables on Christmas Eve in future!

Mathematics Solutions – An Introduction to Dyscalculia Part A by Jan Poustie et al   ISBN 1 901544 45 1

The author has even managed to misread her own telephone number while dictating it to someone else, even though she was looking at the number at the time.

Perhaps an advantage of Dyscalculia is that misreading the bathroom scales leads to the happy but mistaken illusion that one has lost weight!

Forgetting and misreading numbers

These exceptionally frustrating, and time-wasting, aspects of Dyscalculia do not appear to get any easier with adulthood and possibly the stresses of career and family (and desperately trying to finish this book) make the reliability even worse! No matter how hard one tries, one may only be able to remember a few numbers (one may not even be able to remember those reliably) and when under stress the misreading of numbers becomes more common.

Virtually everything can be misread, from the times on the overhead displays at train stations to the dates on the calendar and the numerals on the clock. Recently, while putting the finishing touches to this book, the author looked at her watch three times during a half-hour period, so determined was she that she would buy the printing paper she needed before the shop closed. She arrived at the shopping precinct to find it deserted. Immediately suspicious, she looked at her watch, reading it for once with frustratingly great ease! It was 5 p.m. She had known that she had to be at the shop by 4 p.m. but she had misread the time on three separate occasions, each time reading it as twenty to four, ten to four and so on.

When using kitchen scales Dyscalculia can cause one to use the wrong proportions of ingredients. When buying scales always have everyone present who is going to use them and check that each person is happy with the type bought. Often there is a distortion in the information on analogue scales (especially those suitable for cooking). This is due to the curving of the surface where the information is displayed. This distortion can be very confusing for some people and they may find digital scales much easier to read.

The author's time-honoured method for coping with misreading and miscalculating can be used when the calculation being done is not a very important one. Do the task three times and presume that whichever number comes up the most is likely to be the right one! Not the most reliable of methods sometimes but at least one can move on to the next task instead of spending ages wondering whether one is correct or not!

Conclusion

Difficulties in acquiring mathematical/numeracy skills can result in huge problems in gaining qualifications appropriate to one's intelligence and in reaching one's potential. The two *Mathematics Solutions - An Introduction to Dyscalculia* titles and the other Next Generation mathematics materials were written to help to turn this situation around for the students within our care and to make it possible for them to achieve success.

We can enable our students to reach their potential if we work together to learn about their problems, find solutions for them and provide support for each other. Even though they may never be 'good at maths' they may still be able to achieve examinations in the subject and so be enabled to progress to the next stage of their education or to achieve their life goals.

Students will not reach their potential unless we provide them with appropriate help and support. In order to help them find a way to overcome their difficulties we have to widen our own horizons and become involved in a journey of discovery. Journeys come in all shapes and sizes – from a saunter down a country lane in the family car to a journey by shuttle out into space.

Travelling in the family car may feel safe but going out into space is a threatening prospect because of the dangers of the unknown, unless, of course, like the author you are a 'Trekkie' and so would be fascinated by looking for the odd Vulcan!! Many people, prior to opening this book, may have felt threatened by the whole field of Dyscalculia. Hopefully, having read it, the reader will now feel that although it has not been a 'saunter down a country lane' the subject of Dyscalculia no longer feels like the 'unknown regions of space'.

The first step of our journey is the accessing of knowledge so that we can recognise the student who has problems and understand the difficulties in learning that are present. Here we need to both talk, and listen, to our students (and their parents)

Students can find that qualifications can be very difficult to gain (if not impossible) without appropriate and effective help and support.

Vast amounts of equipment are not necessary though creativity, flexibility, modern textbooks, and appropriate methods and materials are essential.

as well as acquire knowledge of the Specific Learning Difficulties Profile and its impact upon the acquisition and use of mathematical skills.

The second step is to deliver appropriate intervention that will enable our students to overcome their difficulties. This book (and *Mathematics Solutions - An Introduction to Dyscalculia; Part B*) shows that there are plenty of strategies that we can use with students who have specific learning difficulties in mathematics. All students are likely to benefit from intervention, with the smallest amount of improvement likely to be found among those students with the most severe forms of the conditions found within (or alongside) the SpLD Profile. Within the field of specific learning difficulties it is generally accepted that the earlier the intervention the greater the improvement in functioning.

The third step is to enable students to achieve their academic and life goals. Some students will be enabled to progress to their academic mathematical goals; e.g. GCSE mathematics at 'C' grade etc. Others may only wish to obtain a limited mathematical goal which is necessary for their career, while others still may have great difficulty in improving their skills sufficiently in order to cope with basic tasks; e.g. cooking, shopping and DIY.

In the enlightened school, the presence of Dyscalculia does not condemn students to the bottom sets in mathematics, nor does it restrict their opportunities to discover higher mathematics. Even students who experience considerable difficulties in learning mathematics can work in the higher maths sets at secondary-school level if they receive adequate and appropriate help and support. Without help, there is little prospect that such students can achieve such dizzy mathematical heights and it will be made much harder for them to achieve their career and life goals. With help, our students with specific learning difficulties in mathematics can have a bright future – it is up to us to ensure that their future is one which glows rather than one that dimly lights the odd corner.

Even if the numeracy/mathematical difficulties are not caused by Dyscalculia the individual may still need some specialist

Mathematics Solutions – An Introduction to Dyscalculia Part A by Jan Poustie et al   ISBN 1 901544 45 1

mathematics tuition to overcome them. However, the shortage of such specialists for both assessment and teaching may make such provision difficult to obtain. Ideally, individuals need a teacher who both fully understands mathematics in all its complexity and who also understands how to teach mathematics to students whose difficulties are being caused by the presence of the conditions found within, and associated with, the Specific Learning Difficulties Profile.

It is essential that the specialist teacher has a working knowledge of Sharma's techniques no matter what age group they teach. Unfortunately, such people appear to be rare in the UK at present and so we have relatively few specialists who possess the knowledge that is needed to help these students.

We badly need our teachers to be trained in the recognition and remediation of specific learning difficulties in mathematics. Advanced teaching qualifications such as the OCR Diploma SpLD (which now takes the place of the RSA Diploma SpLD) may barely touch upon this area. We appear to need either a new qualification that concentrates on learning difficulties in mathematics or we need to add an appropriate module to qualifications such as the OCR Diploma.

A pilot one-year specialist mathematics course was organised by Mark College in 2000 (for details of it contact Dr Steve Chinn, Mark College, Tel: 01278 641632.)

Many professionals feel that their departments/schools are already overstretched in simply catering for those with literacy difficulties and that they therefore do not have the resources to extend their provision wider. However, in the technological age of the twenty-first century, mathematical skills have become essential.

Mathematical difficulties leave individuals open to ridicule and humiliation when they are not able to do a simple task such as adding a couple of figures correctly or make an appointment on time. Without adequate provision such individuals may have great difficulties in reaching their potential because they struggle to acquire, or lack, the qualifications to enter further education.

The individual with severe difficulties may exist in a world where they understand little, or no, mathematics. When all is confusion, individuals have no hope of explaining their difficulties nor any chance of overcoming them. Their difficulties do not go away and so, when under stress or when tired, they worsen. For the lucky ones, high intelligence, great determination and a huge amount of effort may enable them to survive and even appear good at mathematics during the primary school years. However, once they reach secondary school their standard of mathematics rapidly goes downhill as the demands on memory and non-understood concepts and processes becomes too great. Individuals with advanced literacy skills can be reduced to tears when they know that their mind can soar with reading tasks but soddenly refuse even to float with those based on numeracy.

Although, with age, some of those affected by mathematical difficulties manage to devise coping strategies of their own, many do not. Early appropriate provision will help individuals to overcome their difficulties. However, unless we all learn to recognise such individuals (and professionals become trained in the most effective methods which can help them) many will never have the opportunity to test their wings, let alone reach the sky.

Part 3

Resources

Mathematics Solutions – An Introduction to Dyscalculia Part A by Jan Poustie et al   ISBN 1 901544 45 1

Main Sources of Help and Support

ATTENTION DEFICITS

The ADHD Family Support Group UK
c/o Mrs G Mead, IA High St, Dilton Marsh, Westbury, Wiltshire
BA13 4DL
Tel: 01373 826 045; Fax: 01373 825 158.
Has free ADD/ADHD information pack.

The Hyperactive Children's Support Group
71 Whyke Lane, Chichester, West Sussex PO19 2LD
Tel/Fax: 01903 725182.
Provides a Basic Introductory Pack.

ADDISS
PO Box 340, Middlesex, HA8 9HL
Tel: 0208 905 2013; Fax: 0208 386 6466.
Stocks a wide range of ADD/ADHD books and holds national
conferences.

DYSLEXIA

*All of these organisations provide information; the first three provide
conferences and telephone support as well. Also see pages 138-139 as
some of the organisations mentioned offer assessment and teaching
and training.*

The British Dyslexia Association
98 London Road, Reading, RG1 5AU
Tel: 0118 966 2677; Fax: 01734 351 927; Helpline: 0118 966
8271; World wide web: http://www.bda-dyslexia.org.uk./

Scottish Dyslexia Association
Unit 3, Stirling Business Centre, Wellgreen Place, Stirling,
Scotland FK8 2DZ Tel: 01786 446650.

DYSPRAXIA

*These organisations provide conferences, information and telephone
support.*

Dyspraxia Foundation
8 West Alley, Hitchin, Herts United Kingdom SG5 IEG
Tel: 01462 454 986; Fax: 01462 455 052.
Publishes Praxis II.

Dyspraxia Foundation Adult Support Group
Mary Colley, 7 Sumatra Road, London NW6 IPS

LANGUAGE

AFASIC – Association For All
Speech Impaired Children
69–85 Old Street, London
EC1V 9HX
Tel: 020 7841 8900.
Holds conferences, provides
information sheets and
booklets; also has a helpline.

AUTISTIC SPECTRUM
DISORDER

The National Autistic Society
393 City Road, London EC1V
INE
Tel: 020 7833 2299
Fax: 0171 833 9666
Provides conferences, in-service
training & support. Has several
dedicated telephone numbers
Parent helpline:
Tel: 0870 6008585

Information Service:
Tel: *0207 9033599*
*(for professionals working with
children and adults)*

Has the following websites:
General information:
www.nas.org.uk

Professional researchers:
www.autismconnect.org

Scottish Society for Autistic
Children
Hilton House, Alloa Business
Park, Whins Road, Alloa
FK10 3SA.

CHILDHOOD HEMIGPLEGIA AND ASSOCIATED CONDITIONS

Hemihelp
166 Boundaries Road, London, SW12 8EG
Tel: 020 8672 3179.
Offers help regarding Childhood Hemiplegia to parents and professionals. Produces a newsletter. Helpline:
Monday – Friday 10am–1pm.

Child Head-Injury Trust
Mrs Sue Colville (secretary), The Children's Head Injury Trust, c/o Neurosurgery Department, The Radcliffe Infirmary, Woodstock Road, Oxford OX2 6HE.

OSTEOPATHY

Osteopathic Centre for Children
Harcourt House, Cavendish Square, London
Tel: 020 7495 1231;
Fax: 020 74951232.

General Council and Register of Osteopaths
56 London Street, Reading RG1 4SQ
Tel: 01734 576585.

TWINS

TAMBA (Twins And Multiple Birth Association)
17 Clevedon Green, South Littleton, Evesham, Worcestershire WR11 5TY.

Tel: 020 7435 5443.
Provides conferences, information, support.

The Dyspraxia Association
Aileen Tierney, Chairperson, The Dyspraxia Association, 5 Blackglen Court, Sandyford, Dublin 18
Tel: 01 295 7125.

The Dyscovery Centre
12 Cathedral Road, Cardiff CF1 9LJ.
Tel: 01222 788666.
Provides assessment and a remediation programme.

HOMEOPATHY
Can be helpful in some cases, especially with regard to stress, behaviour and poor sleep.

The Society of Homeopaths
2 Artizan Road, Northampton NN1 4AU
Tel: 01604 21400; Fax: 01604 22622.

OTHER ORGANISATIONS

PATOSS (Professional Association of Teachers of Students with Specific Learning Difficulties)
PO Box 66, Cheltenham, Gloucestershire GL53 9YF.
Membership is open to teachers and other professionals.

Institute of Neuro-Physiological Psychology
Warwick House, 4 Stanley Place, Chester
Tel: 01244 311414.
Provides training for Neuro-Developmental Delay.

NASEN (National Association for Special Educational Needs)
NASEN House, 4/5 Amber Business Village, Amber Close, Amington, Tamworth, Staffs. B77 4RP
Tel: 01827 311500.
Produce a wide range of useful books & hold conferences. They publish three journals 'British Journal of Special Education', 'Support for Learning' and 'Special'. Membership is open to professionals, parents etc.

Tourette Syndrome (UK) Association
PO Box 26149, Dunfermline, Fife KY12 9WT
Provides an information pack.

Checklist for visual problems

	Please circle Never ⟷ Always					

Circle the response you think best describes your student

Symptom

		Never					Always

1. Reading comprehension is good to begin with, but reduces rapidly as reading continues.   1 2 3 4 5 6

2. Complaints of sore eyes or headaches when reading or writing.   1 2 3 4 5 6

3. Complaints of blurred vision, or of words going 'fuzzy' or 'double', 'or swimming about on the page'.   1 2 3 4 5 6

4. Reading comprehension is not as good as IQ would predict.   1 2 3 4 5 6

5. Has difficulty keeping place or line on the page when reading, and needs to use a marker to help.   1 2 3 4 5 6

6. Maths is better than reading (apart from where reading questions is concerned).   1 2 3 4 5 6

7. Letters are reversed (e.g. b/d), and order of letters is confused in words (e.g. was/saw).   1 2 3 4 5 6

8. Has difficulties learning to spell, and errors tend to be phonetic in nature.   1 2 3 4 5 6

9. Has problems copying material from blackboards and OHPs.   1 2 3 4 5 6

10. Loses concentration easily, and is distracted a lot.   1 2 3 4 5 6

If the total score on this checklist comes to more than 15–20, then it is probable that your child needs a behavioural vision examination.

© Copyright Keith Holland.
The reader has permission to photocopy this checklist for use with his/ her students or children in order to identify their visual difficulties.

The signs of visual difficulties are really quite simple to spot, and the use of a standardised questionnaire can make this quite easy. The questionnaire on the previous page has been used by Keith Holland for many years, and is only one of many such designs available that have been in use over the last fifty years.

Note
Keith Holland is a behavioural optometrist based at:
27 St George's Road,
Cheltenham, Glos. GL50 3DT.
Readers can contact the British Association of Behavioural Optometrists (BADO) to find their nearest specialist in this field:
72 High Street, Billericay, Essex CM12 9BS; Tel: 01277 624 916.
Behavioural Optometrists specialise in visually related learning difficulties.

GUIDE TO USING THE 'CHECKLIST FOR VISUAL PROBLEMS QUESTIONNAIRE

By Keith Holland B.Sc., FCOptom., FCOVD, FAAO, DCLP; edited by Jan Poustie.

Two important things to recognise when using any questionnaire are that symptoms will change with time and with fatigue (tiredness), and that the child may not in fact report symptoms unless s/he is asked directly. Many children (who have never previously complained of any visual symptoms), when asked if print goes double or moves about while reading, report 'Yes, it does, but then doesn't it do so for everyone?' This often occurs to the horror of their parents, who have assumed that silence in this area means absence of difficulty! The child's perspective is that they are somehow 'thick' for not being able to cope with what they assume others find it easy to deal with.

This notion that children have (of their inferiority in coping with what they assume others deal with) goes well beyond the realms of vision. It is often a key factor with children who are teased, or who perceive themselves as failing, and they will often have very negative self-images. Their self-image can be unwittingly reinforced by parents and teachers if they constantly emphasise the difficulties, and fail to spot and to highlight the child's strengths and successes which may well be far greater than the difficulties. Adults may also fail to talk with the child about their own difficulties, leaving the child to feel inferior to the parent/ teacher etc., and somehow not living up to the expectations and ideals they perceive have been set for them.

When looking for signs of potential visual difficulties, bear in mind that symptoms will usually be reduced, or even absent, during holiday time, and may take a while to reappear at the start of term again. Visual difficulties are very much a factor of stress and fatigue, and may become worse during exams, or when other factors (possible home difficulties for example) are increased. The child who starts off reading fairly fluently, but whose performance deteriorates after a few lines, or when in the 'body' of a large paragraph, is a definite candidate for further checking.

HOW I FEEL ABOUT MATHS

Name ....

Date ....Class ....

Notes

 0 = Very little (or no) skill in this area.
10 = Usual functioning of peer group.

Put a circle round the number that shows how well you can do each activity.

I am good (or okay) at:
(Can include any activities, hobbies, sports etc. as well any area of the curriculum.)

0   1   2   3   4   5   6   7   8   9   10   ....

0   1   2   3   4   5   6   7   8   9   10   ....

0   1   2   3   4   5   6   7   8   9   10   ....

I have some difficulty with:
NUMBER

0   1   2   3   4   5   6   7   8   9   10   ....

TABLES 2X, 5X AND 10X

0   1   2   3   4   5   6   7   8   9   10   ....

TABLES 3X AND 4X

0   1   2   3   4   5   6   7   8   9   10   ....

TABLES 6X AND 7X

0   1   2   3   4   5   6   7   8   9   10   ....
Continued overleaf.

Mathematics Solutions – An Introduction to Dyscalculia Part A by Jan Poustie et al   ISBN 1 901544 45 1

Notes	
…………………...……	**TABLES 8X AND 9X**
	0 1 2 3 4 5 6 7 8 9 10
	READING (UNDERSTANDING WHAT I HAVE READ)
…………………...……	0 1 2 3 4 5 6 7 8 9 10
	WRITING SUMS DOWN
…………………...……	0 1 2 3 4 5 6 7 8 9 10
	PLANNING and ORGANISATION (of myself, my work, my desk, my room)
…………………...……	0 1 2 3 4 5 6 7 8 9 10
	SELF-ESTEEM (How I feel about myself)
…………………...……	0 1 2 3 4 5 6 7 8 9 10
	WRITING NUMBERS (Neatly, and the right way round)
…………………...……	0 1 2 3 4 5 6 7 8 9 10
	THINKING WHEN I AM DOING MATHS
…………………...……	0 1 2 3 4 5 6 7 8 9 10
	WORKING AT SPEED (IN MATHS)
…………………...……	0 1 2 3 4 5 6 7 8 9 10
	FRACTIONS AND PERCENTAGES
…………………...……	0 1 2 3 4 5 6 7 8 9 10
	ANGLES AND GEOMETRY
…………………...……	0 1 2 3 4 5 6 7 8 9 10

Notes

ADDITION

| 0 | I | 2 | 3 | 4 | 5 | 6 | 7 | 8 | 9 | 10 |

....

SUBTRACTION

| 0 | I | 2 | 3 | 4 | 5 | 6 | 7 | 8 | 9 | 10 |

....

MULTIPLICATION

| 0 | I | 2 | 3 | 4 | 5 | 6 | 7 | 8 | 9 | 10 |

....

DIVISION

| 0 | I | 2 | 3 | 4 | 5 | 6 | 7 | 8 | 9 | 10 |

....

MONEY

| 0 | I | 2 | 3 | 4 | 5 | 6 | 7 | 8 | 9 | 10 |

....

LISTENING (following instructions)

| 0 | I | 2 | 3 | 4 | 5 | 6 | 7 | 8 | 9 | 10 |

....

UNDERSTANDING TIME (how we measure it and how to read a clock)

| 0 | I | 2 | 3 | 4 | 5 | 6 | 7 | 8 | 9 | 10 |

....

WORD FINDING (Being able to remember the word that I want to use)

| 0 | I | 2 | 3 | 4 | 5 | 6 | 7 | 8 | 9 | 10 |

....

WORD LABELLING (Being able to remember the names of things and symbols)

| 0 | I | 2 | 3 | 4 | 5 | 6 | 7 | 8 | 9 | 10 |

....

Other areas of concern: (these can be any concerns; e.g. the person the student shares a table with, passing GCSE mathematics etc.)

| 0 | I | 2 | 3 | 4 | 5 | 6 | 7 | 8 | 9 | 10 |

....

Continued overleaf.

Mathematics Solutions – An Introduction to Dyscalculia Part A by Jan Poustie et al   ISBN 1 901544 45 1

Notes

....   0   1   2   3   4   5   6   7   8   9   10

....   0   1   2   3   4   5   6   7   8   9   10

....   9   4   2   7   10   1

....   6   3   8   0   5

....   +   =   x   –   ÷

Notes to assessor:

1. Always be on the look out for language difficulties. When asking whether there are difficulties, use the word that the student is used to; e.g. if asking whether subtraction is a problem you may need to use the word 'take away' instead of subtraction.

2. It can be useful to show the student the main operation signs (see above) before doing this sheet so that you can check which terms they use for them (and whether the symbols are recognised.)

3. When assessing a student who has considerable difficulties, check that the numbers 1 to 10 are also known first. Also check that they can say the numbers 1 to 10 in their correct order.

4. If the student is seven years old or less then use the 'Clouds' sheets in *Identification Solutions for Specific Learning Difficulties* by Jan Poustie et al, ISBN 1901544 14 1 to determine the student's views.

MEAL PLANNER

TIME	PREPARATION	HOB	OVEN	MICROWAVE

DINNER IS SERVED!

Mathematics Solutions – An Introduction to Dyscalculia; Part A by Jan Poustie et al, ISBN 1 901544 45 1
The reader has permission to photocopy this sheet for use with his/her students, the parents of such students and staff working with these students in order to decide upon appropriate provision for their difficulties.

EASY:
These are the easiest ones to use/read

MIDDLE:
A book that most people should be able to cope with.

MIDDLE/ HARD:

The most difficult books in this group.

HARD: It's a hard mountain to climb – but worth it when you get to the top!)

Useful Resources

There are many resources available to help reinforce mathematical concepts and some that teach the skills too. Few have been designed specifically for students affected by Dyscalculia. This is not meant to be a comprehensive index of resources but it provides information on products that may be useful. Unless otherwise stated all products can be read/used by various types of professionals and by parents. Some of the books are harder than others and so symbols have been used to make it easier for the reader to choose suitable books (see right).

CONTENTS	PAGE
Reference Materials (Maths, including Sharma materials)	170
Reference Materials (Specific Learning Difficulties Profile)	172
Next Generation Mathematics Products *Note: the details of all other products mentioned in this book can be found within each chapter. They are also indexed separately (see page 187).*	175
Lectures	176

Mathematics for Dyslexics – A Teaching Handbook (2nd Edition)
By Steve Chinn and Richard Ashcroft (ISBN 1 86156 043 5, published by Whurr).
A comprehensive guide to Dyslexia and mathematics, this book suggests a wide range of strategies. Ideally, the reader should have a good understanding of maths.

Maths for the Dyslexic – A Practical Guide
By Anne Henderson (ISBN 1 85346 534 8, David Fulton Publishers).
A guide to helping the Dyslexic student overcome difficulties in mathematics. Although intended for parents and teachers, not all parents will find some of the examples easy to follow. It is to be noted that, despite Anne Henderson's experience of students who have Dyscalculia, those of us who have the condition <u>can</u> be both good readers and good spellers, but Anne is right in noting that our time-sense, sequential ability and directional and organisational skills leave a lot to be desired! This book includes a section on the 'Language of Mathematics'.

Dyslexia and Mathematics
Edited by T. R. Miles and E. Miles (ISBN 0 415 04987 3, published by Routledge).
Includes articles by the editors and by Steve Chinn, Mary Kibel, Richard Ashcroft and Anne Henderson. Includes: language, an in-depth look at the effects of the inchworm

and grasshopper way of working mathematical tasks, theoretical considerations, reading and writing in mathematics, older pupils.

Specific Learning Difficulties in Mathematics – A Classroom Approach

By Olwen El-Naggar (ISBN 0 906730 81 3, published by Nasen)

This book is intended to inform and support the class teacher when dealing with students affected by specific learning difficulties in mathematics. It shies away from the use of the terms Dyslexia/Dyscalculia. It includes information on how teachers can use observation of (and discussion with) students to determine their difficulties and provides suggestions for ways in which a range of difficulties can be experienced by the SpLD Profile student and ways in which the teacher can help. It also looks at IEPs.

Elementary Mathematics and Language Difficulties – A Book for Teachers, Therapists and Parents

By Eva Grauberg (ISBN 1 86156 048 6, published by Whurr).

Age range covered: pre-school –14 yrs

A very interesting book to read. Grauberg has used her own personal experience and a great many sources (e.g. research papers) to supplement and support her suggested strategies. The book mainly deals with three areas of difficulty: weakness in symbolic understanding, organisational skills and memory. Some of her suggestions conflict with those of Sharma; e.g. with regard to when written recording needs to occur. (In this case it is only likely to be a problem when the student is affected by both symbolic language difficulties and Developmental Dyscalculia. In such cases the tutor would be advised to blend the two strategies advocated by each specialist whilst remembering that the language needs of the student must be attended to first.) This book is likely to be a challenging read for readers who lack confidence in and/or lack a good understanding of mathematics.

Sharma materials

These are quite complex to read and so are only really suitable for professionals and parents with a strong interest in mathematical learning difficulties. Sharma produces a quarterly magazine in the USA and he is also the editor of *Focus on Learning Problems in Mathematics,* of which at present there are over twenty titles one of which is entitled *Dyscalculia.* Some of his *Math Notebook* magazines and videos, are available in the UK via: Berkshire Mathematics (Mrs P. Brazil, Chazey Bank, The Warren, Mapledurham, Reading RG4 7TQ). There are over forty *Math Notebooks,* those which are likely to be of special interest to the reader are *Dyslexia, Dyscalculia, and some Remedial Perspectives for Mathematics Learning Problems; Cuisenaire Rods and Mathematics Teaching; Prerequisite and Support Skills for Mathematics Learning.; and Mathematics as a Second Language, Parts 1 and 2.* (Part 2 includes vocabulary lists for 5–11 years.). A very useful video which is available from Berkshire Mathematics, is *Numeracy 1 – Teaching Number Relationships.* One can order Sharma materials direct from Professor Sharma and/or pay a subscription in order to obtain *Maths Notebook* on a regular basis. (All payments to Professor Sharma have to be made using American dollars.) Professor Sharma's address is: Center for Teaching/Learning Mathematics, PO Box 3149, Framingham, Massachusetts 01701– 3149, USA, Tel: 001 508 877 7895.

Content applies to: primary school to adult.

An Introduction to Mathematics and Language

By Jan Poustie (ISBN 1 901544 96 6, published by Next Generation).
Difficulties in using and understanding mathematical language can dramatically reduce the student's ability to acquire mathematical skills. Written by a Specific Learning Difficulties Specialist who is also affected by Dyscalculia (and by the mathematical language difficulties that can accompany it) this guide is a must for everyone interested in this field. It provides a wealth of information on what to do plus provides information on Help & Support agencies and useful resources. The problems are explained, strategies suggested and solutions found. It contains two A4 full-colour laminated maths posters.

Content applies to: primary school to adult.

Mathematics Solutions – An Introduction to Dyscalculia, Part B: How to Teach Students who have Specific Learning Difficulties in Mathematics

By Jan Poustie (ISBN 1 901544 72 9, published by Next Generation).
The problems are explained, strategies suggested and solutions found. It provides a wealth of information on what to do, useful resources, teaching strategies and a recommended lesson format, including:

Helping the student,	Prioritising provision,
Teaching tips,	Place value,
Passing examinations,	How to achieve success,

Levels of knowing mathematics (Professor Mahesh Sharma)
Understanding and developing the prerequisite skills for mathematics.

Content applies to: pre-school to adult.

Identification Solutions for Specific Learning Difficulties, Part A:

A Manual for Understanding, Identifying and Referring for Diagnosis those who have Specific Learning Difficulties in the areas of literacy, behaviour and language.
By Jan Poustie et al (ISBN 1 901544 14 1, published by Next Generation.)
This is the second edition (updated, extended and indexed) of the nationally acclaimed *Solutions for Specific Learning Difficulties: Identification Guide*. It is a must for those who want to:

▸ be able to identify the causes of learning difficulties.

▸ know more about the field of specific learning difficulties, the conditions within the SpLD Profile and how to help those affected by them.

Comments about the 1st edition:
'A valuable resource for parents, teachers and other professionals.'
(Violet Brand, International speaker on Dyslexia)
'A definitive guide. A valuable resource. If you only buy one book around the subject of Specific Learning Difficulties make it this one.'
(from a review by Gill Dixon in the Dyspraxia Foundation's *Midline* magazine.)

Developmental Dyspraxia (2nd Edition)

By Madeleine Portwood (ISBN 1853465739, published by David Fulton Publishers)
Contains a Motor Screening Test, materials to improve visual-perceptual and motor co-ordination function .

Attention Deficit/Hyperactivity Disorder- A Practical Guide for Teachers
By P. Cooper and K. Ideus (ISBN 1 85346 431 7, published by David Fulton Publishers, London.)
A clear and concise guide to classroom practice for teachers.

Understanding Attention Deficit Disorder - A parent's guide to A.D.D. in children
By Dr C. Green and Dr K. Chee (ISBN 0 09 180844 8, published by Vermilion).
A very useful introduction to ADD for parents and professionals. Contains information on how to recognise ADD, practical advice, medication, sources of help and self-help for ADD adults.

The World of the Autistic Child
By Bryna Siegel (ISBN 0 19 507667 2, publisher Oxford University Press). Contains much information on recognition and aspects of the condition. Has a large section on classroom intervention strategies.

The Autistic Spectrum - A Guide for Parents and Professionals
By Lorna Wing (ISBN 0 09 475160 9, Publisher Constable and Company Ltd.).
Available from the National Autistic Society (see page 161). An excellent comprehensive and practical guide for parents and professionals. Shows how people with autism experience the word, the reasons for their disturbed behaviour and resistance to change. Explains ways of teaching students.

Autism and Asperger Syndrome
Edited by Uta Frith (ISBN 0 52138608 X, publisher Cambridge University Press).
Contributors to this book: M. Dewey, Uta Frith, C. Gillbert, F. Happé, D. Tantam and Lorna Wing. Includes the first ever translation of Asperger's paper, shows how much adaptation, learning and personal development is possible if there is a sensitive understanding of the precise problems involved. Looks at the syndrome from childhood to adulthood.

Psychological Aspects of Hemiplegia
By Robert Goodman (from Archives of Disease in Childhood – March 1997, Vol 76, No. 3 pages 177-178 available from the BMJ publishing group, BMA House, Tavistock Square, London WC1H 9JR Tel: 0171 383 6305).

Brain Gym– A Teacher's Edition
By P. and G. Dennison (ISBN 0 942143 02 7).
Some of these exercises have been found to be useful by some students. Suitable for professionals/parents/affected adults. There are Brain Gym books for parents too.

A Teacher's Window into the Child's Mind
By Sally Goddard (ISBN 0 9615332 5 0).
Explains how the different primitive and postural reflexes can affect learning. It suggests strategies/programmes that can be used inside/outside of the classroom.

Childhood Speech, Language and Listening Problems

By P. McAlleer Hamaguchi (ISBN 0 471 03413 4, published by John Wiley & Sons, Inc.). An excellent practical guide for parents and teachers. After defining each problem it offers some solutions and explains the meanings of the terms used by speech and language therapists. Includes recognition of the difficulties and how they affect the child academically and socially, and tips for helping the child at home.

Speech and Language Difficulties

By B. Daines, P. Fleming and C. I. Miller (ISBN 0 906730 87 2, published by NASEN, see page 162 for details).
Provides background information to the problems language-impaired students face in the classroom and useful strategies to help them.

Assessment and Management of Central Auditory Processing Disorders in the Educational Setting

By Teri James Bellis (ISBN 1 56593 628 0, published by Singular Publishing Group, Inc., available from the UK branch of this company).
A very good book on this relatively new topic to the UK educational scene. It explains the science of CAPD, its assessment and management and how to develop a programme to help those who have this condition.

British Dyslexia Association Publications

For address see page 161.
Dyslexia Handbook: provides up-to-date information on Dyslexia.
Dyslexia – Early Help, Better Future: a very simple to follow short video.
Dyslexia in the Primary Classroom: a video and manual aimed at staff development for teachers. It highlights the problems and suggests appropriate teaching strategies. '
Dyslexia: Signposts to Success: a guide for adults who have Dyslexia.

Content applies to: primary to adult.

Planning and Organisation Solutions

By Jan Poustie (ISBN 1 901544 81 8, published by Next Generation).
This manual explains the different types of planning and organisational models available and the huge variety of ways in which they can be used to improve academic work in writing, spelling , language, maths etc.

> 'It provides an excellent outline of the problems and the solutions. Both teachers and parents will find it valuable with the range of solutions presented. The chapter on Mind Maps® is splendid – this is much more relevant to these children/students.'

(Violet Brand, International speaker on Dyslexia.)
Contains: a wealth of photocopiable resources.

Clock language

Age Suitability: Primary.

Students with language/mathematical difficulties can have great problems in learning to tell the time. This very colourful and attractive product enables parents/teachers to teach the student the foundation skills needed for him/her to be able to read the time. The clock can be used for both teaching the language of time and to teach how to read the time using the terms 'Past' and 'To'. Language covered includes:

- ➤ Fractions related to time (halves, quarters, three-quarters)
- ➤ Clockwise and anticlockwise
- ➤ 'To' and 'Past'; e.g. 15 minutes to/quarter to.

Take Off with Number

Age suitability: 7 years to adult.

It reduces mathematical anxiety and improves planning, organisation, sequential, classifying, times tables and number skills. It contains a travel version of the Rummikub® game, Manual and the Rummikub Activities Book. It is available in two formats. The 'Private' version is easier to use as it contains a simplified version of the manual. The 'Educational' version contains a more complex manual which includes:

1. How to teach some aspects of language.
1. A maths language assessment tool relating to the language of position.
2. Photocopiable assessment sheets and lesson plan.

A pack containing just the manual and the activities book is also available for those who already possess the Rummikub® game or for those who require the Classic version of the game. (The Classic version has larger Rummikub tiles and is suitable for those with visual/handling difficulties. It is available from toyshops.)

Take off with Number is for the student who is afraid/ anxious when dealing with numbers and/ or is disorganised.

Basic Number

Age Suitability: 7 years to adult.

This product has been designed to improve number/numeral correspondence up to 20, pattern recognition, numeral reading and writing, and number bond skills. (Number bonds are the pairs of numbers that equal 10 or 20; e.g. 7+ 2 = 10,   12 + 8 = 20.) It contains an instruction booklet (which explains how to do number arc and number bonds work) and a set of wooden numerals (contains thirty-two wooden numerals, height 8 cms). The set has two of each of the numerals 3, 5, 6, 7, 8, 9; three each of the numerals 2 and 0 and twelve of the numeral 1 and two each of the open and closed forms of the numeral 4).

Tablesgraphics(Set 1)

Age suitability: all.

This sturdy, fully laminated, product covers the 6X, 7X, 8X, 9X tables. It provides a unique, fun and multisensory way to learn times tables. Contains a manual and a set of playing cards.

Age suitability: all

Breakthrough to Number

Note: expected publication date Autumn 2001

This product is being designed for use with students who have severe problems in understanding number; i.e. simple addition and subtraction. People interested in trailing this product should contact Jan Poustie (her details are on page 176.)

Various specialists provide lectures on learning difficulties in mathematics. Key people are as follows:

Name	Lecture area	Contact details
Professor Mahesh Sharma	Dyscalculia	See page 171–172
Dr Steve Chinn	Dyslexia and maths	See page 139
Anne Henderson	Dyslexia and maths	E-mail: Anneh123@aol.com
Jan Poustie	Dyscalculia and the SpLD Profile conditions	Tel: 01823 289559 Fax: 01823 289566 E-mail: jan.poustie@virgin.net Website: janpoustie.co.uk

The following Interactive Lectures/Workshops/INSETs are available from Jan Poustie
Please contact her (via the one of the methods shown above) for further details. The lectures are suitable for professionals, parents and adults affected by the various conditions.

The Recognition of Dyscalculia
Topics covered: The different forms of Dyscalculia, How the other conditions in the SpLD Profile affect the learning of mathematics, natural learning styles, some practical solutions.

Mathematics and Language
Topics covered: Factors causing language difficulties, receptive and expressive language, mathematics as a foreign language, mathematical schema, word problems, using language to help the learner, understanding the concepts, teaching tips, what it is like to have the prolem, Mind Mapping for mathematics.

How to teach the student who has Dyscalculia
Topics covered: Tools, concepts and models. Prerequisite skills for mathematics, how to use games to improve mathematical skills, basic sub-skills for mathematics.

Recognising the Specific Learning Difficulties Profile
Topics covered: Dyslexia, Specific Language Impairment, Autistic Spectrum Disorder, Central Auditory Processing Disorder, Dyscalculia and the various forms of Attention Deficits and Dyspraxia.

Identifying Dyscalculia in the Early Years
This is part of a series of three modules which cover pre-school and reception. Very practical and interactive sessions which are arranged by the host in an early years environment (or with access to early years equipment).
Comment from a previous attendee:
  '*These courses should be a must to anyone with or caring for young children. Very interesting and well-delivered with lots of participation on our part. I have enjoyed the course immensely.*'

abstract concepts, strength of ASD students 118, 120, 124

accounts, difficulties in keeping associated with Dyscalculia 149-50

Acquired Dyscalculia 15-17, 27, 30, 38

Acquired Dyslexia 101

ADHD (Attention Deficit Hyperactivity Disorder) 105, 113
   see also Attention Deficits

AFASIC (Association for All Speech-Impaired Children) 81, 161

algebra, difficulties associated with SpLD Profile conditions 7, 50, 141

alliteration, as tool in remediation of Specific Language Impairment 87

analogue clocks 7, 96, 151

aphasia 81

application of knowledge, difficulties arising from Dyspraxia and Autistic Spectrum Disorder 48

area method of multiplication 24, 25-6

arithmetic IQ 142

Articulatory (Verbal) Dyspraxia 23, 43, 57-8, 67, 90, 93, 99
   see also Dyspraxia

articulatory difficulties see expressive language difficulties

Ashcroft, Richard 34, 48, 58, 104

Asperger Syndrome 44, 90, 115, 123-4, 126, 130
   see also Autistic Spectrum Disorder

assessment for mathematical learning difficulties
   assessors 138-9
   provision resulting from 142-6
   SpLD Profile conditions, tests for 136-8
   tests, overview of 139-41
   what and when to assess 133-6
   see also Statement of Special Education Needs

associated movements, Dyspraxia 73

Aston Index 75, 76, 137

atopic conditions, link with Specific Learning Difficulties Profile conditions 35

Attention Deficits (ADD) 105–110
   associated with distractibility 108, 150, 163

associated with SpLD Profile conditions 21, 29, 30, 32, 41, 47, 49-50, 67, 88, 115
   associated with slow response rates 18

Attention Deficits Hyperactivity Disorder (ADHD) 105, 113, 114

behavioural elements 41-3, 113, 114, 116, 117-18, 119, 120-23, 123-5, 126-32 see also behavioural difficulties
   bullying associated with 96
   effects of on author 3
   erratic work associated with 8
   forms and causes of 44, 105-7
   impact on learning 107-11
   mathematical difficulties arising from 47
   memory difficulties arising from 51, 52, 58, 103
   'Not as Specified' (NOS) Attention Deficits 105
   overview 37
   photocopying of worksheets as tool in remediation of 65
   sources of help and support 161
   tests for 135-6

auditory closure activities 80

Auditory Decoding Deficit 75

auditory dysfunctioning
   auditory processing difficulties 51-2, 93-4, 136
   auditory stimulation 77-80
   classroom environment, importance in remediation of 76-7
   overview 75-6
   Right Ear Advantage 76
   staggered spondaic difficulties 76
   see also Central Auditory Processing Disorder; receptive language difficulties

auditory sequential memory 75, 86-7, 136-8

auditory stimulation
   auditory strategies 78-80
   lack of 77
   management of disorders 78
   musical instruments, learning to play 45, 76, 77-8, 93-4

Austistic Spectrum Disorder (ASD)
   associated with directional confusion 55

Mathematics Solutions – An Introduction to Dyscalculia Part A by Jan Poustie et al   ISBN 1 901544 45 1

associated with SpLD Profile conditions 19, 29, 30, 41, 58

behavioural elements 41-4, 50, 89, 113-14, 116-32

bullying associated with 96

conflict 121

difficulties in making inferences 118-19

hyperacusis associated with 114-15

mathematical difficulties arising from 22-3, 48, 49, 136

memory difficulties arising from 52, 103

originality of thought 120-1

overview 37, 40, 44

sensory information (disorganised) 119

sources of help and support 161

autism see Autistic Spectrum Disorder

baby (Primitive) reflexes 45

BAS tests 91, 100, 137, 140, 141-2

Behaviour Inhibition Disorder see Attention Deficits

behavioural difficulties

causes of, and overview of remediation strategies 113-14

classroom, managing student in 115-17, 124-6

effects on body signals and learning 41-3

gullibility and sexuality 126-7

key points in dealing with 118-24

Managing the student in the classroom 115-124

'overload' situations, strategies for coping with 127-9

overview 41-2

practical demonstrations of difficulties 129

referrals and supportive agencies 130

'risk assessments', conducting 130

sensory information, unusual sensitivity to (hyperacusis) 72-3, 114-15

support, offering 131-32

topic/task choice and strategies 117-18

see also Attention Deficits; Autistic Spectrum Disorder; Dyspraxia

behavioural optometry 54, 63, 163-4

Bellis, Teri James 78

blurred vision 163-4

Blythe, Peter 45

body language, difficulties associated with Specific Language Impairment 81, 88

body signals, impact of behavioural conditions on 42-3

Brain Gym exercises 62-3

brain

corpus callosum 45, 75-6, 93

deficiency of white matter in leading to Non-verbal Learning Deficit 39

'executive function' of 119

impact of Chronic Fatigue Syndrome on chemistry of 38

impact of diet on 43

limbic system 105-6

link with Dyscalculia 19, 26, 27-8

neural pathways 45, 73-4, 106

Brand, Violet 174

breast milk, DHA in 73-4

'brushing', of Primitive (baby) reflexes 45-6

budgeting, difficulties associated with Dyscalculia 149

bullying 12, 96-7

calculators, difficulties associated with Dyscalculia 7, 22, 149

calendars, difficulties associated with Dyscalculia 20, 148, 151-2

carers, responding to 'overload situations' 127-130

carrels, study 125

case studies 57-8, 91-6, 115-17

categorisation difficulties, associated with Specific Language Impairment 88

Central Auditory Processing Disorder (CAPD)

associated with Attention Deficits 41, 106, 107, 109

mathematical difficulties arising from 31, 32, 50

memory difficulties arising from 51

Neuro-Developmental Delay as causal factor in 44-5

overview 37
receptive language difficulties associated with
56, 85
research into 28
slow response rate associated with 23
see also auditory dysfunctioning
checking of work, difficulties associated with
Dyscalculia 21
Childhood Hemiplegia 15, 16, 27, 38-9, 48, 52,
101, 162
Chinn, Steve 10, 32, 48, 58, 139, 157, 176
Chronic Fatigue Syndrome (ME/Post Viral
Fatigue Syndrome)
attention and sequencing difficulties arising
from 49
comprehension difficulties associated with 56
leading to Acquired Dyslexia 101
link with Dyscalculia 15, 16, 27, 31
mathematical difficulties arising from 48
overview 38
reading and writing difficulties associated with
54-5
visual-spatial difficulties associated with 52, 57
classification skills, difficulties associated with
Dyslexia 103
classroom
environment 12, 76-7, 78, 114
managing student in 115-26
recognising Dyscalculia in 17-26
see also school, impact of Dyscalculia in
clocks, difficulties associated with SpLD Profile
conditions 7, 96, 148, 150-2, 154-5
'clumsiness', associated with visual-spatial
difficulties 52
clustering of information, as learning tool 87,
138
cluttering of speech 85
colour
changing background as a tool in remediation
of Dyspraxia 62, 65, 71-2
coloured lenses 54
coloured stickers, use on wall calendars
152-3
comorbidity of SpLD Profile conditions see

Specific Learning Difficulties (SpLD) Profile
comprehension difficulties see receptive language
difficulties
computer programs, as tool in remediation of
SpLD Profile conditions 65-6, 74, 89, 99, 111,
121, 149-50
concentration see Attention Deficits
conceptualisation, difficulties associated with
SpLD Profile conditions 14, 18, 48, 58, 104,
139
concrete apparatus 7, 13, 14, 24, 56-7, 109
conflict, over behavioural problems 120, 125
Constructional Dyspraxia 47
contextual clues, as tool in remediation of
auditory dysfunctioning 80
conversation, difficulties associated with Specific
Language Impairment 89, 94
cooking, difficulties associated with Dyscalculia
7, 9, 148, 152-3
Corkish, Norma 37
corpus callosum 45, 76, 93
counselling, as tool to combat anxiety over
mathematics 13
cranial osteopathy 105
Cuisenaire Rods 11, 50, 58, 79, 84, 173
cutlery, difficulties associated with Graphomotor
Dyspraxia 64

daydreaming 8, 42, 47, 77, 105, 113
day-to-day tasks, impact of Dyscalculia on
147-8
denominators and numerators, confusion over
55
Developmental Co-ordination Disorder (DCD)
see Dyspraxia
Developmental Dyscalculia 15, 16, 19, 25, 27,
28-9, 57-8, 90, 93, 111
Dysymbolia 31
Forms of 28 - 34
Graphic Dyscalculia 31
Ideognostic Dyscalculia 31
Lexical Dyscalculia 30 - 31
Operational Dyscalculia 32
Practognostic Dyscalculia 29 - 30

Verbal Dyscalculia 29
  see also Dyscalculia
Developmental Dyslexia 27-8, 36, 102
  see also Dyslexia
Developmental Dyspraxia 41, 42-3, 44, 59-60
  see also Dyspraxia
diagnosis see identification of learning difficulties
diaries 152
dictation, as tool in remediation of Dyspraxia
  70
diet, role in remediation of behavioural
  conditions 42-3, 73-4, 106-7
Digit Tests 136-8
Direct Dyslexia (Hyperlexia) 101
directional confusion 55-6, 102
disorganised sensory information, difficulties
  associated with Autistic Spectrum Disorder
  119
distractibility, associated with Attention Deficits
  109, 150, 163
Dixon, Gill 174
DIY, difficulties associated with Dyscalculia 9
docosahexonic acid (DHA) 73
dysarthria 85
Dyscalculia
  assessing for 117, 133-45
  associated with Specific Language Impairment
    90, 93
  benefits of intervention 156
  comprehension difficulties associated with 56
  definition, widening of 27-32
  Dyscalculia Spectrum 30
  historical use of term 15-17
  lectures on 176
  living with 3, 147-55
  memory difficulties arising from 52
  planning and organisational 49
  recognising 17-26
  size-grading, difficulties associated with 29,
  30, 58
  video concerning 173
  see also Developmental Dyscalculia
Dyslexia 101-104
  assessment for 136

  associated with directional confusion 55
  associated with SpLD Profile conditions 29,
    30, 40-41, 59, 90, 97
  characteristics of 101-3
  development of research into 27-8
  Dyslexia Early Screening Test (DEST) 137
  Dyslexia Screening Test (DST) 137
  Dyslexia Spectrum 30
  erratic work associated with 8
  forms of 101
  language difficulties associated with 54
  mathematical difficulties associated with 7,
    22-3, 48, 104
  inherited nature of 44
  lectures on 176
  link with corpus callosum malfunction 76
  memory difficulties arising from 51, 52, 104
  overview 36
  planning and organisational difficulties arising
    from 49
  slow response rate associated with 23
  sources of help and support 161
  video concerning 173
  writing difficulties associated with 55
  see also Developmental Dyslexia
dysphasia see Specific Language Impairment
(Dysphasia)
Dysphonetic Dyslexia 101
Dyspraxia 59-74
  assessment for 130, 136-7
  associated with directional confusion 55
  associated with SpLD Profile conditions 20,
    29, 30, 40-41, 59-60, 90, 93, 94, 107
  associated with visual-spatial difficulties 52
  behavioural elements 41-3, 113, 116-17
  bullying associated with 96
  comprehension difficulties associated with 56
  dietary supplements as a tool in remediation
    of 73-4
  effects of 3
  Graphomotor Dyspraxia 63-7, 71
  link with travel sickness 35
  linked with Non-verbal Learning Deficit 39
  mathematical difficulties arising from 22-3, 29,

30, 31, 47-8
Occulomotor Dyspraxia 40-41, 53, 56-7, 60-63, 151
overview 36
perceptual difficulties associated with 71-2
planning and organisational difficulties arising from 49, 60
postural difficulties associated with 60
relationship difficulties associated with 127
remediation through learning to play a musical instrument 77
sensory difficulties associated with 72-3, 114
sources of help and support 161-2
Verbal (Articulatory) Dyspaxia 23, 43, 57-8, 67, 90, 93, 99
writing difficulties associated with 54, 55

environment see classroom: environment
examinations, stress associated with 26, 110, 111, 122, 155, 164
'executive function' of brain 119
expectations, limitations imposed by 12
expertise, primary/secondary school teachers 14
expressive language difficulties 37, 54, 81, 82, 85, 90, 95, 134

facial expressions, confusion concerning 88-9
fear, of mathematics 8, 23
'fidget breaks', as a tool in remediation of Attention Deficits 60
fidgeting, associated with Attention Deficits 105, 109
fine motor skills 36, 37, 59-60, 63, 67, 70
see also motor skills
finger counting, linked to Dyscalulia 18
fractions, difficulties associated with Specific Language Impairment 95
Fragile-X 39-40
fragmentation of tasks, associated with Dyscalculia 20-21
Frith, Uta 125
furniture, significance of in remediation of Graphomotor Dyspraxia 66

genetically inherited syndromes 39-40, 44
geometry, difficulties associated with SpLD Profile conditions 20, 36, 39, 53, 54, 61
gifted students, behaviours of 107
Gillet, P. 78
'glare', reducing 62, 65
global (qualitative) learning style 9, 10-11, 108, 110, 123, 133, 172
glossary of terms, as a tool in remediation of auditory dysfunctioning 77
'glue ear' 80, 93-4
grammar, difficulties associated with Specific Language Impairment 82-5
Graphomotor Dyspraxia 63-7, 71
Grauberg, Eva 173
grey areas, in SpLD Profile 40, 41-2, 113, 116
gross motor skills 36, 57-8, 59-60, 63, 67
see also motor skills
gullibility, associated with Attention Deficits and Autistic Spectrum Disorder 126-7

handwriting difficulties 61, 62, 63, 72, 121
see also writing difficulties
headaches 52, 61, 62, 163
Henderson, Anne 172, 176
higher-level language experience, lack of 98
Higher-Level Language Impairment (HLL) 89-91
holidays, behavioural changes seen in 93
Holland, Keith 53, 163-4
homeopathy 105, 162
homework 14, 18, 118
hyperactivity 106-7
see also Attention Deficit Hyperactivity Disorder
hyperacusis 72, 114-15, 129
Hyperlexia (Direct Dyslexia) 101

identification of learning difficulties
assessment for 133-45
behavioural conditions 41-3
causes of 9-11, 12-14
combined conditions 40-41

Dyscalculia 17-26
    indicators 7-9
    see also Statement of Special Education Needs
Individual Education Plans (IEPs) 144
inferences, difficulties associated with Autistic
    Spectrum Disorder and Attention Deficits
    118-19
Integration Deficit 75
    see also auditory dysfunctioning
integration of parts, difficulties arising from
    Constructional Dyspraxia 47
intelligence, masking SpLD Profile conditions
    34, 91-2, 100, 160
Intelligence, high 158
inversion of numbers, associated with Dyspraxia
    72
irony, confusion concerning associated with
    Specific Language Impairment 88

Jira, intensive listening exercises intervention
    programme 77

kinaesthetic learning techniques 11, 45, 75, 104
Kosc, Ladislav 133, 134

language
    adapting to students' needs 117-18, 168
    of mathematics, difficulties associated with
        SpLD Profile conditions 8, 23, 49, 134
    as key to Specific Learning Difficulties Profile
        35
    see also expressive language difficulties;
        receptive language difficulties; Specific
        Language Impairment
learning style, relationship to teaching style 5, 9-
    12, 13-14, 109, 117-18
    see also natural learning styles; qualitative
        (global) learning style; quantitative
        (sequential) learning style
liaison, importance of in diagnosis and
    remediation of SpLD Profile conditions 130
limbic system, brain 105-6
literacy skills
    impact of Childhood Hemiplegia on 16-17

impact of delayed motor skills upon 44-6
    impact of Developmental Dyslexia on 27-8
location, importance of in remediation of
    Graphomotor Dyspraxia 67
logic of mathematics, difficulties linked to
    Dyscalulia 17, 19-20, 24, 31
long-term memory difficulties associated with
    Attention Deficits 109
Loveless, Eugene 28, 133
'lowest', explaining mathematical meaning of 83
Luria (1966) 19-20, 28
magic squares 25-6, 34
mammalian brain 113
    map-reading difficulties 9, 16, 18, 39, 53, 55,
        61, 62, 71
mathematics
    assessment tests 133-6, 138-45
    causes of difficulties in 9-14
    identification of difficulties in 7-9
    impact of SpLD Profile conditions on learning
        of 47-58
    language of 8, 23, 49, 134
    logic of 17, 19-20, 24, 31
    'Mathematics Communication' strategy 133-4,
        141, 143
    skills, impact of Specific Language Impairment
        97-8
    see also Dyscalculia
McGlown, David 45
McKinlay, Ian 48, 59
ME see Chronic Fatigue Syndrome (ME, Post-
    Viral Fatigue Syndrome)
meals, difficulties involved in preparation of 7, 9,
    148, 153-4
Meares-Irlen Syndrome 38, 52
memory
    difficulties associated with SpLD Profile
        conditions 47, 51-2, 58, 99, 103, 109, 124
    visual hooks 87
    see also auditory sequential memory; short-
        term memory difficulties
mental arithmetic 137-8, 140
metabolic functioning of brain 73-4
misalignment problems 23, 61

Mathematics Solutions – An Introduction to Dyscalculia Part A by Jan Poustie et al   ISBN 1 901544 45 1

miscounting, linked to Dyscalulia 17
misdialling on telephone 8, 147, 149, 154
Misreading numbers 153-4
mixed diet, importance of 43, 106
motor coordination skills
    assessment for 137
    difficulties with 52, 54, 56-7, 99
    impact on literacy skills of delay in acquiring
        44-6
    see also fine motor skills; gross motor skills
multiplication 22, 23, 24-5, 49, 140, 141, 165-7
    see also times tables, learning of
multisensory teaching techniques, in remediation
    of Specific Language Impairment 100
musical instruments, learning of as tool in
    remediation of SpLD Profile conditions 45,
    76, 77-8, 93-4

Nash-Wortham, Mary 67
National Autistic Society 128
natural learning styles 10, 11, 110
    see also qualitative (global) learning style;
        quantitative (sequential) learning style
Near-vision Dysfunctioning 23, 52, 53, 57
neural pathways 45, 73, 106
Neuro-Developmental Delay (NDD) 44-6, 75-6
neuromaturation see Neuro-Developmental
    Delay (NDD)
Non-verbal Learning Deficit (NLD) 39, 52
'Not as Specified' (NOS) Attention Deficits 105
number bonds 18, 24, 70, 175
number stories 21, 69, 81
numbers, memory difficulties associated with
    Dyscalculia 147-9, 153-4
numerators and denominators, confusion over
    55

occulomotor difficulties, leading to 'swimming
    text' 57
Occulomotor Dyspraxia 40-41, 53, 60-63, 151
organisation (see planning and organisation)
originality, associated with Autistic Spectrum
    Disorder 120-1
osteopathy 162

'overload' situations, strategies for coping with
    127-9

paper, feel of 66
paraphasic substitutions 22
Parent Partnership Officer, LEA 117
penhold, in relation to remediation of
    Graphomotor Dyspraxia 65
perceptual difficulties 54, 55, 71-2, 123, 133,
    135, 163-4
perseveration of inappropriate procedures
    associated with Dyscalculia 21-2
personality, impact on visual functioning 53-4
phonological difficulties 68, 85, 94, 101, 102
Phonological Dyslexia 101
physiotherapy 13
pictorial-based learning techniques 14, 80
planning and organisation difficulties 20, 36, 39,
    47, 49, 60, 99, 102, 103
playgroup leaders, skills of 92
Portwood, Madeleine 59, 72, 73-4, 113
Post Viral Fatigue Syndrome (PVFS) see Chronic
    Fatigue Syndrome (ME/Post Viral Fatigue
    Syndrome)
posture 60, 66-7
Postural (movement control) reflexes 45
praise, importance of 125
prepositions, difficulties in use of 82
pre-school children, assessment for SpLD Profile
    conditions 136
Primitive (baby) reflexes 45-6
pronunciation difficulties 68, 85, 94, 101, 102
puberty, impact on Attention Deficits students
    119

qualifications, achieving 157-60
qualitative (global) learning style 9, 10-11, 47,
    107-8, 110, 123, 133, 172
quantitative (sequential) learning style 9, 11,
    133, 172
questioning
    strategy, of Mahesh C. Sharma 83-4
    typical of Asperger Syndrome students 122-3

REA (Right Ear Advantage) 76

reading difficulties associated with SpLD Profile conditions 55

receptive language difficulties
  associated with auditory processing difficulties 136
  associated with Autistic Spectrum Disorder 119
  associated with combination of SpLD Profile conditions 56-7
  associated with Dyslexia 104
  associated with Specific Language Impairment 37, 81, 82, 85-7, 90, 94, 95

referrals and supportive agencies 130, 161-2

relationships, difficulties associated with Autistic Spectrum Disorder 120

repeated addition method of multiplication 24-5

repetition, linked to Dyscalulia 17

reptilian brain 113

resources
  lectures, sources and subjects 176
  mathematics, reference materials concerning 172-4
  Next Generation Products 175
  overview 3-4
  photocopiable 163-9
  SpLD Profile conditions, reference materials concerning 174

response rate, slowness of associated with Dyscalculia 18, 23

reversal of letter 163

reversal
  of concepts 22-3
  of numbers 72, 163

Reverse Digit Tests 137-8

revision, importance of 14

Rey-Osterrieth Complex Figure Test 137

Right Ear Advantage (REA) 76

Rinaldi, Wendy 89

'risk assessments' 130

Ritalin, as tool in remediation of Attention Deficits 106

ritualistic behaviours, associated with Autistic Spectrum Disorder 120

role-play 90

routine, importance of to ASD and ADD students 121-2

saccadic eye movements (tracking) 61

sarcasm, confusion concerning associated with Specific Language Impairment 88

'savants' 125

scales (weighing), difficulties associated with Dyscalculia 155

school, impact of Dyscalculia in 7-9, 17, 147
  see also classroom

Scotopic Sensitivity Irlen Syndrome see Meares-Irlen Syndrome

Segar, Mark 127

self-esteem 12, 23, 42, 96, 164

Semantic-Pragmatic Disorder 87-9

sensory channels of learning 11, 124-5

Sensory Integration Disorder see Dyspraxia

sensory 'overload' (hyperacusis) 72-3, 114-15, 129

sensory information (disorganised) 119

Sensory stimulation (least amount of) 125

sentence order, difficulties associated with Specific Language Impairment 81

sequencing difficulties 49, 102, 104, 135

sequential (quantitative learning style) 9, 11, 133, 172

sexuality, risks associated with Attention Deficits and Autistic Spectrum Disorder 126- 7

Sharma assessment tools 138-9

Sharma, Mahesh C. 3, 4, 5, 10, 28, 34, 48, 50, 58, 83, 133-5, 172-3, 176

short-term memory difficulties 51-2, 102, 103, 104, 110
  see also memory

shyness, confused with Specific Language Impairment 91-2

singing, as tool in remediation of SpLD Profile conditions 45, 76, 93

slow response rate associated with SpLD Profile conditions 23

sound therapies, in remediation of Central

Auditory Processing Disorder 45

spatial difficulties 16-17, 36, 52-4, 88, 135, 148, 150-51

special advisors, LEA 114

Special Education Needs Co-ordinator (SENCO/ AENCO) 115, 117

specialist tuition, shortage of 157-8

Specific Language Impairment (dysphasia)
  associated with auditory dysfunctioning 79
  associated with SpLD Profile conditions 19, 41, 57-8, 70, 109
  bullying, associated with 96-7
  case studies 91-6
  expressive language difficulties associated with 54, 82, 85
  grammatical difficulties 82-5
  higher-level language experience, lack of 98
  Higher-Level Language Impairment (HLL) 89-91
  mathematical difficulties arising from 47, 97-8
  memory difficulties arising from 51
  overview 36-7
  planning and organisational difficulties arising from 49
  receptive language difficulties associated with 56, 85-7
  Semantic-Pragmatic Disorder 87-9
  slow response rate associated with 23
  sources of help and support 161
  summary 99-100
  terms used to describe 81
  word confusion 98-9
  word-finding/labelling difficulties, associated with 81

Specific Learning Difficulties (SpLD) Profile
  associated conditions 38-40 see also
    Childhood Hemiplegia; Chronic Fatigue Syndrome; genetically inherited syndromes; Meares-Irlen Syndrome; Non-verbal Learning Deficit
  behavioural conditions, associated with 41-4
    see also Attention Deficits; Autistic Spectrum Disorder (ASD)
  comorbidity of 40-42 see also Attention Deficits; Autistic Spectrum Disorder (ASD); Central Auditory Processing Disorder; Dyscalculia; Dyslexia; Dyspraxia; Specific Language Impairment
  delayed motor skills and literacy 44-6
  impact on numeracy and mathematical skills 47-58
  lectures on 176
  overview 35-8
  Specific Learning Difficulties Profile Dyscalculia 27 - 33

spectacles, as a tool in remediation of Occulomotor Dyspraxia 63

speech
  delayed onset of associated with Dyspraxia 69
  therapy 70, 88, 95, 100, 145

spelling difficulties associated with Articulatory Dyspraxia 69, 70

SpLD Profile see Specific Learning Difficulties (SpLD) Profile

staggered spondaic difficulties 76

Statement of Special Education Needs 115-17, 141-5

stress
  associated with Attention Deficits 111
  associated with Specific Language Impairment 91, 93, 94-5
  difficulties associated with Dyscalculia 26, 157
  impact on SpLD Profile conditions 160
  as major cause of behavioural difficulties 121-2
  visual difficulties, associated with 53-4, 164
    see also examinations

successful student management 125-6

sub-skill (prerequisite skills) functioning 26, 134, 137, 138, 173

'sugar highs and lows' 106-7

support, behavioural problems 130-32

Suzuki method 77-8, 94

'swallow reflex', difficulties associated with Articulatory Dyspraxia 68

'swimming' text 57, 163-4

symbolic language difficulties 52, 124, 173

'Take-off with Numbers' teaching pack 13, 175
teaching strategies and style, relationship to
learning style 5, 9-12, 13-14, 109, 117-18
   see also natural learning styles; qualitative
      (global) learning style; quantitative
      (sequential) learning style
telephone, difficulties associated with Dyscalculia
   8, 147, 149, 154
textbooks, outdated nature of some 11
'time out breaks', importance of for carers 132
time, difficulties associated with 7, 20, 88, 96,
   148, 151-2, 155, 175
times tables, learning of 24, 58, 104, 111, 134-5,
   137, 140, 165-6
      see also multiplication
Tourette Syndrome 115-6
traffic-lights' cards 128
Transfer to secondary school 144
transition times, between (pre-school)/schools
   89-90, 91-2, 153
transitivity skills 137
travel sickness, link with Dyspraxia 35
Tuberous Sclerosis 120
Turner, Martin 39
twins, Attention Deficits associated with 105

UADD (Undifferentiated Attention Deficit
   Disorder) 105

Verbal (Articulatory) Dyspaxia 23, 43, 57-8, 67,
   90, 93, 99
      see also Dyspraxia
vicious circle of Specific Language Impairment
   99-100
video recording, of lectures 77
visual-perceptual difficulties 54, 55, 71-2, 123,
   133, 135, 163-4
visual-spatial difficulties 16-17, 36, 52-4, 88, 135,
   148, 150-51
vocabulary, difficulties associated with Specific
   Language Impairment 81
voice creation, mechanics of 67-8

wall calendars 151-2

watches 151-2
white space, difficulties associated with 61, 71
WISC tests 91, 137, 139-40, 142, 143
withdrawal from school, in remediation of
   behavioural conditions 13, 43
word confusion, associated with Specific
   Language Impairment 98-9
word-finding/labelling difficulties 79, 80, 81, 89,
   98, 104, 134
word-processors, as tool in remediation of
   Graphomotor Dyspraxia 65
workplace, impact of Dyscalculia on 148
WRAT (Wide Range Achievement Tests) 133,
   140-41, 142, 143
writing
   difficulties, associated with SpLD Profile
      conditions 54-5, 68-9 see also handwriting
   style, in relation to Graphomotor Dyspraxia
      67
   tools, importance of in remediation of
      Graphomotor Dyspraxia 65

A Guide to Coping Specifically for People with Asperger Syndrome (Mark Segar) 127

A Teacher's Window into the Child's Mind (Sally Goddard) 173

Accelerated Learning in the Classroom (Alistair Smith) 145

Action for ME 38

ADDISS 161

ADHD Family Support Group UK 110, 161

AFASIC (Association for All Speech-Impaired Children) 161

An Introduction to Mathematics and Language - Problems, Strategies and Solutions (Jan Poustie) 47, 49, 99, 173

Appleford School, Wiltshire 138

area method of multiplication 25

Assessment and Management of Central Auditory Processing Disorders in the Educational Setting (Teri J. Bellis) 78, 174

Association for All Speech-Impaired Children (AFASIC) 161

Aston Index 75, 76, 137

Attention Deficits, sources of help and support 161

Attention Deficit/Hyperactivity Disorder – A Practical Guide for teachers P. Cooper and K. Ideus) 173

Auditory Processes (P. Gillet) 78

Autism and Asperger Syndrome (ed. Uta Frith) 126, 173

Autistic Spectrum Disorder, sources of help and support 161

BAS tests 91, 137
  BAS II Number Skills Worksheet 140, 141, 142

'Basic Number' (Next Generation) 175

behavioural optometry 54, 63, 163-4

Brain and Behaviour Clinic, London 39

Brain Gym exercises 62-3

Brain Gym – A Teacher's Edition (P. and G. Dennison) 173

Breakthrough to Number (Jan Poustie) 175

British Association of Behavioural Optometrists (BADO) 54, 164

British Dyslexia Association 161

British Dyslexia Association Publications
  Dyslexia Handbook 174
  Dyslexia – Early Help, Better Future (video) 174
  Dyslexia in the Primary Classroom (video and manual) 174
  Dyslexia: Signposts to Success 174

CALSC 103

Carroll diagrams 103

Center for Teaching/Learning Mathematics 134

Child Communication and Learning 89

Child Head-Injury Trust 162

Childhood Hemiplegia, sources of help and support 162

Childhood Speech, Language and Listening Problems (P. McAleer Hamaguchi) 174

'Clock Language' (Next Generation) 150, 175

'Clouds' sheets, *Identification Solutions for Specific Learning Difficulties* (Jan Poustie) 168

'Contact-a-family' 132

'Count and Add' (computer program) 111

cranial osteopathy 105, 106

'Crystal Forest 2000' computer program (Shertson) 74

Cuisenaire Rods 11, 50, 58, 79, 84, 171

Cuisenaire Rods and Mathematics Teaching (Mahesh C. Sharma) 171

Developmental Dyspraxia (2nd edition, Madeleine Portwood) 72, 106, 136, 137, 172

'The Developmental Test of Visual Perception' 71

'Diagnosis and Remediation of Learning Problems in Mathematics' (Sharma course) 133

Digit Tests 137-8

Dyscalculia (Focus on Learning Problems in Mathematics, edited Mahesh C. Sharma and Eugene J Loveless) 171

Dyslexia
  Dyslexia and Mathematics (ed. T.R. Miles and E. Miles) 170

Dyslexia, Dyscalculia, and Some Remedial Perspectives for Mathematical Learning Problems (Mahesh C. Sharma) 32, 171

Dyslexia Early Screening Test (DEST) 137

The Dyslexia Handbook 2000 101

The Dyslexia Institute 139, 145

Dyslexia Screening Test (DST) 137

sources of help and support 161

Dyspraxia

The Dyspraxia Association 161-2

The Dyspraxia Foundation 72, 161

Dyspraxia Foundation Adult Support Group 161

sources of help and support 161-2

Early Communication Skills (Lynch and Cooper) 78

The Early Years Centre 126

Edington and Shapwick School, Somerset 138

Elementary Mathematics and Language Difficulties - A Book for Teachers, Therapists and Parents (Eva Grauberg) 171

'Elite Manager Week' diary (Collins) 151

FM Radio Link system 78

Focus on Learning Problems in Mathematics (Mahesh C. Sharma) 135, 171

'Gaining Face' (computer program) 89

General Council and Register of Osteopaths 162

Get Ahead (Vanda North and Tony Buzan) 110

Graded Activities for Children with Motor Difficulties (James Russell) 45

Hearing Support Service, LEA 78

Helen Arkell Centre, Surrey 139

Helix pie chart stencil 36

Hemihelp 162

'How to teach the student who has Dyscalculia' (lecture by Jan Poustie) 176

Hyperactive Children's Support Group 161

Identification Solutions for Specific Learning Difficulties; Part A (Jan Poustie et al.) 35, 40, 43, 45, 48, 52, 53, 54-5, 59, 62, 63, 72, 75, 113, 135, 145, 168, 174

'Identifying Dyscalculia in the Early Years' (lecture by Jan Poustie) 176

independent study carrels 125

INNP Neuro-Developmental Delay programme (NHS) 46

Institute of Neuro-Physiological Psychology 162

Institute of Optometry 54

Intelligence Testing with WISC III 139

Irlen lenses 54

Lander Software 111

Language

Mathematics as a Second Language - Part Two Mathematics Word Problems (Mahesh C. Sharma) 134, 171

An Introduction to Mathematics and Language (Jan Poustie) 172

'The Language of Position Teaching Pack' (Next Generation) 56

LDA 103, 137

LEA

Parent Partnership Officer 117

special advisors 114

Special Education Needs Support Team

Lego® 47, 82

Listening Skills (Maths Key Stage 1 and 2, The Questions Publishing Company) 79, 86

Literacy Solutions (Jan Poustie) 2, 36, 53

low-plus lenses 63

magic squares 25-6, 32

Mark College 104, 139, 157

Mathematics

Math Notebook (Sharma) 171

'Mathematics and Language' (lecture) 176

Mathematics as a Second Language - Part Two Mathematics Word Problems (Mahesh C. Sharma) 134, 171

'Mathematics Communication' strategy 133-4, 141, 142

Mathematics for Dyslexics - A TeachingHandbook

(2nd edition Steve Chinn and Richard Ashcroft) 32, 145, 170

Mathematics Solutions - An Introduction to Dycalculia, Part B: Teaching Tips for Specific Learning Difficulties in Mathematics and Resources (Jan Poustie) 1, 2-3, 26, 134, 155, 174

'Mathematics and Language' (lecture by Jan Poustie) 176

'Maths Blaster' (computer program) 111

'Maths Circus' (computer programs) 99

Maths for the Dyslexic - A Practical Guide (Anne Henderson) 170

Numeracy 1 – Teaching Number Relationships (video) 171

The Maths Notebook (Mahesh C. Sharma) 32, 172

ME Association, the 38

meal planner, resource sheet 169

Mind Maps® 79, 103, 110

Movement Assessment Battery for Children (Henderson and Sugden) 136-7

Music Solutions for Specific Learning Difficulties (Jan Poustie) 77

NASEN (National Association for Special Educational Needs) 162

The National Autistic Society 161

Newcomen Centre, Guy's Hospital, London 130

Next Generation Publishing mathematics products 175
    see also Poustie, Jan

NFER-Nelson Publishing 89, 145

NSPCC 132

'The Nuffield Centre Dyspraxia Programme' 70

Number Shark (computer program) 149

Number Triangle test 135

OCR Diploma 157

Osteopathic Centre for Children 162

Parent Partnership Officer, LEA 117

PATOSS (Professional Association of Teachers of Students with Specific Learning Difficulties) 162

Picture Exchange Communication System (PECS) 129

pie chart stencil 36

Planning and Organisation Solutions (Jan Poustie) 49, 60, 79, 103, 110, 124, 174

Polygon clocks 151

Portwood Motor Screening Test 136

Poustie, Jan 138, 173, 174, 175, 176

Praxis II (The Dyspraxia Foundation) 72

Prerequisite and Support Skills for Mathematics Learning 171

Pyramid Education Consultants Inc. 129

The Psychological Association 136, 137

Psychological Aspects of Hemiplegia (Robert Goodman) 173

Quickbooks (computer accounting program) 150

Quicken (budgeting software) 149

'Recognising the SpLD Profile - An Overview' (lecture by Jan Poustie) 176

'The Recognition of Dyscalculia' (lecture) 176

referrals and supportive agencies, behavioural problems 130

'Reflex Stimulation Programme' (Blythe and McGlown) 45

resources
    lectures, sources and subjects 176
    mathematics, reference materials concerning 172-4
    Next Generation mathematics products 175
    photocopiable 163-9
    SpLD, reference materials concerning 174

Reverse Digit Tests 137-8

Rey-Osterrieth Complex Figure Test 133, 137

RSA Diploma SpLD 157

Rummikub® 103, 175

Sasco wall planner 152

Scottish Dyslexia Association 161

Scottish Society for Autistic Children 161

'Sesame Street' (TV programme) 82

Sharma Certificate in the Diagnosis and Remediation of Mathematical Learning Difficulties 135, 145

Sharma materials 171

The Society of Homeopaths 107

The Society of Osteopaths 162

Special Education Needs Co-ordinator (SENCO/ AENCO) 115, 117

Specific Language Difficulties, sources of help and support 161

Specific Learning Difficulties in Mathematics - A Classroom Approach (Olwen El-Naggar) 171

Speech and Language Difficulties (B. Daines, P. Fleming and C. I. Miller) 174

Stile 'Maths Language' pack 82

SULP (Social Use of Language Programme) 89

Syndrome of Non-verbal Learning Disabilities (Byron Rourke) 39

'Tablegraphics Set 1' (Next Generation) 124, 175

Take Time (M. Nash-Wortham) 45

'Take-off with Number' teaching pack (Next Generation) 13, 175

'talking calculators' 149

'talking clock' (RNIB) 151

'talking watch' (Argos and RNIB) 151

TAMBA (Twins and Multiple Birth Association) 105, 162

Taskmaster 103

The Autistic Spectrum – A Guide for Parents and Professionals (Lorna Wing)

The World of the Autistic Child (Bryna Siegel) 173

Thinking Goes to School (Furth and Wachs) 62

Tourette Syndrome (UK) Association 162

'traffic-lights' cards 128

Understanding Developmental Dyspraxia (Madeleine Portwood) 72

Understanding Attention Deficit Disorder – A parent's guide to A.D.D. in children (Dr. C Green and Dr. K. Chee) 173

Venn diagrams 103

video resources (Mahesh C. Sharma) 173

visual problems, checklist for 163-4

wall calendars (Boots five column version) 152

WISC tests 91, 100, 137
  WISC III^{UK} - Arithmetic 139-40, 142, 143

WRAT (Wide Range Achievement Tests) 133
  WRAT 3 - Arithmetic 140-41, 142, 143, 145

Year Planner (Sasco) 152